Faculty Tenure

A Report and Recommendations
by the
Commission on Academic Tenure
in Higher Education

A Report and Recommendations
by the

Commission on Academic Tenure
in Higher Education

William R. Keast
Chairman

John W. Macy, Jr.
Cochairman

FACULTY TENURE

Jossey-Bass Publishers
San Francisco • Washington • London • 1973

FACULTY TENURE
A Report and Recommendations by the Commission on Academic Tenure in Higher Education
by the Commission on Academic Tenure in Higher Education

Library of Congress Catalogue Card Number LC 72-11625

International Standard Book Number ISBN 0-87589-162-4

Manufactured in the United States of America

JACKET DESIGN BY WILLI BAUM

FIRST EDITION

Code 7305

The Jossey-Bass
Series in Higher Education

Preface

The Commission on Academic Tenure in Higher Education was established during 1971 and worked under a grant from the Ford Foundation. The commission was jointly sponsored by the Association of American Colleges (AAC) and the American Association of University Professors (AAUP), two organizations with a long history of joint activity in the development of policies relating to higher education. In particular, the AAC and the AAUP were the framers of the 1940 Statement of Principles on Academic Freedom and Tenure, the fundamental document on the subject. The 1940 statement was a restatement and expansion of the 1925 Statement on Academic Freedom and Tenure, prepared by a conference of educational organizations, including the AAC and the AAUP, convened by the American Council on Education. The 1925 statement, in turn, had replaced the original 1915 Declaration of Principles drawn up by the Committee on Academic Freedom and Tenure of the AAUP and endorsed by that association in 1915–1916.

By 1970, the 1940 Statement of Principles on Academic Freedom and Tenure had been officially endorsed by eighty-one professional organizations. It had been incorporated, explicitly or by reference, in detail or in principle, in the policies of most of the institutions of higher education in the United States. However, at the end of a troubled decade on American campuses, a fresh inquiry into academic tenure seemed called for—particularly since two prestigious national commissions, formed to search out the causes of the widespread campus unrest of the 1960s and to propose remedies, had identified the operation of the tenure system as a possible cause. One of these commissions, the Special Committee on Campus Tensions, under the chairmanship of Sol M. Linowitz, concluded:

> *Tenure policies—concerning a faculty member's right to hold his academic appointment until retirement once competence has been demonstrated (except when extreme malfeasance has been demonstrated by due process)—need to be appraised. The justification for tenure is the crucial protection it gives to academic freedom. Professors who espouse unpopular views must be free from reprisal. Tenure was not devised in the spirit of trade union systems to guarantee job security. But it has come to serve this function too, at a cost. It sometimes has been a shield for indifference and neglect of scholarly duties. At a time when an increasing number of teachers, especially in community colleges and state colleges, are organizing for collective bargaining, the committee recognizes that a challenge to the present concept of tenure is no small matter, that the issues involved are complex and difficult to resolve, and that a satisfactory solution must maintain effective safeguards for academic freedom. Nonetheless, we urge the American Association of University Professors and the Association of American Colleges . . . to reexamine existing policies. Standards for awarding tenure—a matter of institutional autonomy—need broadening to allow greater consideration of teaching ability. Scholarly communities must be protected as effectively as tenure now protects individual professors.[1]*

The President's Commission on Campus Unrest (the Scranton Commission) made a similar recommendation: "As one means of improving the quality of teaching in higher education, we urge re-

[1] *Campus Tensions: Analysis and Recommendations,* Report of the Special Committee on Campus Tensions, S. M. Linowitz, Chairman (Washington, D.C.: American Council on Education, 1970), pp. 42–43.

consideration of the practice of tenure. Tenure has strong justification because of its role in protecting the academic freedom of senior faculty members. But it also can protect practices that detract from the institution's primary functions, that are unjust to students, and that grant faculty members a freedom from accountability that would be unacceptable for any other profession."[2]

In 1971 the AAC and the AAUP created the Commission on Academic Tenure as a separate, autonomous unit. It was to design and carry out its own program of investigation and make its report directly to the academic community and the general public, without reference to the sponsors. This agreement was expressly understood by all members of the commission and has been scrupulously observed. *Faculty Tenure,* therefore, presents the views of the commission and not those of the AAC or the AAUP or the Ford Foundation.

The task of the Commission on Academic Tenure was to consider the operation of the tenure system in higher education, to evaluate the criticisms of academic tenure made during recent years, to consider alternatives to tenure in effect or proposed for adoption, and to recommend needed modifications or improvements in the tenure system if it is to be retained.

The commission met for the first time in September 1971. It completed formal work on recommendations in late June 1972. The commission study was conducted through a series of meetings of the entire commission; through visits by task forces of the commission to fourteen campuses and university centers throughout the United States; through extensive correspondence and consultation with faculty, administrative officers, students, members of governing boards, and officers of state systems of higher education; and through the work of a small Washington staff.

The commission visited the following campuses, chosen to provide diversity in size, location, control, purpose, and support: Atlanta University Center (Atlanta University, Clark College, Morehouse College, Morris Brown College, Spelman College); California State College at Los Angeles; City College of the City University of New York; Cornell University, Ithaca, New York; Hampshire College, Amherst, Massachusetts; Lewis and Clark College, Portland, Oregon;

---

[2] *Report of the President's Commission on Campus Unrest,* W. Scranton, Chairman (Washington, D.C.: Government Printing Office, 1970), p. 201.

Tarrant County Junior College, Fort Worth, Texas; University of
Nebraska at Omaha; University of South Florida, Tampa; University
of Wisconsin at Madison. At each of these institutions, members of the
commission interviewed officers of the central administration, deans,
and department chairmen; tenured and nontenured faculty; officers of
faculty organizations; students; and, in some cases, members of boards
of control, officers of multicampus systems, and leaders of collective
bargaining groups.

Because certain dimensions of tenure—history, legal aspects,
and implications for collective bargaining trends—require concentrated
and expert treatment, Walter Metzger of Columbia University, Victor
Rosenblum of Northwestern University, and William McHugh of
American University have prepared special chapters on these topics.
The commission is especially grateful to these scholars for their contributions.

The staff, in addition to reviewing the literature on tenure,
received special assistance from the Office of Research of the American
Council on Education, which prepared a computer report on faculty
attitudes on tenure and related matters. The data from this study are
presented in Chapter Seven. Also, at the commission's request, the
Higher Education Panel of the ACE administered a wholly new survey
of current institutional policies and practices relating to tenure. The
results of this survey are presented in Chapter Six.

The commission was assisted in its work by many individuals
and organizations. It wishes especially to record its gratitude to Frederic
Ness, F. L. Wormald, John Gillis, and other members of the staff of
the Association of American Colleges; Bertram Davis, Jordan Kurland,
Margaret Rumbarger, and other members of the staff of the American
Association of University Professors; Todd Furniss, Alan E. Bayer,
Jeffrey Dutton, Barbara Blandford, and other members of the staff of
the American Council on Education; scores of persons on the campuses
visited, whose interest, candor, and concern made these visits especially
valuable; the approximately two hundred faculty members, administrators, students, members of governing boards, and officers of state
education agencies who generously responded to the commission's
request for their views on academic tenure with written statements,
many of them extensive and detailed; Jacob Samit, director of field
services, Colleges and Universities Department, American Federation

of Teachers, who presented the federation's views to the commission; Allan M. West, deputy executive secretary, National Education Association, who supplied to the commission a detailed draft statement of the association's position on tenure; John A. Ferguson, deputy director of the commission; and Susan E. Lippek, the commission's administrative and research assistant.

Austin   WILLIAM R. KEAST
January 1973

Contents

xv

SPECIAL TOPICS

SUPPORTING DOCUMENTS

7. Faculty Attitudes and Tenure   227

    Appendix: 1940 Statement of Principles on
          Academic Freedom and Tenure   249

    Glossary of Terms   255

    Selected Bibliography   259

    Guide to Recommendations   270

    Index   273

Commission on Academic Tenure in Higher Education

WILLIAM R. KEAST (chairman), *professor of English and director, Center for Higher Education, University of Texas at Austin*

JOHN W. MACY, JR. (cochairman), *former president, Corporation for Public Broadcasting*

DAVID ALEXANDER, *president, Pomona College*

HENRY L. BOWDEN, *partner, Lokey and Bowden, Atlanta*

WILLIAM B. BOYD, *president, Central Michigan University*

JOSEPH P. COSAND, *professor of higher education, University of Michigan (from January 1972 to February 1973 served as deputy commissioner for higher education, U.S. Office of Education)*

RALPH F. FUCHS, *emeritus professor of law, Indiana University*

LOUIS H. HEILBRON, *partner, Heller, Ehrman, White, and McAuliffe, San Francisco*

EVA JEFFERSON, *student, Boalt Hall School of Law, University of California, Berkeley*

PAUL OBERST, *professor of law, University of Kentucky*

ROSEMARY PIERREL SORRENTINO, *professor of psychology, Brown University*

Special Contributing Authors

WALTER P. METZGER, *professor of history, Columbia University*

VICTOR G. ROSENBLUM, *professor of law, Northwestern University*

WILLIAM F. MCHUGH, *professor of law, The American University*

Faculty Tenure

A Report and Recommendations
by the
Commission on Academic Tenure
in Higher Education

Academic Tenure Today

Academic tenure (see glossary) is a characteristic aspect of faculty service in American higher education. A survey conducted for the commission in April 1972 revealed that tenure plans are in effect in all public and private universities and public four-year colleges; in 94 percent of the private colleges; and in more than two thirds of the nation's two-year colleges, public and private (see Chapter Six, Table 3). An estimated 94 percent of all faculty members in American universities and colleges are serving in institutions that confer tenure.[1]

What has come to be regarded as the "standard" tenure plan is embodied in the 1940 Statement of Principles on Academic Freedom and Tenure, developed by the Association of American Colleges and

[1] W. T. Furniss, *Faculty Tenure and Contract Systems—Current Practice,* ACE Special Report (Washington, D.C.: American Council on Education, 1972), p. 1.

the American Association of University Professors. Here, tenure is viewed as a means of ensuring academic freedom and of providing sufficient economic security to make the academic profession attractive to men and women of ability—both objectives being indispensable to the successful fulfillment of the social purposes of higher education. The 1940 statement provides that "after the expiration of a probationary period" faculty members should have "permanent or continuous tenure" and that their service should be terminated "only for adequate cause, except in the case of retirement for age or under extraordinary circumstances because of financial exigencies." The statement provides further that the terms of academic appointments should be stated in writing, that the probationary period of full-time service should not exceed seven years, that teachers should enjoy full academic freedom during the probationary period, that a dismissal or a termination for cause should occur only under full academic due process, and that terminations because of financial exigency should be "demonstrably *bona fide*." The 1940 statement has been supplemented and extended by AAUP statements on dismissal proceedings, renewal and nonrenewal of faculty appointments, notice of nonreappointment, professional ethics, and related matters. These statements have had wide influence on institutional practice.

Tenure Policies and Practices

The 1940 statement is a statement of principles, not a prescription of substantive institutional practice. It was designed to provide guidance in institutions that differ greatly in objectives, organization, governance, and tradition. The supplementary statements, similarly, set forth recommended procedures, leaving great latitude for variation from one institution to another. There are, consequently, great variations in tenure policies and practices—despite the widespread endorsement or adoption of the 1940 statement and despite the existence of tenure arrangements in most American colleges and universities. It is quite inaccurate, indeed, to refer to "the tenure system" in American higher education, since "system" implies more uniformity and consistency than exist in institutions today.

On every aspect of tenure, institutional policies and practices vary: definition of tenure; its legal basis; criteria for appointment, reappointment, and award of tenure; length of probationary period; categories of personnel eligible for tenure; relationship between tenure and rank; procedures for recommending appointments and awarding tenure; procedures for appeal from adverse decisions; procedures to be followed in dismissal cases; role of faculty, administration, students, and governing board in personnel actions; methods of evaluating teaching, scholarship, and public service; and retirement arrangements. In all these and many more, the range of variation among the 2600 institutions of higher education (and sometimes even within institutions —from division to division or even from department to department) is enormous.

Some institutions have formal tenure policies and procedures; many do not. Some institutions provide explicit statements concerning qualifications and criteria for reappointment and award of tenure; many, perhaps most, do not.

In some institutions personnel policies are communicated clearly and authoritatively to the faculty; in others there is widespread ignorance, confusion, or difference in interpretation, not only among the younger faculty but often among the senior faculty and administrators responsible for personnel actions.

In some institutions an effort is made to assist the young faculty member to develop as a teacher and scholar; in many, the young teacher is given virtually no assistance or information about his strengths or shortcomings until the time of final decision on reappointment.

A few institutions exercise close control over the proportion of tenured faculty; most, at least until recently, have not had policies governing the relative size of the tenured and nontenured groups.

In some institutions personnel actions originate with and generally follow the recommendations of departmental personnel committees or other faculty groups; in others the chairman or dean makes the effective recommendation, with or without formal consultation with the faculty; in still others the president or other principal administrative officer plays the central role.

In some institutions methods have been established for obtaining student evaluations of faculty performance—sometimes formally, sometimes informally; sometimes in a uniform manner, sometimes with wide variation from department to department or even from one individual to another. In other institutions there is no serious attempt to reflect student opinion in personnel decisions.

This situation is not new. Reporting in 1959 on a survey of eighty institutions in California, Illinois, and Pennsylvania carried out in 1955–56, Byse and Joughin observed that in the seventy-seven schools with tenure arrangements, "Tenure is embodied in a bewildering variety of policies, plans, and practices; the range reveals extraordinary differences in generosity, explicitness, and intelligibility. Large or small, public or private, nonsectarian or religiously affiliated, there is no consensus concerning either the criteria or the procedures for acquiring and terminating tenure."[2] In 1962, Paul Dressel found a similar variety in tenure policies and practices among thirty-one major universities.[3] And B. N. Shaw came to similar conclusions on the basis of his study of ninety-one state colleges and land-grant universities in 1969.[4]

The results of the survey of tenure carried out for the commission in the spring of 1972 by the Higher Education Panel of the ACE are given in Chapter 6. On the basis of this survey, the following observations can be made about current tenure policies and practices in the colleges—approximately 85 percent of the total—that have tenure plans:

1. There is wide variation among types of institutions in the percentage of the faculty who held tenure appointments in the spring of 1972. The median for all institutions was 41–50 percent on tenure. The median for all universities and for public two-year colleges was 51–60 percent on tenure, for all four-year colleges 41–50 percent, and for private two-year colleges 31–40 percent. Forty-five percent of all institutions had more than 50 percent of their faculties on tenure. Twenty-five percent had more than 60 percent on tenure.

2. Both initial and succeeding contracts during the probationary period are for one-year periods in most four-year and two-year colleges,

---

[2] C. Byse and L. Joughin, *Tenure in American Higher Education: Plans, Practices, and the Law* (Ithaca, N.Y.: Cornell University Press, 1959), p. 133.

[3] P. L. Dressel, "A Review of the Tenure Policies of Thirty-One Major Universities," *Educational Record*, 1963, *44*, 248–253.

[4] *Academic Tenure in American Higher Education* (Chicago: Adams, 1971), pp. 89–99.

both public and private. In universities, nearly two thirds use one-year initial and renewal contracts; about one third award contracts for two or more years.

3. In general, the *maximum* probationary period ranges from three to seven years. (It is important to distinguish the maximum allowable probationary period from the probationary period actually used; no data are available on the latter point, but promotion and termination very commonly occur before the maximum probationary period has elapsed.) The median term is six years for all institutions, seven years in private universities, four years in public two-year colleges. Eighteen percent of all institutions use a maximum period of three years or less; 28 percent use a maximum of four years or less.

In general, private institutions use much longer probationary periods than do public institutions; in 64.5 percent of the private universities, for example, the maximum is seven years, but only 36.7 percent of the public universities set a seven-year maximum. The shortest probationary periods prevail in the public two-year colleges: almost half these institutions set the maximum at three years or less; 65 percent, at four years or less.

4. There is great variation among types of institutions in allowing credit for prior service to reduce the probationary period. More than half of all institutions allow no credit for prior service, and public institutions as a group are much less likely to grant credit than private institutions. The institutions that allow no credit are predominantly the two-year colleges (69.7 percent of the public and 73.7 percent of the private) and the public four-year colleges (69.4 percent). The practice in these two-year colleges is apparently related to their use of a relatively short (three- or four-year) probationary period; but this does not explain the practice of the public colleges, where the median probationary maximum is six years. Universities, public and private, and private four-year colleges are more generous in granting credit for prior service, but from 33 to 41 percent even of these institutions do not do so. When credit for prior service is granted, the usual limit is three years, although 21 percent of the public universities allow credit for four years or more.

5. In institutions that use conventional faculty ranks (virtually all universities and four-year colleges, but only about half the two-year colleges), professors and associate professors are universally eligible for

tenure. Eligibility for tenure in the ranks of assistant professor and instructor is more variable. Assistant professors may receive tenure in most institutions, but less commonly in private universities (58 percent), public universities (70 percent), and private two-year colleges (79 percent) than in private (84 percent) and public (90 percent) four-year colleges and in public two-year colleges (100 percent). Instructors are eligible for tenure in one third of all institutions. Private universities and four-year colleges are only about half as likely to make instructors eligible for tenure as are their public counterparts.

6. Tenure is awarded generously. Forty-two percent of the institutions responding to this particular question granted tenure to *all* faculty members considered for tenure in the spring of 1971. Two thirds of the institutions granted tenure to 70 percent or more of those under consideration. Tenure is awarded most liberally in two-year colleges and least liberally in universities: more than half of the public and nearly two thirds of the private two-year colleges granted tenure to all those under consideration; only 15 percent of the public and 10 percent of the private universities did so.

7. Most institutions—94 percent—place no limit on the proportion of their faculty who may be tenured. Of the few who impose some limit, most are private, and more often four-year colleges than universities; the two-year colleges are least likely to limit the proportion of tenured faculty.

8. When a probationary appointment is not renewed or when tenure is denied, nearly half (47 percent) of all institutions always provide written reasons for the action to the faculty member; 16 percent never give written reasons.

9. Procedures under which a faculty member may appeal a decision not to reappoint him or not to award him tenure are available in 87 percent of all institutions. Appeal procedures are most common in public institutions and in two-year colleges. Nearly one fifth of the private four-year colleges and 16 percent of the private universities lack such appeal procedures.

10. Between September 1969 and April 1972, appeals from adverse personnel decisions were made in slightly less than half of all institutions. Appeals were made in three quarters of the universities, two thirds of the public four-year colleges, just under half of the private four-year colleges, about 45 percent of the public, and just under a

fifth of the private two-year colleges. About 13 percent of all institutions with tenure plans had more than three appeals during this period. Appeals were most frequent in universities and public four-year colleges; nearly a fifth of the private universities and public colleges had seven or more appeals.

Tenured and Nontenured Faculty

To these observations about institutional tenure policies and practices it is possible to add some conclusions about tenured and nontenured faculty, based on the responses to a 1969 survey of 60,000 faculty conducted by the Carnegie Commission and the American Council on Education. Relevant data from this survey are presented in Chapter 7.

The overall percentage of faculty who reported that they were on tenure in 1969—just under 50 percent—agrees generally with the returns from the 1972 Higher Education Panel survey. (It should be noted, however, that this percentage includes all faculty. The percent of full-time faculty on tenure would be somewhat higher.) The largest faculty group was in the thirty-six to fifty age bracket in all types of institutions; next largest was the group thirty-five and under. Approximately one third of all faculty members were thirty-five or under in 1969. In the 1970s and 1980s, colleges and universities face the formidable task of adjusting the aspirations of a relatively young faculty to declining rates of enrollment growth, stable or declining budgets, and program shifts.

Though the proportion of tenured faculty in 1972 appears to be just about what it was in the early 1960s, the prospects for the future are very different. The relative youth of most present faculties means that retirements will occur at a slower rate and fewer tenure positions will open up. Budgets are expected to remain tight; and enrollments—although they will continue to grow—will grow at a sharply reduced rate. If institutions continue to award tenure to 60 to 80 percent, or more, of eligible faculty, and if faculty size does not grow proportionately, many will find themselves, within a few years, with tenure staffs so large that promotion for younger faculty will be increasingly difficult. The effort to bring increased numbers of women and minority-group members into the higher teaching ranks may be frustrated. Institutions will lack the vigor and freshness of a substantial junior faculty. This

will be a major problem in the administration of faculty personnel
programs during the 1970s; several of the commission's recommendations are designed to help deal with it.

Educational Developments

Tenure, like so many other things these days, does not work as
well as it once did. Whether it can be made to work is a large question,
upon which the future of higher education may in a fundamental way
depend. If tenure is to be made to work, it is esssential first to examine
the context in which the greatest deficiencies in its operation arose or
came sharply into view. Such an examination, though necessarily
brief and touching only the highlights of immensely complex developments, will make clear that the major problems attributed to academic
tenure are in fact broader problems arising from the revolution in
higher education during the last twenty years, from certain unresolved
differences of opinion in our society about educational purposes and
priorities, and from permanent difficulties in problems of organizing
professional service in institutional settings. It will also make clear
that—in view of the radically altered circumstances of colleges and
universities in the 1970s—reform in the operation of faculty personnel
programs as a whole and of tenure plans in particular should have the
highest priority.

Since World War II, and especially since the late 1950s, higher
education in the United States has been transformed. Specifically,
higher education has been democratized; a universal opportunity for
higher education, or something closely approaching it, has become
a stated national policy. No such fundamental change in the theory or
extension of higher education has ever occurred in this or any other
country. During this educational revolution the following developments
have been of greatest significance for tenure and faculty personnel
policy in general:

First of all, the total number of college and university teachers
grew enormously—grew more, indeed, in percentage terms than did
student enrollments. Graduate schools became less selective; new
graduate programs, many of relatively low quality, were started. A
booming market and a selective service system that made "going on
to graduate school" a way of life brought into college and university
faculties many who had only a marginal commitment to academic life

and no serious induction into the standards of the academic profession.

At the same time, new institutions were established and existing institutions were expanded and transformed at an unprecedented rate, often with no clear plans or objectives to support a serious faculty selection and development program; policy formulation and planning were postponed or thought to be unnecessary. As a result of this expansion, the demand for faculty was so great and the supply so meager that standards were often lowered, existing qualifications for appointment were frequently waived, the academic-rank structure was deeply compromised by the inflation (the rank of instructor virtually disappeared, and hordes of assistant professors were appointed without terminal degrees). In this situation, tenure largely lost its significance. It became an inducement to be used in recruiting and retaining faculty. The habits that persist to this day were established: tenure became virtually automatic; no limit was set on the proportion of faculty with tenure; selection was minimal; tenure was conferred at an earlier age and after shorter probationary periods. Tenure was too often taken for granted and in consequence lost much of its value; it largely ceased to be thought of as the very heart of the academic personnel system. Gresham's Law found its expression in the currency of the academy. Only a relatively small number of fortunate institutions were able to avoid these effects of inordinate growth.

In addition, the reward system in American higher education came increasingly to emphasize graduate teaching and research. Though the reasons for this are numerous and complicated, compelling influence was exerted by massive federal programs, the bulk of them designed to support graduate training and research. The great new wave of teachers was imbued with the notion that the acme of academic life is graduate study, that the best undergraduate students are those who want to go on to graduate school, that the best institutions are graduate institutions, and that advanced courses and increasingly specialized training should be provided even in the most improbable settings.

Concurrently, as immense numbers of students hit the colleges and universities, the deficiencies in American undergraduate education, always serious and never satisfactorily resolved even after the intense experimentation and debate of the 1930s, became the focus of national debate. Since higher education was now to be accessible to all, its quality was of concern to everybody. If the educational system was to provide instruction for all, then teaching effectiveness—hitherto only a hoped-for by-product of the American way of preparing college and university faculty—would have to be given new emphasis. Since higher education was becoming a right, and since its mounting costs were increasingly and obviously borne by every taxpayer, students and parents, reinforced in their demands by a growing consumerism, insisted more emphatically upon good teaching; and "accountability" became a watchword in educational debate. What good teaching is, how curricula should be organized, how and by whom teaching effectiveness could be measured—all these remained as unclear as ever. But an intense polarization between teaching and research developed, manifesting itself in obvious and subtle ways on every campus. To make matters worse, the tendency to regard teaching and research as incompatible opposites was merged with a whole series of other problems agitating the society and finding their most intense expression on American campuses: the notorious generation gap (the older professors tended to be the researchers and graduate teachers); the Vietnam War (the controversy over war research reinforced antagonism to research generally in the minds of many students); the demand for "relevance"; the new antiestablishmentarianism; the growing distrust of institutions and authority.

The wonder is not that the tenure system—like the educational system in general—should have shown weaknesses and deficiencies under the pressure of these conditions. So did other institutions in the society—the health-care system, the law-enforcement system, the information system, the welfare system, to name but a few. The wonder is that the tenure system survived at all—that many excellent teachers and scholars were brought into the profession and rewarded for their excellent performance; that much excellent teaching was done; that profound changes were made in American higher education; that the fundamental values of academic freedom and institutional integrity continued to be honored and sought.

Alternatives

A substantial number of institutions—most of them junior and community colleges—operate not under a tenure plan but under some form of contract system. In the 1972 Higher Education Panel survey,

32 percent of all two-year schools reported that they employ faculty only on a term-contract basis, without provision for tenure; 6 percent of the private four-year colleges use contracts exclusively. Together, this group constitutes some 15 percent of all institutions—11 percent of the private and 20 percent of the public (see Chapter Six, Table 3). These institutions, which though numerous are mostly small, employ about 5 or 6 percent of all faculty members in American colleges and universities.

All two-year colleges using contract systems reported that they limit the initial contract and any succeeding contract to one year. All the four-year colleges using contract systems also limit the initial contract to one year; 71 percent of them also limit succeeding contracts to one year, but 29 percent reported that succeeding contracts could be for two- or three-year terms.

Contract plans, although broadly similar in using very short-term contracts and in affording opportunities for contract renewal, differ greatly in detail. Among the more interesting variations are the following: (1) Evergreen State College, Washington, usually grants three-year contracts to its faculty members. A portfolio containing examples and descriptions of the faculty member's work as a teacher-scholar is maintained for use in evaluating performance. A favorable evaluation leads to a new three-year contract; an unfavorable evaluation leads to a notice of nonrenewal one year in advance of the expiration of the contract. (2) Franklin Pierce College in New Hampshire has instituted a system of three-year "rolling" contracts. A faculty member is first awarded one or more one-year contracts during a probationary period of not more than seven years. If he survives the probationary period, he is granted a three-year contract and is evaluated annually; if the evaluation is positive, his contract is extended. Thus, a faculty member on a three-year contract is evaluated at the end of the first year. If the evaluation is positive, he receives a new contract for three years. If the evaluation is negative, he has the remaining two years of the contract in which to remedy his deficiencies. If he receives another negative evaluation at the end of the second year, the third year of the contract is terminal; if positive, he is awarded a new three-year contract. The process is continuous. (3) Goddard College, Vermont, operates under a contract system in which, after an initial one-year appointment, faculty contracts are lengthened to three and then to five years. Toward the end of the contract period, a committee on faculty evaluation and retention reviews the performance of the faculty member and makes a recommendation to the president for renewal or nonrenewal. This committee, comprised of faculty and students, ordinarily reviews those faculty members with three- and five-year contracts in the fall of the final year and those with one-year contracts in the winter. The committee has great flexibility in determining the procedures to be used in the evaluation process (whether through interviews, surveys, self-evaluations, or some other procedure). (4) Governors State University in Illinois is developing a cyclical arrangement under which initial appointments will be for two or three years, and faculty members will be eligible thereafter for five- to seven-year contracts, with annual evaluations. A successful evaluation will lead to a renewal for five to seven years. (5) Hampshire College in Massachusetts uses "growth contracts." Original appointments and reappointments may be from one to seven years, although in practice they have usually been for three years. If the faculty member wishes to remain at Hampshire, he so requests and his performance is evaluated more than one year before the expiration of his contract. Each faculty member prepares a "growth" contract proposal, in which he requests a specific term appointment and outlines activities he wants to undertake and the goals he expects to achieve. The acceptability of the proposal, as well as satisfactory evaluation of past performance, determines whether or not the faculty member receives a contract. The process is repeated as the next contract approaches its expiration date. Obviously, the possibilities for variation are practically limitless. Many other proposals are put forward in the literature cited in the Bibliography.

From the data in Chapter Six, certain generalizations can be made about the way that contract systems operate. First, contracts seem to be renewed almost as a matter of course. In 1971, more than nine out of ten contracts were renewed in 87 percent of all institutions; and in 66 percent of the four-year private colleges on contract systems, all expiring contracts were renewed. Only a small fraction of all contract schools—less than 5 percent—renewed less than 80 percent of the contracts. We do not know whether 1971 was a "typical" year for these institutions, but the point is striking nonetheless.

Second, despite the common assertion that academic due

process is provided for in these institutions, only 19 percent reported that they have procedures under which a faculty member can appeal a decision not to renew his contract. Of course if virtually all contracts are renewed, there may be little need for an appeal procedure. Nevertheless, the absence of appeal procedures stands in sharp contrast to the availability of appeal procedures in 87 percent of all colleges and universities with tenure plans.

Third, none of the private two-year schools now using contracts reported plans to establish a tenure system; 15 percent of the public two-year colleges and 29 percent of the private four-year colleges, however, intend to substitute a tenure system for their current contract system—suggesting some dissatisfaction with contract arrangements.

Since many of the institutions using contract systems are new, small, and deliberately experimental, it is too early to assess their performance, even if it were clear what the nature of the experiment was in each case, how it could be evaluated, and what part the contract arrangement played in the outcome. Until some serious research is done, especially on a comparative basis, appraisal of the virtues of contract systems will continue to be largely a matter of opinion. The commission believes that individual and comparative studies of typical alternatives to tenure should be undertaken. Since institutional studies are necessarily long-term affairs, significant conclusions are not to be expected in the near future.

Pros and Cons

In the current debate about academic tenure, old arguments have been repeated, earlier arguments have been adapted to new contexts, and new arguments have emerged from concerns not central in earlier periods of crisis in the history of tenure. It may be well to list here the major lines of argument for and against tenure.

The following arguments are frequently made against tenure:

1. Since academic freedom must be assured to all teachers, even if they do not have tenure, academic tenure cannot be essential to academic freedom; what is essential is academic due process. Tenure is merely a "condition of employment," one among several that might be used.

2. Tenure imposes an inflexible financial burden upon institu-

tions; in times of financial stringency like the present, that burden may become intolerable.

3. The tenure system, especially in times of financial crisis, diminishes the institution's opportunity to recruit and retain younger faculty. In this respect, the system operates to the disadvantage of new entrants into the profession and makes it especially difficult to expand the representation of women and members of minority groups in faculties.

4. The tenure system leads to diminished emphasis on quality undergraduate teaching, because tenured professors prefer to concentrate on advanced and graduate education and on their own research and because, in the bestowal of tenure, research accomplishment is more easily measured than good teaching. The professional reward system, in the tenure context, thus fails to serve institutional and social needs.

5. The tenure system encourages the perpetuation of established departments, disciplinary specialties, and schools of thought within departments; it tends to exclude new approaches and subject matter in higher education.

6. Tenure, by ensuring permanence of appointment, diminishes accountability, fosters mediocrity and "deadwood," and makes it excessively difficult for an institution to rid itself of an incompetent or irresponsible professor.

7. The tenure system forces an institution to make permanent appointments before it has had adequate time to assess an individual's competence; conversely, it puts the young faculty member under undue pressure to demonstrate his qualifications in too brief a period of time.

8. Tenure plans encourage controversy and litigation about nonrenewal of probationary contracts and denial of tenure; such contests are becoming increasingly common.

9. The tenure system provides a cloak under which irresponsible political activity, often encouraging or supporting campus disruption, can be carried out.

10. Tenure commits the institution to the individual but not the individual to the institution; tenured professors are free to leave for a better job elsewhere, regardless of how damaging their departure may be to the institution.

11. The tenure system, by concentrating power in the hands of professors on permanent appointments, diminishes the role of students and younger faculty in college and university affairs.

In addition, certain advantages alleged for contract systems are used in the arguments against tenure:

1. The contract commits the faculty member to the institution for the period of his contract and thus eliminates what is alleged to be the "one-way-street" aspect of tenure, which allows the faculty member to leave the institution whenever he wants to.

2. Potential nonrenewal of contracts provides an incentive to good performance and thus eliminates "deadwood."

3. Contracts permit greater flexibility in institutional planning, budgeting, and program development by allowing expansion and contraction of the faculty to fit changed institutional circumstances, such as supply of students, interest in different programs, or available dollars.

4. Contract arrangements conduce to educational flexibility by enabling the institution to terminate the contracts of those who do not respond to current needs and to appoint those others who do.

The following arguments are commonly made in support of tenure:

1. Tenure is an essential condition of academic freedom: it assures the teacher that his professional findings or utterances will not be circumscribed or directed by outside pressures, which could otherwise cost him his position; and it assures students and the public, who support and rely upon the teacher's professional integrity, that the teacher's statements are influenced only by his best professional judgment and not by fear of losing his job.

2. Academic tenure creates an atmosphere favorable to academic freedom for all—the nontenured as well as the tenured—because the tenured faculty form an independent body capable of vigilant action to protect the freedom of their nontenured colleagues. The fact that probationary faculty members have academic freedom without tenure does not prove that tenure is irrelevant to academic freedom.

3. Academic tenure, by creating a faculty with a strong long-term commitment to the institution, contributes to institutional stability

and esprit. It thus promotes collegiality, joint responsibility for professional and institutional standards, and effective institutional governance.

4. Tenure assures that judgments of professional fitness will be made on professional grounds and not on grounds of competitive personal advantage.

5. By forcing institutions at a definite time to decide on whom to confer tenure and whom to let go, the tenure system helps institutions avoid continuing on their faculties those who are agreeable but not outstanding and whose term appointments might otherwise be renewed regularly out of generosity, friendship, or neglect.

6. Tenure is an important means of attracting men and women of ability into the teaching profession; by minimizing competitive economic incentives, it encourages teachers to concentrate on their basic obligations to their students and their disciplines.

7. Tenure has an economic value that helps offset the generally lower financial rewards of higher education, thus enabling institutions to compete for professional talent—especially in such fields as law and medicine, which have highly developed markets outside the colleges and universities.

Moreover, certain questions or doubts about contract systems imply advantages for tenure:

1. In contract systems, faculty members on temporary contracts recommend each other for reappointment or for nonrenewal. Two tendencies seem likely, both dangerous to standards and quality. Faculty members may vote for each other in the hope of improving their chances for reciprocal favor when it is their turn to be considered. Or they might vote against each other in the hope of diminishing future competition. Good academic practice has always prohibited probationary faculty members from voting on each other's reappointment or advancement to tenure. The dangers this tradition seeks to avoid might become in contract operations a constant condition and might lead to mutually supportive mediocrity on the one hand or to factionalism on the other.

2. With personnel decisions thus exposed to the constant pressures of self-interest, it seems likely that the substantive role of administrative officers will increase and that of the faculty will decrease. Perhaps that is why contract arrangements are appealing to many

administrators. But a faculty reduced to dependence and docility can scarcely be relied upon to perform higher education's vital tasks; administrative judgment on questions of professional competence is not invariably good; and a deepening of faculty-administration distrust and polarization should be avoided, not encouraged.

3. Prolonged exposure to the uncertainties of contract renewal and all that goes with it seems likely to have damaging effects on faculty morale and performance. The commission's investigations have confirmed what common sense suggests—probationary periods create anxiety. One virtue, and not a small one, of the tenure system is that the time of anxiety is of determinate length; at last a final decision is made. But under a contract system the probationary period is permanent. The human costs of such an arrangement are incalculable. They are not likely to be borne by academics. Increasingly in our society means are being found and enforced to reduce individual exposure to the hazards of job termination. Faculty unionization is increasing rapidly, and it would be naïve to suppose that faculties will long accept the uncertainties of regular contract review without seeking the protection of collective bargaining. The drive for job security will surely lead to virtual tenure, based on seniority or some like principle, or to some system similar to civil service.

4. It is not reasonable to believe that contract arrangements can be expected, in and of themselves, to produce better teaching or greater devotion to it. Much is made of periodic reviews and evaluations; but who is to make them, using what criteria, enforced through what principles of legitimacy? (These questions must of course also be asked about tenure plans, and the commission in later sections makes proposals designed to help answer them effectively.) There will be good teachers, as well as poor teachers, under the contract system or any other system; some will get better and some will get worse. But the problems of definition and measurement of good teaching will remain to be solved, as will the question of fair procedure. Moreover, when teachers must always think about getting a new job somewhere else, will they not tend to concentrate a good deal of their time and energy on things that will enhance their prospects outside the institution? What reason is there to suppose that everyone under contract arrangements will automatically devote himself wholeheartedly to the institution and his students? One of the great problems in higher

education generally is the tug between outside interests, on the one hand, and commitment and performance within the institution on the other. This problem, it is reasonable to predict, may be exacerbated and made permanent under contract conditions, particularly when market conditions are poor for faculty, and especially for those most able in their disciplines.

5. Contract arrangements do not necessarily conduce to innovation. The question is, of course, what sort of innovation, for what ends, as determined by whom? These questions are not often asked or answered. Too often, innovation is not satisfactorily distinguished from mere novelty; and the immensely complex problems of institutional stability and change, of continuity and renewal, are pushed aside. But these are problems with which any personnel system must deal, and there is no evidence that valuable innovations in education are most likely to come from those whose positions in the institution are in jeopardy. Indeed, the Harvard Committee on Governance came to precisely the opposite conclusion after examining the history of "intellectual and curricular innovation" at Harvard:

> *It is observably the case that most of the major experimental changes in Harvard education—the "case system" at the law and business schools; the interdisciplinary programs such as comparative literature and American civilization in the Graduate School of Arts and Sciences; and a long series of developments in the colleges, from the creation (in the waning years of the Eliot elective system) of history and literature as an undergraduate interdisciplinary honors concentration to the formulation and launching of general education—have derived from the thinking, the time and the energies of tenured faculty members.*[5]

6. As to flexibility in institutional arrangements, especially in budget matters, faculty contracts would seem to offer hope to the institution struggling to meet its commitments with limited and perhaps diminishing resources. But questions of fair procedure have to be solved if legal action is to be avoided, and choices have to be made among those whose contracts might be terminated for financial reasons.

---

[5] *Discussion Memorandum on Academic Tenure at Harvard University* (Cambridge, Mass., 1971), p. 17; italics in the original.

Seniority is likely to play a major role in these determinations, just as tenure status does in cases of financial exigency in other institutions. Financial exigency, if it is to be dealt with in a fair manner, presents about the same problems in either system. Of course, if "flexibility" means greater opportunity for arbitrary action, then the advantage claimed for contracts may rather be a danger both to the individual and the institution.

7. Finally, the assumption that in contract systems academic freedom is assured for all through due-process procedures is simply not proven. The absence in most of the institutions of any procedures for appeal in nonrenewal cases suggests indeed that due-process procedures do not in fact exist and that academic freedom is not adequately protected.

These are only the most important of the arguments pro and con, or those that have figured most prominently in recent discussions. As Chapter Three makes clear, most of the arguments have appeared in earlier debates. Indeed, the most detailed and cogent presentation of arguments against academic tenure is to be found in Fritz Machlup's 1964 presidential address to the AAUP, "In Defense of Academic Tenure." A few of the arguments against tenure are new; of particular force today is the argument, new to discussions of tenure, that the tenure system tends, under conditions likely to prevail for the next decade or so, to limit opportunities for women and members of minority groups to enter and advance in the academic profession, thereby frustrating institutional purposes and national social policy. But just as this new argument springs from a changed social context, so the more traditional criticisms of academic tenure have acquired new significance or new force as a result of the enormous changes in American higher education since World War II, and especially in the decade of the 1960s, and a new urgency because of the outlook for higher education in the 1970s and 1980s.

Some of the criticisms of tenure are valid, as knowledgeable and candid proponents of tenure have always admitted. No system involving the judgment of persons can ever be foolproof; tenure decisions have on occasion been wrong and will continue to be. People change as they grow older; the powers and energies of some will decline, and some will decide to coast and take it easy. Institutions wishing to upgrade themselves have in fact found their efforts impeded by the presence of certain tenured faculty members, who were perhaps competent enough by the earlier standards but mediocre by the new. Though it is too much to hope that such problems as these can be completely solved, they can be ameliorated, and several of the commission's recommendations are designed with this in mind.

In the judgment of this commission, the weaknesses that have brought academic tenure under needed scrutiny are not imperfections in the concept itself but serious deficiencies in its application and administration—deficiencies resulting in large measure from fundamental changes in American education during the last two decades. These deficiencies, we are convinced, are remediable, by reform in institutional policy and practice and professional standards and priorities. Our recommendations (see Chapter Two) are intended to promote such reform. Since tenure is central in academic practice, improvement must be sought in all sectors that influence our colleges and universities. Our recommendations are therefore directed to faculties, administrators, members of governing boards, students, legislators, professional and educational associations, government agencies, and collective bargaining groups. Since colleges and universities are social institutions, reform must have a broad social base. But the fundamental task of improving the tenure system must be carried out within individual institutions and, basically, by faculties themselves, in a new effort to express the radical purpose of tenure: to create the most favorable institutional setting for professional teaching and scholarship, in freedom and responsibility.

II

Academic Tenure
Tomorrow

Academic tenure is fundamental in the personnel policies of most American colleges and universities today. In the judgment of this commission, it should continue to be the characteristic form for organizing professional teaching and scholarly service in American higher education. The commission affirms its conviction that academic tenure, rightly understood and properly administered, provides the most reliable means of assuring faculty quality and educational excellence, as well as the best guarantee of academic freedom. So central is academic freedom to the integrity of our educational institutions—and to their effectiveness in the discovery of new knowledge, in conservation of the values and wisdom of the past, and in the promotion of critical inquiry essential to self-renewal—that academic

21

tenure should be retained as our most tested and reliable instrument for incorporating academic freedom into the heart of our institutions. The commission urges institutions with tenure plans to retain them and to work toward necessary improvements. It urges institutions that may be considering the abandonment of tenure to consider carefully the long-run consequences of such a step. And it invites institutions without tenure plans to consider whether their full development as centers of academic excellence would not be promoted by the adoption of a strong and reliable tenure system.

Many of the grave problems that have beset American higher education in recent years are bound up, as we have seen, with deeper changes in higher education itself and in the relations between education and society. These problems—for example, the relative priority to be given to graduate and professional education on the one hand and the education of undergraduates on the other—cannot be resolved by any such simple change in academic personnel practice as the modification or abolition of tenure. Problems of this order will yield, if they yield at all, only to more thoughtful analysis, broader social consensus, and greater diversification and quality of educational effort.

But some deficiencies in our system of higher education *are* associated with tenure. The question of the priority to be accorded graduate versus undergraduate education admittedly requires a deep analysis of our purposes as a society; nevertheless, the tenure system as it operates in too many institutions makes progress toward that analysis more difficult. For there is a characteristic bias in tenure operations, whereby the more advanced forms of education are deemed superior and deserving of special consideration in the personnel-selection process. But here—and examples can easily be multiplied—it is not the principle of tenure that produces the difficulty. There is nothing inherent in the concept of tenure that necessitates this result. The broad biasing effect arises from many causes. One of the most important causes is the much heavier federal support since World War II for graduate and professional training than for undergraduate education. Tenure, in this context, incorporates certain educational responses to these causal factors and tends to give them more enduring effect.

In the judgment of this commission, therefore, the problems with which tenure is clearly implicated arise not from anything in the principle of tenure itself but from deficiencies in the operation of the tenure system in individual institutions. The commission believes that a strong commitment to making tenure work, combined with measures to improve its operation in different institutional settings, can reduce many of the deficiencies that critics of tenure have noted. A simple reaffirmation of the value of tenure, however, will not do. For many institutions, a fundamental rethinking of personnel policies and the criteria and procedures for their application will be necessary. The principle of tenure itself will not long survive unless reform of its abuses and elimination of weaknesses in its operation are vigorously pursued —with the faculty, which has the most at stake, taking the lead.

On the other hand, the commission sees no ground for believing that the alternatives to tenure that are now in use or that have been proposed can deal more effectively with these problems than would a strengthened and renewed system of tenure. And we are convinced that no alternative that has been proposed will eliminate the deficiencies identified in the operation of the tenure system, will not involve new and serious problems of other kinds, and can be relied upon to protect academic freedom and the continued integrity of institutions of higher education.

1. The commission recommends that academic tenure, as defined in this report, be recognized, because of its positive value in maintaining both academic freedom and the quality of faculty, as fundamental in the organization of faculty service in American higher education.

The commission urges all institutions to take prompt and vigorous measures to improve the operation of present tenure plans in order to correct deficiencies which have become increasingly apparent in recent years and thus to strengthen academic tenure for the future.

The detailed recommendations that follow are intended to assist institutions in their efforts to develop better academic personnel practices. The commission's proposals advocate (a) new emphasis on institutional responsibility, (b) attention to some neglected elements of an effective tenure system, (c) recognition of tenure problems as related to the professional development of the faculty, (d) specific means of strengthening institutional tenure plans in normal operations, (e) consideration of a number of special problems of current concern, and

(f) measures for needed information and research to assist colleges and universities in improving and maintaining effective faculty personnel programs.

Institutional Responsibility

If the tenure system is to be strengthened, the major responsibility rests with each college or university itself. Procedural standards and general guidelines for good institutional practice are available. The urgent task is for individual institutions to improve the internal administration of faculty personnel programs. It is here that substantive decisions are made; it is here, therefore, that improvements in personnel practices can be achieved or that present deficiencies will be perpetuated. Improvements will require a clearer definition of the respective roles and responsibilities of faculty, students, administration, and governing boards, a more vigorous acceptance of these responsibilities, and a new level of cooperation in fulfilling them. On the other hand, institutions will be able to reform their own policies and practices and discharge their full responsibility for the effectiveness of personnel programs only if such external agencies as legislatures and courts afford them the necessary scope.

Faculty. In the academic profession, as in other professions, it is the professionals (the faculty, led by its tenured members) who decide on admission to the profession, on fitness to continue, and on advancement through the professional reward system. Within the institution the faculty, acting directly or through its representatives, makes the crucial decisions or recommendations concerning appointment, reappointment, and award of tenure, and concerning salaries, promotions, and other emoluments. This is the prevailing situation in higher education, even though legal authority is exercised by governing boards, usually on the basis of recommendations by college and university presidents.

Since faculties make the basic personnel decisions, improvement in faculty personnel programs, and particularly in the tenure system, depends essentially on improvement of faculty decision-making performance. The commission's recommendations are largely directed to establishing institutional conditions conducive to responsible faculty decisions, and to helping faculties recognize the importance of their personnel decisions for the institution as a whole and for the future of the academic profession.

2. The commission recommends that the faculty of each institution, as its professional center, play a major role in developing the institution's tenure policies by recommending them for administrative review and adoption by the governing board and by keeping them under continuing scrutiny. The institution's procedures for implementing tenure policies should place primary responsibility upon the faculty for substantive decisions in all individual cases of appointment, reappointment, award of tenure, review and appeal, and application of sanctions. In fulfilling its central responsibility in personnel matters, the faculty should be guided by the highest professional standards and by an informed and objective sense of the mission and needs of the institution.

Probationary Faculty. Academic personnel decisions, especially those involving promotion and the award of tenure, have traditionally been primarily the responsibility of the tenured faculty. The commission recommends no fundamental change in this practice, which is consonant with the general scheme of organization in institutions operating under tenure plans and with the basic theory of the profession. The commission, then, fully recognizes and endorses the commonly accepted principle that nontenured faculty in competition for a limited number of tenure appointments should be disqualified on grounds of interest from formal participation in the decisional process.

Members of the faculty on probationary appointments have of course played an important role, sometimes a formal one, in recruitment and initial appointment of junior faculty members. Some department chairmen and departmental personnel committees have developed informal methods of securing the views of the nontenured staff on reappointment and tenure decisions affecting their peers. But the opinions of probationary faculty members are too often unsought or are secured and utilized in ways that are likely to diminish their value. That value can be very high; for members of the probationary faculty, working closely together, have opportunities to assess each other's work often not available to the tenured faculty, and their perspectives on educational and personnel questions can provide a valuable supplement or corrective to the views of the senior staff. The probationary faculty usually agree on who are the superior teachers, the most original scholars, the most stimulating colleagues among their number, and they are usually very keen in identifying time-servers, attractive mediocrities, and mere opportunists.

3. The commission urges institutions to develop methods of consulting nontenured members of the faculty in connection with decisions on reappointment and bestowal of tenure, and of reflecting in the ultimate recommendations the opinions of nontenured faculty.

Students. Concerning the proper role of students in faculty personnel decisions there are of course sharp differences of opinion among faculty members. Nearly 60 percent of faculty members believe that promotion should be based in part on formal student evaluations of their teachers; only 20 percent, however, favor giving students a formal role in the decision process, while 25 percent favor informal consultation and 54 percent believe that students should have a minor role or none at all (see Chapter Seven, Table 8).

The commission believes that students have a contribution of potentially great importance to make to the personnel process, one that could provide values and information not so readily available from any other source and that could contribute significantly to the students' own understanding of the educational process and the nature of educational institutions.

In addition to their role in helping to develop and execute a program for the evaluation of teaching, students can assist in the personnel process in two distinct ways, which need to be considered separately because the arrangements for student participation in them may well differ. One is in the development of institutional policies and criteria for appointment, promotion, and the award of tenure. The other is in decisions in individual cases. Students can and should have a role in both situations; it would seem artificial and futile to involve students in the formulation of policies and criteria and then deny them any role whatsoever in the consideration of specific cases. But full and formal participation may be more appropriate or easier to arrange in the former than in the latter, depending on the institution's own character and traditions. Nevertheless, the commission believes that the student contribution to the effectiveness of the personnel program should be expanded and given greater weight.

4. The commission recommends that students should participate in a serious and significant way in developing and reviewing institutional tenure policies, including the development of criteria for appointment and the award of tenure and of methods by which teaching effectiveness is to be assessed.

The commission recommends that students should have a participant but not a controlling role in making recommendations concerning initial appointment, reappointment, and the award of tenure.

Administration. Though there is much confusion and controversy about the proper role of administrative officers in faculty personnel decisions, their fundamental responsibilities certainly include these: ensuring that the faculty does in fact fulfill its professional responsibility in personnel decisions, including initiative in review and revision of criteria and procedures; ensuring that appropriate and comprehensive personnel policies are developed and securing their approval by the governing boards; ensuring compliance with institutional policies and standards; providing leadership in promoting changes in personnel policies as new circumstances require them; informing board, faculty, and students about current personnel operations and longer-term prospects; ensuring that a faculty staffing plan is developed, adhered to, and kept up to date.

In too many institutions administrative officers—deans, academic vice-presidents, presidents—perform what should be essentially a faculty role in personnel matters, especially in the award of tenure. Promotion and tenure decisions are often made by administrators with little or no consultation with faculty, except for the department chairman. This practice has two grave perils. On the one hand, decisions made in this way are not likely to be professionally sound: few administrators, however expert they may be in their own disciplines, possess the competence for sound individual decisions in the many fields taught in a modern college or university. On the other hand, this practice permits or requires the faculty to abrogate its own responsibility for making professional decisions; the result is a faculty whose only stake in the tenure process is the individual security of its members. Such a faculty does not see itself as custodian of professional values and standards in the institution and therefore does not bend its efforts to making the system work. And the process is self-reinforcing. In difficult cases, faculties or chairmen often shift the burden to the dean or vice-president, relying on him to bail them out of decisions that were faulty in the first place. Administrators, after a certain amount of this, come to mistrust faculty judgment or courage and increasingly make substantive decisions themselves; in time the faculty role is attenuated to grumbling about administrative intervention. The question is not so much one of technical authority and power, but of the proper definition of the respective responsibilities of the several elements in the academic community.

5. *The commission recommends that, in strengthening institutional operations, administrative officers emphasize their role in ensuring that a formal personnel policy, appropriate to the institution's own objectives, is developed and kept under review; in securing full compliance with the institution's standards and procedures in all personnel recommendations that come before them for review; in promoting the participation of students and junior faculty in the personnel process; in establishing a faculty development program and resources for its implementation; in stimulating fresh thought in the institution on faculty personnel matters; and in protecting academic freedom. Administrative officers should give special attention to ways in which faculties can be brought to discharge their full responsibility for the achievement and maintenance of high professional standards in all personnel decisions.*

Governing Boards. It is sometimes said that the most important decision a governing board ever makes is the selection of a president. So far as the board's substantive decision making is concerned, this may well be true. But the board's actions in faculty personnel matters, and especially in tenure questions, may well have, in sum, more enduring impact upon the institution.

The distinction between the de jure and de facto distribution of authority in American institutions of higher education is nowhere more evident than in the role of the governing board in faculty appointment and promotion. Though governing boards have the sole legal power to make appointments and confer tenure, they normally devolve that power upon the president and faculty, retaining only the formal exercise of authority and intervening in a substantial way only in crises. This distribution of real authority is fundamental: it is the only secure basis on which, according to the distinctive American practice, genuine professional standards can be maintained in institutions under lay control. In no well-administered college or university would a governing board substitute its own judgment in particular cases for that of the faculty and administration, any more than a lay board of a well-administered hospital would select a new chief of medicine except upon the recommendation of its professional director and staff.

But this necessary feature of American institutions of higher education has produced problems in practice. These problems are well symbolized by the fact, familiar to every administrator and board member, that at any board meeting the actions conferring tenure—and thereby defining the future of the institution's program and the long-term allocation of its resources—are customarily handled in a completely perfunctory way, virtually without discussion, in contrast to the length and intensity of debate devoted to such topics as the placement of a parking structure, the naming of a building, or the award of a construction contract. Boards of control often do not know or apparently care what the institution's personnel policies are or what their rationale is. They often have no means of knowing how policies are applied and what procedures have been used to ensure that the recommendations coming to them rest upon careful consideration and sound professional judgment. College and university administrators, to whom boards customarily and correctly entrust the supervision of the institution's personnel program, are often at fault here in failing to keep the board informed about personnel policies and their application, about the present and future status of staff plans, about the impact of new social imperatives and legislation. Not uncommonly this is because senior administrators have not themselves devoted the time and attention to personnel policies and their application to be able to explain them to their boards, or because of a desire to avoid board interference.

The result of all this is not simply the frustration often felt by board members at their remoteness from central concerns of the administration. More important, these conditions produce a tendency, when problems arise, for board members to take symptoms for causes. In relation to academic tenure, this tendency leads to calls for the abolition or attenuation of tenure as a means of giving new emphasis to undergraduate teaching, or appointing more women or blacks on the faculty, or getting rid of irresponsible professors. As a result, casual intervention in individual cases, producing conflict and danger to both academic freedom and board responsibility, becomes more probable.

Governing boards need not and must not usurp the responsibilities of faculty and administration in order to play a more vital role in strengthening institutional personnel programs.

6. *The commission believes that governing boards should insist upon the development of strong personnel policies and a staffing plan that will enable the institution to reach its objectives. They should require regular reports on the operation of the plan, including present and projected distribution of faculty by rank, age, sex, ethnic background, field of study, and the like. They should establish with the administration methods through which they can be kept informed of the manner in which the institution's tenure policies and criteria are embodied in particular personnel recommendations. They should ensure that personnel policies, especially as they affect tenure, are kept continuously under review and that needed revisions are brought promptly to the attention of the board.*

Institutions and State Systems. More and more states are moving to state-wide coordination or administration of higher education. The forms of organization above the level of the individual campus vary greatly. At one extreme there are loose coordinating boards which establish or recommend only the most general policies, leaving the several institutions largely free to direct their own affairs. At the other extreme are single boards of control having authority over several institutions, or several campuses of a single institution, or even all colleges and universities in a single state. Just as the patterns of organization vary, so does the resultant distribution of authority between the individual institution and the system-wide board or central administration.

This is not the place to review the complex reasons for the rapid development of these larger schemes of organization, to discuss their relative merits, or to appraise their effects. With respect to the specific question of tenure and to personnel policy generally, however, the commission believes that this trend in American education carries significant dangers and that steps must be taken to avoid them. Whatever their other virtues, all such system arrangements increase the bureaucratization of higher education, removing policy formulation and decision making to an ever greater distance from the individual faculty member. They add one or more additional layers of administration and control, making operations cumbersome, introducing delay, fragmenting responsibility, and creating new opportunities for replacing deliberation and decision with the circulation of memoranda and routine compliance reports between distant points. Many institutions are now much too large and heavily bureaucratized to permit personnel decisions to be carefully made and reviewed. Additional layers of administration are bound to make matters worse; for as lines of authority and responsibility get longer, they become weaker, and faculties themselves will lose the responsibility they must have if the tenure system is to work, or will feel less obligation to exercise the responsibility they have. Detailed system-wide personnel codes and criteria will surely lead to institutional homogenization and a lowering of quality.

This commission believes that where state-wide or multiunit operations are in effect, the principle of sound personnel policy should be to hold the role of the system's central administration to the minimum and to assign the maximum responsibility and authority for personnel policy and practices to the individual institution and to appropriate units within it.

7. *The commission recommends that where several institutions operate under a single governing or coordinating board and a central system administration, faculty personnel policies be stated in general terms, sufficient to achieve the minimum necessary system-wide uniformity, but giving the individual institutions in the system maximum latitude to adopt rules and procedures appropriate to their individual missions, traditions, and needs, and to bear the responsibility for the effectiveness of their personnel programs.*

The commission believes that academic tenure must rest upon a judgment of competence for permanent service in a particular institutional setting and that this judgment must be made by the faculty in relation to the institution's own program and aspirations; therefore, where "system" operations prevail, tenure should be held in the institution and not in the system as a whole.

8. *The commission recommends that in "system" or state-wide or multicampus operations, tenure should be explicitly granted in a particular institution and not in the system as a whole.*

Multiunit systems, it is said, permit more rational allocation of faculty and other resources among institutions and therefore allow specialization and concentration of programs, with the strengthening that may result from minimizing competition and eliminating mediocre programs. In pursuit of this goal, it may be desirable to transfer faculty among institutions. However, arrangements for program consolidation or termination and the resulting transfer of faculty should be made with great care, so that the interests of institution and faculty alike will be protected and so that institutional responsibility for tenure decisions will not be compromised.

9. To cover cases in which transfer of faculty from one institution to another may be desirable, the commission recommends that the system administration and the individual institutions develop procedures that will protect both the tenure and freedom of the faculty member, and which will permit the responsible exercise of professional evaluation and judgment by the faculty to which transfer is contemplated.

Institutions and the Courts. Cases arising from institutional decisions in faculty personnel matters have been taken to the courts in constantly increasing numbers during recent years. The courts have served as a necessary forum for resolution of fundamental problems relating to the rights and responsibilities of both faculty members and institutions, often putting academic practice on a new and sounder basis. But the amount of litigation about personnel decisions, and its rapid increase, is alarming. Even in a notably litigious era, marked by a heightened sensitivity to personal freedoms and new problems in balancing the claims of individuals with those of social and governmental institutions, the increase in court cases involving educational personnel issues is a symptom of a growing malaise in higher education. This is especially true with respect to the position of the nontenured faculty. A large number of recent court cases, including the Roth and Sindermann cases recently decided by the Supreme Court, have been brought by nontenured faculty alleging violation of constitutional guarantees in decisions affecting them. The number of these cases points to grave deficiencies in institutional policy or its application and to serious deterioration in the fabric of institutional personnel relations.

In the judgment of this commission, while legal action to protect individual, professional, and institutional interests may be essential as a last resort, regular recourse to the courts testifies to the absence or failure of institutional and professional standards and procedures. Frequent resort to court determination of personnel questions will surely erode institutional and faculty autonomy, thus jeopardizing the ability of faculties and institutions to govern themselves in the interest of their students and society generally. We believe that institutions must work to secure and maintain the environment essential to their own effectiveness. They must take positive measures to realize their own futures, rather than allowing them to be determined by default, through external processes that are bound to be slow, costly, unpredictable, and above all inappropriate to the unique function of colleges and universities in our society.

10. The commission urges colleges and universities to develop their own internal policies and procedures for dealing fairly and effectively with faculty personnel problems (such as nonrenewal of probationary appointments, denial of tenure, and dismissal), so as to minimize reliance on the courts.

On the other hand, the entire higher education community, while accepting its responsibility for so conducting its affairs as to make reliance on the courts necessary only in the most unusual or intractable cases, has an obligation to press for self-restraint on the part of courts and other agencies. If institutions are to develop sound personnel programs, their responsibility must not be diminished or usurped by outside agencies. It would be a grave disservice to higher education if the courts were to impose rules that would replace internal institutional processes of professional judgment and decision. Apart from their indispensable role as final arbiter in individual cases, the courts can function most significantly in support of higher education by setting standards of reasonable procedure to which institutions must adhere.

The same principle applies to legislatures and to administrative and regulatory agencies, federal and state. Statutes and administrative rulings on faculty personnel matters are becoming ever more explicit and detailed. Such topics as the length of the probationary period, the professional qualifications for appointment and promotion, faculty workloads, sabbatical leave policy, appointment, renewal and nonrenewal procedures, and criteria for tenure have all been dealt with in specific detail in legislation proposed in state after state. In like manner, regulations of federal agencies in such matters as the representation of women on college and university faculties have taken forms which appear to many to infringe upon institutional autonomy. No doubt much of this is in response to the conviction that institutions cannot be depended upon to manage their own affairs or to their laggard or reluctant answers to urgent social problems. But a permanent answer to these problems, consistent with the crucial role colleges and universities are expected to play in our society, will surely not be found by shifting responsibility for basic personnel policy decisions away from the colleges and universities. That will lead only to further weakness, further erosion of institutional vigor, and further loss of independence. The best role for legislative bodies and administrative agencies is to set broad objectives and standards of institutional performance and allow the maximum latitude to institutions to develop their own methods of achieving them.

11. The commission urges the higher education community, including national associations, to call vigorously to the attention of courts, legislatures, and administrative agencies the importance, in dealing with academic personnel matters, of preserving for institutions of higher education and their faculties a specific zone of responsibility and authority for policy decision, as being essential for their proper functioning in the service of society.

Neglected Elements of an Effective Tenure System

Teaching Effectiveness. Writing in 1966 on "The Professor and His Roles," Logan Wilson remarked, "There is a rising tide of grumbling everywhere, and especially in the larger universities, about the lack of attention to effective teaching and the absence of systematic means of teacher improvement."[1] The observation, though not new in 1966, is even more true today; the tide of grumbling has become a flood of loud complaint.

The commission is not persuaded that the quality of teaching in American colleges and universities is generally inferior, and it has found no evidence that tenured teachers are less effective than those without tenure. In discussions of the problem, *teaching effectiveness* is often ill defined; complaints frequently assume a particular view of

[1] In C. B. T. Lee (Ed.), *Improving College Teaching* (Washington, D.C.: American Council on Education, 1967), p. 104.

the "best" teaching style, or involve a judgment about the relative value of graduate versus undergraduate teaching, or assume that effectiveness in teaching is to be judged only by classroom performance.

Nonetheless, the commission is persuaded that though all institutions insist upon evidence of teaching ability as a condition of reappointment, tenure, and subsequent rewards, and most assert that teaching is the most important criterion in personnel decisions (see Chapter Seven, Table 8), few institutions have developed reliable methods to evaluate teaching ability and to promote its improvement. As a result, other criteria predominate in personnel decisions. This is injurious to students, to faculty development, and to the success of the institution's program. It is demoralizing to junior faculty members, many of whom believe that, whatever the institution's official proclamations may be, teaching ability is not in fact held in high esteem and is not given as much weight as other factors in appointment and promotion decisions. Many young teachers, therefore, become cynical about the profession and divert their energies, in self-protection, away from teaching and their responsibility to their students. In addition, the lack of reliable methods of evaluating and improving teaching permits some tenured faculty to decline in teaching skill, to fail in adapting their techniques to new generations of students, and to escape the consequences of their deficiencies as teachers when it comes to salary increases, further promotion, and other rewards.

General and permanent changes in this situation are largely beyond the power of individual institutions, nor could they be brought about simply by abolishing the tenure system. The "academic revolution," as Riesman and Jencks have aptly named it, has proceeded too far for that. A new commitment to high-quality teaching will require fundamental changes in graduate school programs, reform in federal program priorities, and an enhanced firmness of institutional purpose, to name but a few of the more basic conditions. But institutions can do much more than they are now doing to improve teaching and to give greater recognition to it in the faculty development and evaluation process. And if national professional associations would provide more stimulation and assistance, institutions could do still more.

Kenneth Eble's appraisal of the situation is sound:

The profession has argued for years that it cannot very precisely reward or even stimulate effective teaching without knowing what effective teaching is. Lacking that knowledge, it cannot very well identify good prospective teachers or attract them into the profession or help develop teaching skills. But we are not that short of useful information about teaching effectiveness, and the widespread use of student evaluations is generating more. We have little to lose in putting that information to work in examining what the teacher does and how what he does might be done better.[2]

This is not the place for a review of research on the improvement and evaluation of college and university teaching. The literature is vast and growing rapidly. An excellent review of the literature has recently been provided by Jerry G. Gaff and Robert C. Wilson.[3]

12. The commission recommends that each institution develop methods of evaluating the teaching effectiveness of both its nontenured and its tenured faculty, and procedures for reflecting these evaluations in pertinent personnel actions.

The commission recommends that professional associations continue and expand their efforts to improve college teaching, especially at the undergraduate level, and to develop more reliable methods for its evaluation, and urges them to disseminate the results of these studies to faculty members and institutions.

Role of Students in Assessment of Teaching. In the judgment of this commission, student opinions about the quality of the teaching they receive can be of great value. Specifically, they can help the institution reach sound personnel decisions and carry out an effective career-development program. Student assessment of teaching has been undertaken in a serious and often sophisticated way on many campuses, and the general trend is toward even greater use of student opinion.

[2] K. E. Eble, *The Recognition and Evaluation of Teaching* (Salt Lake City: Project to Improve College Teaching, 1970), p. 20.

[3] "The Teaching Environment," *AAUP Bulletin,* 1971, 57, 475–493. In addition, three publications by K. E. Eble resulted from his work as director of the Project to Improve College Teaching, jointly sponsored during 1969–71 by the Association of American Colleges and the American Association of University Professors. These are *The Recognition and Evaluation of Teaching* (1970), *Career Development of the Effective College Teacher* (1971), and *Professors as Teachers* (1972).

But student evaluation of teaching has not yet been fully utilized as a significant resource for the improvement of the educational process and as an important ingredient in personnel decisions.

Student ratings of courses and teachers have always been made. An informal network for circulating such information is a constant and influential element in the educational process; more formal student-organized course-evaluation books, often containing extremely penetrating observations, have achieved great popularity among students. Personnel decisions have generally included some reference to student opinions and attitudes, but on the whole, at least until recent years, they were gathered in a haphazard and probably unreliable manner.

Even now, in institutions that have adopted more formal and systematic methods for collecting student opinions about teaching effectiveness, it is not clear that student evaluations are taken seriously when personnel decisions are made. The reason is, in part, that dependable, generally accepted methods of student evaluation have not been achieved. The commission found a widespread suspicion among students and younger faculty members that their institutions—although they profess to attach great importance to student opinion about teaching and devise elaborate, sometimes overelaborate, systems for registering it—largely disregard student opinion in the decision-making process. The problem is therefore not just one of developing reliable instruments for gathering student opinion about teaching, difficult as that may be. It is also one of changing faculty attitudes and habits to ensure that their decisions reflect, to whatever degree is appropriate in each individual case, the weight of that opinion. And if the evaluation is to work in the long run and not be just a passing device for minimizing campus tensions, ways will have to be found to enable students to see that their views are not only sought but are taken seriously.

Obviously students should not expect a perfect correlation between their assessment of teachers and the outcome of personnel decisions affecting them. Many other criteria will be at work. Even with respect to teaching effectiveness, student opinion provides only one of several bases for judgment. If a teacher consistently given superior ratings by students is not reappointed or awarded tenure, or if a teacher rated only average or marginal is reappointed or promoted, there should be countervailing factors shaping the decision. These factors, and the rationale for the weight given them, ought to be explicable to students. But if a pattern emerges in which student opinion consistently runs one way and actual decisions another, there is reason to conclude either that the student evaluation is regarded as unreliable or that student opinion of teaching effectiveness is not in fact being taken seriously. In either case, correction needs to be made.

Faculty cooperation in developing and administering a student evaluation program and in using it seriously will be easier to achieve if the evaluation techniques are simple and if procedural requirements are minimized. There is a proper skepticism about the statistical refinement of some evaluation techniques, and proper doubt of the value of ratings expressed in numbers carried to two or three decimal places. The teaching process does not lend itself to that sort of quantification, and faculties are not likely to take seriously any procedure that offers a specious exactitude. Due allowance must be made for different sorts of teaching situations and for the necessities imposed by different subjects. The important parts of the teaching process that do not occur in the classroom—course planning, preparation of study materials, development of assignments, examinations—must not be neglected in evaluation, though here student opinion may be less relevant or less reliable. Efforts should also be made to get follow-up evaluations by students some time after they have had a particular course or teacher, when they have a different perspective and a broader base for evaluation.

13. The commission recommends that institutional procedures for the assessment of teaching effectiveness include an explicit and formal role for students. There should be a systematic arrangement for the periodic collection and evaluation of student opinions of the teaching effectiveness of every faculty member. Taking into account necessary variations for specific programs and teaching situations, the evaluation procedure should be as far as possible consistent throughout the institution. The institution should regard student evaluation of teaching as having a high priority and should commit energy and funds to the development and improvement of its techniques for student evaluation.

If student evaluation is to be useful, each institution must develop means to ensure that student opinion of teaching effectiveness is in fact consistently given serious weight in decisions about reappointment, nonreappointment, the award of tenure, and subsequent person-

nel actions. Each institution should evolve ways to enable students to see that their assessments have indeed been taken into account.

Evaluation of Scholarship and Research. Every member of the academic profession must have scholarly, research, or creative ability, in some degree, if knowledge is to progress and if instruction is not to become merely the transmission of accepted doctrine or technique. Depending on their particular missions, institutions will continue to vary enormously in the weight they assign to scholarly or research ability in the selection and advancement of their faculties. But even institutions committed wholly to relatively elementary teaching will prefer to have faculties whose scholarly qualifications and interests, if they do not prompt them to make original contributions of their own, will enable them to approach their subjects in a scholarly manner, to make reliable assessments of developments in the fields in which they teach, and to inculcate a spirit of inquiry in their students.

With respect to the evaluation of scholarly, research, or creative ability, the commission's investigations have identified these major concerns:

1. Evaluation too often stresses quantity rather than quality. Review committees are impressed by the number of publications rather than by their significance. Extrinsic signs such as the general reputation of journals or publishers are often substituted for a positive assessment of the work itself. Nontenured members of faculties, believing that largely quantitative tests of publication prevail, lose confidence in the evaluation process and are often prompted to undertake quick projects that will expand their bibliographies, rather than to work on more difficult or more long-term problems.

2. In fields such as the drama, creative writing, and musical composition, where the modes of "publication" are essentially different from those in other disciplines, appropriate differential standards for judging the practitioner's qualifications are inherently difficult to develop, and the attempt is frequently not made. Probationary faculty in these fields often feel themselves at a severe disadvantage, believing that members of personnel committees drawn from other disciplines apply largely irrelevant criteria to their work. Similar problems arise in such fields as nursing and social work, architecture and engineering, where professional performance is crucial.

3. Faculty appointive bodies frequently assess scholarly or

research competence merely in terms of the current standards of the discipline at large (sometimes, indeed, the standards of the discipline at an earlier time), without giving serious attention to the specific needs and objectives of the institution. In some institutions, broad scholarly competence may be more important than highly specialized ability; emergent fields or emphases may require special support; replacement of a specialist in a given field may be unwise in light of the institution's changed priorities; appointment or promotion in a given area, even if it conforms to new developments in a discipline, may unbalance the educational program or imply additional commitments the institution is not prepared to make. Standards and emphases current in the discipline at large must be modulated in personnel actions to take account of specific institutional goals for the future.

14. The commission recommends that faculties develop more sophisticated and reliable methods of judging scholarly competence and promise. There is widespread concern that the evaluation of scholarship too often stresses quantity rather than quality, by mere counting of titles or reliance upon the general reputation of journals or publishers. Evaluation by qualified scholars in pertinent disciplines, both within and outside the institution, should be sought. The weight to be given to scholarship in particular instances should be related to the institution's own objectives and needs, and should not simply be based on conceptions generally prevalent in the discipline.

Academic Citizenship. The criteria for the award of tenure have customarily included, in addition to teaching and research, a category of "service," variously defined and evaluated. Account is often taken of valuable professional service outside the institution, such as counsel to community agencies and groups, membership in professional organizations, or assistance to government. Even more often, evaluation of the candidate for tenure includes consideration of his service to the institution itself, above and beyond his normal teaching and research responsibilities. Too often such institutional service is defined, by formal policy or in the practice of appointive bodies, in relatively trivial terms. The number of committees on which a candidate has served or his willingness to accept more than his share of departmental administrative work is sometimes given too much weight, perhaps obscuring a lack of distinction or promise in the more exacting tasks of teaching and scholarship. Vague terms such as "colleagueship" or "cooperativeness," important as these concepts may be if given serious professional content, are sometimes employed to reward the agreeable mediocrity and to exclude the more distinctive teacher-scholar.

If criteria for appraising an individual's present and future capacity for service to the institution are pitched at such a low level, the full measure of faculty contribution to the life of the institution will not be reflected in the appointment and promotion process. A college or university is neither a mere collectivity of teachers and scholars nor an assortment of committee members and would-be administrators. Full academic citizenship includes the individual's capacity for stimulating colleagues and students beyond the confines of classroom and laboratory, his ability to initiate and assist in the development of new educational programs, his capacity for serious and responsible participation in institutional governance. Evidences of academic citizenship of this sort should be sought by those responsible for recommendations on tenure. The probationary period should be organized in such a way as to give the faculty member opportunities to develop and manifest these broader qualifications.

15. The commission recommends that the positive attributes of academic citizenship be given significant weight in tenure decisions and that institutions define academic citizenship in terms which emphasize contribution to the institution as an environment for learning rather than mere proficiency in administrative service.

Faculty Responsibility and Codes of Conduct. The opinion is widespread that college and university faculties have not acted vigorously enough to discipline their own members for breaches of proper academic conduct. Some attacks upon academic tenure have been based upon the allegation that tenured members have themselves been guilty of serious offenses against standards of professional conduct or have been unwilling to take effective action to discipline colleagues who have.

The academic profession, like every other, has properly relied upon individual commitment to professional standards, guided and supported by academic traditions and collegial interaction, as the principal means of maintaining good professional performance by its members. In addition, broad general standards have been developed for the guidance of individual faculty members. The 1940 statement provides a basic definition of the obligations of the college or university teacher (see Appendix). Further statements on professional responsibility have been promulgated by the AAUP, notably its 1966 Statement on Professional Ethics.[4] The profession as a whole has understandably felt that detailed specifications of acceptable and unacceptable conduct are unworthy of a profession, unworkable in practice, subject to administrative abuses, and inconsistent with institutional autonomy and diversity. More needs to be done, however.

The locus of responsibility for the specification and enforcement of professional standards has been assumed to be the individual institution. The preamble of the AAUP Statement on Professional Ethics makes this clear: "In the enforcement of ethical standards, the academic profession differs from those of law and medicine, whose associations act to assure the integrity of members engaged in private practice. In the academic profession the individual institution of higher learning provides this assurance and so should normally handle questions concerning propriety of conduct within its own framework by reference to a faculty group."

This is a wise and useful observation, but it states the problem rather than solving it. If indeed the academic profession as a whole lacks the authority to discipline members who violate professional standards of conduct, then the individual institution must bear that responsibility. And "the institution," as far as professional standards are concerned, should be its faculty, acting not as professors of separate disciplines but as a collective body of members of a single profession. The institution is not, in these matters, the administration or the governing board, whatever their role may be in providing legal validation of disciplinary procedures. The faculty of the institution, therefore, must be the source for the definition and clarification of standards of professional conduct and must take the lead in ensuring that these standards are enforced.

By and large, and with results far better on the whole than is recognized, institutions and faculties have been able to rely on individual self-discipline and the informal correctives of collegial association. But the vast and rapid growth of the profession in recent years has surely weakened the force of professional tradition. And the re-

---

[4] *AAUP Bulletin,* 1969, *55,* 86–87.

flection on campuses of broader social turmoil has presented acute
problems of professional conduct, for which broad general professional
standards and traditional reliance upon individual self-discipline have
been inadequate.

Resort has sometimes been made to external legal procedures,
with risk to the proper autonomy of the profession. More often, unilateral administrative action, with danger to academic freedom, has
been taken in the absence of effective faculty initiative to discipline
itself. And most ominously, assaults upon academic freedom from
within the institution by or with the toleration of members of faculties
themselves have gone unpunished.

In this situation there is a special urgency for faculties to accept
their full corporate responsibility for the integrity of the profession.
That responsibility cannot be avoided, it should not be assumed by
others, and it must be fulfilled. The authors of the 1915 Declaration
of Principles, with remarkable prescience, defined the issue:

*It is . . . inadmissible that the power of determining when
departures from the requirements of the scientific spirit and
method have occurred should be vested in bodies not composed
of members of the academic profession. Such bodies necessarily
lack full competency to judge of those requirements; their intervention can never be exempt from the suspicion that it is dictated
by other motives than zeal for the integrity of science; and it is,
in any case, unsuitable to the dignity of a great profession that the
initial responsibility for the maintenance of its professional standards should not be in the hands of its own members. It follows
that university teachers must be prepared to assume this responsibility themselves. They have hitherto seldom had the opportunity,
or perhaps the disposition, to do so. The obligation will doubtless, therefore, seem to many an unwelcome and burdensome
one; and for its proper discharge members of the profession will
perhaps need to acquire, in a greater measure than they at present
possess it, the capacity for impersonal judgment in such cases,
and for judicial severity when the occasion requires it. But the
responsibility cannot, in this committee's opinion, be rightfully
evaded. If this profession should prove itself unwilling to purge
its ranks of the incompetent and the unworthy, or to prevent the*

*freedom which it claims in the name of science from being used
as a shelter for inefficiency, for superficiality, or for uncritical and
intemperate partisanship, it is certain that the task will be performed by others—by others who lack certain essential qualifications for performing it, and whose action is sure to breed suspi-
cions and recurrent controversies deeply injurious to the internal
order and the public standing of universities.*[5]

This commission believes that faculties should be authorized
and encouraged to develop codes of professional conduct for the guidance of their members and as the basis for sanctions against those
whose conduct falls below professional norms. Such codes should reflect
the broad precepts embodied in such existing formulations as the 1940
Statement of Principles and the 1966 Statement on Professional Ethics
and should attempt to articulate the traditional sentiments of academic persons as to the demands of their calling. Obviously such codes
should not attempt to enumerate every sort of prohibited professional
conduct. A middle ground between undue specification and pious
generality should be sought. The very effort to provide a statement of
professional standards will serve to dramatize the faculty's own responsibility for its integrity and that of the institution.

The commission calls attention to the following as recent
examples of faculty efforts to frame codes and procedures for faculty
self-discipline: Harvard University: The University Committee on
Governance, *Tentative Recommendations Concerning Rights and
Responsibilities* (Cambridge, April 1970) and *Tentative Recommendations Concerning Discipline of Officers* (Cambridge, March
1971); University of California, "Code of Professional Rights, Responsibilities and Conduct of University Faculty, and University
Disciplinary Procedures," adopted by the Assembly of the Academic
Senate, 15 June 1971 (reprinted in Appendix C of Carnegie Commission Report, *Reform on Campus,* 1972); Stanford University
Chapter of the American Association of University Professors, *Report
on Faculty Self-Discipline* (Palo Alto, January 1971).

   *16. The commission recommends that the faculty of each in-
stitution assume responsibility for developing a code of faculty conduct*

---

[5] Quoted in L. Joughin (Ed.), *Academic Freedom and Tenure* (Madison: University of Wisconsin Press, 1969), pp. 169–170.

and procedures and sanctions for faculty self-discipline, for recommending adoption of the code by the institution's governing board, and for making effective use of the code when it has been approved.

Staff Planning. Staff planning is a seriously neglected element of college and university personnel policy. Many problems attributed to the tenure system are in fact the result of poor staff planning. By staff planning we refer simply to the projection, on a departmental and institution-wide basis, of the staff requirements of the institution for a future period, say five to ten years, on the basis of what is known or can be realistically estimated about enrollment, budget, and other resources; program changes; and availability of personnel—all assessed in relation to the goals of the institution as a whole.

The importance of proper staff planning to the effective operation of a tenure system should be obvious. Since tenure is a long-term commitment, it introduces a rigidity into the personnel system that would not be present if, say, individuals could be hired and released on a short-term basis. The critical problems to be resolved by good staff planning include the following:

First, to assure a reasonable spread of age in each faculty unit, so that retirements occur at a fairly regular rate rather than in bunches. Careful recruitment of new faculty and their assimilation into the institution will be facilitated if retirements can be spread out.

Second, to assure that positions for junior appointments will be available at a steady rate and that tenure openings occur regularly enough and in sufficient numbers to provide attractive opportunities for probationary faculty.

Third, to ensure that the proportion of those holding tenure is not so large that new faculty cannot be brought into the institution in sufficient numbers to infuse new vitality into the group, nor so large as to impose an impossible budgetary burden on the institution.

Fourth—and of increasing urgency today—to ensure that opportunities are open for the recruitment of more women and minority-group faculty members, and for their advancement to tenure status.

Fifth, to ensure that the institution has the flexibility, in the disposition of its staff positions, to undertake new programs if it should decide to do so, to expand or contract units in response to changes in demand or interest, and to meet other contingencies.

Serious staff planning has not been carried out in most institutions. During the great expansion of the 1950s and 1960s, planning for most institutions scarcely seemed necessary or even possible. Enrollments were always rising, additional funds always seemed to be available, new programs were being created almost automatically, and qualified faculty were hard to find and keep. Institutions had little time or inclination to think about the long-term future when they were struggling to accommodate mounting numbers of students and coping with campus unrest and turmoil. Today the situation is reversed: the rate of enrollment increase—or even enrollments themselves—is falling steadily, budgets are tight, and faculty supply is up in relation to demand.

A vivid illustration of the kind of problem institutions face as a result of the largely unplanned growth of recent years is provided by Frederick E. Balderston in his study of financial crisis in education:

> To illustrate the issue of aging of faculty, let us assume that the institution has gone through a period of expansion in which mostly junior people were added to the faculty, so that at the beginning of the decade 50 percent of the faculty was nontenured, 10 percent consisted of associate professors, and 40 percent were (youngish) full professors. Now let ten years pass, with no change in the total number of faculty positions. In each year, let us say, one fifth of the nontenured faculty come up for promotion to associate professor, of whom three fourths make it and one fourth are replaced by new assistant professor appointments; one fourth of the associate professors come up for promotion to full professor and three fourths of them make it; the rest remain as associate professors; and among the full professors (because the faculty is young), nobody reaches retirement age.
>
> By the end of the tenth year, here is the situation: the rank distribution is 10 percent assistant professors, 15 percent associate professors, and 75 percent full professors.[6]

The proportion of the faculty with tenure will now be 90 percent. The age distribution of the tenure faculty will be very lopsided. There will be virtually no openings for promotion to tenure for the nontenured

[6] "Varieties of Financial Crisis," in L. Wilson (Ed.), *Universal Higher Education: Costs, Benefits, Options* (Washington, D.C.: American Council on Education, 1972), pp. 92–93.

faculty. The addition of new members to the faculty will have been reduced to a trickle. Because the chance of advancement is so poor, the institution will find it difficult to attract good people. The high proportion on tenure will not only be an increasingly difficult financial burden, as salaries and retirement subsidies continue to rise for this expanding group, but will make it virtually impossible to reallocate faculty positions among departments if that should be needed. It will be virtually impossible to increase the representation of women and minority groups in the faculty. The institution has become "tenured-in."

With variations that do not alter the chief features of the case, this illustration could easily be reproduced on one campus after another. Much of the pressure to abolish or modify the tenure system arises from this kind of situation. In the commission's judgment, the proper approach is through staff planning and better administration of the tenure system.

17. The commission recommends that each institution develop a staffing plan and a procedure for reviewing and modifying it on an annual basis. The plan should be developed through joint faculty-administration consultation, and should be based on the institution's most careful and realistic estimates of enrollments, budget support, program development, and other relevant variables for a period of five to ten years in the future. For each teaching unit (department, division, college) and for the institution as a whole, the staffing plan should project the age and tenure patterns of the present faculty, scheduled retirements, and other factors likely to influence the composition and distribution of the faculty, with due allowance for contingencies.

The staffing plan should serve as the basis for budget projections, as a guide to the options open to the institution in the recruitment and retention of faculty, as the basis for formulation of policy to govern the award of tenure, and as the basis for communication with faculty members on their prospects for reappointment and appointment to tenure.

18. The commission recommends that staffing plans provide explicitly for a substantial increase, in virtually all institutions, in the tenure component of women and members of minority groups.

Serious work is beginning to be done in developing techniques for staff planning; in projecting the consequences of alternative appointment, promotion, and retirement policies; and in inventing models that can be used to make such projections. For example, David S. P. Hopkins of the Stanford University Academic Planning Office has prepared a paper on "The Influence of Appointment, Promotion, and Retirement Policies on Faculty Rank Distributions" (June 1972). At the University of Rochester, Kenneth E. Clark and William H. Meckling have developed a model of faculty flow to support their report to the Academic Council on "Appointment and Promotion Procedures at the University of Rochester" (February 1972).[7] Work of this kind should be widely disseminated. Education associations, on local, regional, and national levels, could perform a valuable service by bringing institutional studies to the attention of the education community generally and by themselves undertaking studies of staff planning problems and methods.

A staff plan must not be merely a *pro forma* endorsement and perpetuation of current staffing patterns. It should reflect a careful reassessment of current programs and their staffing requirements in light of the institution's objectives and responsibilities. It should provide flexibility for future program change and innovation, most appropriately on the assumption that there is not likely in the immediate future to be a significant *net* increase in resources to support such change.

Accordingly, the staffing plan should provide for a pool of positions, not allocated to any teaching unit, which can be used for the development of new programs, responses to changes in enrollment patterns, and other future contingencies. As positions are allocated from this pool, the pool should be replenished from positions that become available through attrition of the current faculty. In large institutions it may be desirable to retain a position pool under the supervision of deans of the larger schools and another pool under central administrative control.

19. The commission recommends that in formulating its faculty staffing plan, each institution develop policies under which an appropriate number of tenure positions, when they become vacant, are

---

[7] The commission is grateful to President Robert L. Sproull of The University of Rochester and to Dean Albert H. Hastorf and David S. P. Hopkins of Stanford University for providing copies of these documents.

available for allocation to any unit where they may be needed, or for temporary suspension, or for elimination.[8]

In developing and keeping current a realistic staffing plan, each institution will have to face the question of the proper ratio of the tenured to the nontenured faculty. Each institution should develop a policy on this matter that is appropriate to its particular mission and its circumstances and resources, with special attention to the age, rank, and tenure composition of its present faculty, the institution's growth prospects, its program plans, and its resource-allocation policies.

The establishment and maintenance of ratios of tenured and nontenured faculty will not be easy. On campuses that are beginning to face up to this problem, misunderstanding and controversy have marked the effort. Older faculty members who began their academic careers before World War II are familiar with tenure ratios and quotas and with departmental organization tables that specified the number of positions at each rank; they grew up with them. These constraints were commonplace in virtually all institutions, and faculty expectations were adjusted to the limits set by institutional staffing patterns. But these practices were abandoned during the expansion period of the late 1950s and 1960s, and the faculty who predominate in American colleges and universities today regard the imposition of tenure ratios or the limitation on numbers at each rank as a newfangled and improper restriction on faculty advancement. Newfangled it assuredly is not. Attention to the balance between tenure and nontenure positions and to an appropriate mix of faculty ranks is simply the revival of standard institutional practice, under conditions of increasing stability which closely parallel those in which the practice arose. But the new attention to ratios, quotas, and faculty mix may result in inequities unless insti-

---

[8] Cf. Carnegie Commission, *The More Effective Use of Resources: An Imperative for Higher Education* (New York, 1972), p. 103: "A sixth way of getting flexibility is to require that all positions vacated through resignation, retirement, or death be allocated back to the central administration, rather than being kept by the individual department or school, so that the central administration may determine where the need for reassignment is greatest. It is important that positions vacated on the initiative of the department not revert, however; else the department may be inclined to keep people it really does not want and should not have."

tutions proceed carefully, with full faculty consultation and advice, in developing their staffing plans. Sudden imposition of quotas may operate unfairly upon probationary faculty who have been led to believe that earlier guidelines correctly define their expectations. Fixed numerical ratios for the institution as a whole will operate with differential effect, often damaging to the academic program as well as to individual faculty members, upon departments of different size and different age composition. The commission urges institutions to develop staffing ratios and new tables of organization and rank with full consideration of these problems.

The commission urges institutions to express their decisions as to the ratio of tenured and nontenured faculty as ranges or limits rather than as fixed percentages. The commission also recommends that the chosen ratios be applied with sufficient flexibility to different instructional units of the institution (departments, divisions, separate schools) to take account of significant differences among them in size, current variations in age composition and tenure mix, varying research and teaching responsibilities, and similar considerations.

The commission believes that an institution probably should not allow more than one half to two thirds of its faculty to be on tenure appointments. This caveat is likely to be especially important during the decade of the 1970s, in view of the relative youth of most faculties and of stabilizing trends in faculty size and financial resources. A larger proportion of tenured faculty is likely to curtail opportunities for the appointment and retention of younger faculty, with undesirable effects on institutional vitality; to impede the development of new programs and interdisciplinary work, for which new faculty will be needed; and to diminish opportunities for the recruitment and promotion of increased numbers of women and members of minority groups.

20. The commission recommends that each institution develop policies relating to the proportion of tenured and nontenured faculty that will be compatible with the composition of its present staff, its resources and projected enrollment, and its future objectives. In the commission's nearly unanimous judgment, it will probably be dangerous for most institutions if tenured faculty constitute more than one half to two thirds of the total full-time faculty during the decade ahead. The institution's policy in this matter, which should be flexible enough to allow for necessary variation among subordinate units, should be used as a guide in recruitment, reappointment, and the award of tenure. Special attention should be given to the need to allow for significant expansion of the proportion of women and members of minority groups in all faculties, especially in the tenured ranks. In achieving its policy goals as to the proportion of its faculty on tenure, institutions will need to proceed gradually in order to avoid injustice to probationary faculty whose expectations of permanent appointments may have been based on earlier, more liberal practices.

Professional Development

Many problems attributed to academic tenure are in fact generic problems of the deployment, maintenance, and improvement of professional skill in an institutional setting. They are bound to occur no matter what form of employment contract is in use. In any college or university, ways must be found to foster the professional development of the faculty. This involves such purposes as the following: encouraging faculty interest in good teaching and in rewarding it, promoting improvement in teaching methods, maintaining at a high level the faculty members' interest in new generations of students and minimizing boredom and fatigue, helping faculty members keep abreast of new developments in their disciplines, providing opportunities for interaction with colleagues in other institutions, providing opportunities for periodic refreshment and retooling, assisting those who want to change fields or develop new lines of teaching or investigation, encouraging those who want to take on administrative responsibilities and helping them prepare themselves for such assignments, providing the means by which those who have served in administrative positions can make a successful transition when they return to regular faculty service. These and related objectives should be the goals of a professional-development program.

In any profession, responsibility for the development, improvement, and maintenance of professional skills must be borne primarily by the professional himself. That must of course continue to be the basic theory of the academic profession. But it is increasingly clear that all professionals need opportunities and assistance in their efforts, and everyone needs stimulation and encouragement. Continuing professional-education programs are now common in medicine, law, and engineering; in at least some states regular participation in such mid-career programs is a condition of continuation of licenses to practice. In the academic profession, special conditions make continuing professional-development programs especially important. The adjustment of general expertise in a discipline to the demands of its effective expression in a specific institution is a fundamental problem. From it stems the need to orchestrate the variety of individual talents and interests and the multitude of roles the institution makes available. And this must be done over extended periods of time, with subtle adjustments for institutional continuity and innovation on the one hand and for individual aging and shifts of interest on the other. Professional development as both teacher and scholar should be a major concern of faculties, administrations, and governing boards.

Provision for the professional development of the faculty has been largely casual and unplanned in most institutions. Continuing development of skill in the faculty member's own discipline has rightly been regarded as fundamental and has received major attention and resources—in sabbatical-leave programs, federal and foundation research support, institutional support for research in the form of released time, and provision of assistance and equipment. Little has been done at a comparable level to support development in other activities, notably teaching, or to design and execute programs to deal with problems of aging, shifts in interest, periodic retooling, return from administrative service, and others listed above. The commission believes that institutions must devote thought and resources to these matters in strengthening their faculty personnel programs.

A particularly useful analysis of career development and suggestions for institutional programs are contained in Kenneth E. Eble's report *Career Development of the Effective College Teacher,* a product of studies undertaken for the joint AAC-AAUP Project to Improve College Teaching.[9]

21. The commission recommends that institutions develop plans to promote the maintenance and improvement of faculty teaching

[9] Washington, D.C.: American Association of University Professors, 1971. See also Eble's *Professors as Teachers* (San Francisco: Jossey-Bass, 1972), pp. 109–130.

and scholarly skills. Such plans might include new policies for the use of sabbatical and other leaves of absence, released time for development of new courses, in-service seminars, and professional programs conducted in association with other institutions.

The commission believes that efforts to assist the probationary faculty member to develop as a teacher and scholar are of cardinal importance. Evaluation for reappointment and the award of tenure should grow out of a positive program designed to induct younger faculty into the full responsibilities of the profession and to help them realize their individual potentialities.

22. The commission urges institutions to develop more continuous and affirmative means of assisting faculty members, especially those on probationary appointment, to improve their teaching, scholarship, and professional performance. Department chairmen should meet periodically with junior faculty to develop individual goals for participation in the work of the department and to review progress and performance. The commission urges faculties to consider, among other techniques, the assignment of probationary faculty to one or more senior faculty as advisors and consultants, on a rotating basis; the institution of regular class visits to probationary and tenured faculty alike; the development of seminars and colloquia on teaching and scholarly problems; and the organization of teams of senior and junior professors responsible for a course or several sections of a course, with full collegial exchange and sharing of responsibilities.

Strengthening Institutional Tenure Plans

Formal Policy Statement. The commission believes that each institution should adopt and disseminate a formal written statement of its faculty personnel policy. In many institutions important elements of a comprehensive policy statement are of course already in existence, whether in traditional practice or through explicit formulation. But few institutions have developed and published policy statements of sufficient breadth. Far too many are forced, in the absence of carefully framed statements of policy, to rely upon emergency or ad hoc responses to unanticipated problems. Such problems are becoming increasingly common; many can now be anticipated and prepared for.

Policies currently in effect in the institution should be reviewed and where necessary revised as part of the development of a more comprehensive statement. The policy statement should be recommended for adoption by the governing board after appropriate consultation among faculty, administration, students, and members of the board.

After adoption, the policy statement should be kept under continuous review. The commission believes that a standing committee should be appointed to carry out this review and to recommend modifications as experience shows them to be needed.

The commission realizes, of course, that the availability of a carefully developed and comprehensive statement of institutional faculty personnel policy will not of itself assure effective operation of a tenure plan. Policies must be interpreted so that everyone in the institution fully understands them, and they must be followed. Faculty members and administrative officers must join conscientiously to ensure that good policies are not modified, frustrated, or sabotaged in application. But though stated policies cannot guarantee effective functioning of a personnel plan, they can afford the indispensable basis for good practice. The process of developing a formal statement and keeping it under review will identify critical problems which must be confronted and dealt with in the academic community; the major issues to which a formal policy statement will be addressed are crucial to the health of the educational process, and many of them have gone too long unexamined. The existence of a stated policy is likely to reduce the amount of ambiguity in personnel actions and to diminish the effect of caprice, the casual variations of power, or the selective application of available tradition.

Explicit policies carry the danger of crippling detail and stultifying procedural rigidity. It is essential, if academic institutions are to preserve a flexibility already gravely threatened, that policies and procedures be stated with sufficient generality to allow for essential differences among subordinate units, while at the same time enunciating institutional standards of general application. The dictum that "less is more" is probably a wise guide in framing general policy statements, especially in a society increasingly rule-bound and increasingly anxious to anticipate every contingency. Good sense and an attempt to preserve or recover the civil traditions of the academy can make the

development of personnel policy an example of educational statesmanship rather than an exercise in pettifoggery.

*23. The commission recommends that every institution develop
a formal statement of its faculty personnel policy, with appropriate
provision for variations to meet the special needs of individual departments and other units. The statement should specify the institution's
policies on each of the following topics:*

*(1) Categories of faculty and other staff members eligible for
tenure.*

(2) Maximum length of the period of probationary service.

*(3) Length and number of appointments for the faculty mem-
ber during the probationary period.*

*(4) Amount and kind of prior service in other institutions
that may be credited toward fulfillment of the probationary requirement.*

*(5) Criteria for reappointment and for award of tenure
(including professional educational and service requirements) and the
methods of evaluation and documentation to be used in applying these
criteria.*

*(6) Procedures for the initiation, consideration, and approval
of recommendations on reappointment and appointment to tenure.*

*(7) Dates for notification of reappointment, nonreappoint-
ment, and appointment to tenure.*

*(8) Procedures for appeal from decisions not to reappoint
during the probationary period or not to grant tenure.*

*(9) Methods of continuing evaluation of faculty performance
after tenure has been granted.*

*(10) Faculty conduct and processes for dealing with violations,
with specific reference to the institution's code of faculty responsibility.*

*(11) Measures that may be employed in cases of inadequate
or improper faculty performance; the procedures to be followed in
cases that might lead to the application of sanctions; and the procedures
for review and appeal of decisions applying sanctions.*

*(12) Procedures to be used in determining whether financial
exigency exists which might lead to termination of faculty appointments, and, upon determination of financial exigency, the method of
deciding which faculty positions are to be eliminated.*

(13) Procedures for identifying disability which might lead

to termination of faculty appointments, and the method of review and appeal from decisions to terminate for disability.

(14) Age of mandatory retirement, the options for service beyond the mandatory retirement age, and the provisions for early retirement.

(15) Policies on fringe benefits, leaves of absence, sabbatical leaves, and related matters.

(16) Policies relating to the retention or modification of tenure for those holding administrative posts, and policies relating to the return to full faculty service of those who have served in administrative positions.

(17) Policies relating to the maintenance of personnel files and regulations governing access to them.

Communication. Faculty personnel policy cannot be effective unless it is communicated. In their campus visits, members of the commission were surprised by the frequency with which faculty members who were interviewed—not only younger members of the faculty, whose futures are at stake, but often also senior members, who bear a major responsibility for applying institutional policy—were ignorant of the precise provisions of institutional policy, or disagreed about them because they had to rely largely upon hearsay or rumor.

If tenure is to be strengthened, a new appointee to the faculty should understand the criteria applied during the probationary period. Knowing what is expected of him, the faculty member can then apply his best energies to his professional development. The institution has a particular obligation to indicate whether the individual's chances for reappointment or the award of tenure are dependent upon special conditions, such as the variable needs of departments, the availability of vacancies, institutional regulations on the proportion of tenure faculty, or financial problems.

During their developmental phases, many institutions have found it desirable to make changes in their criteria for award of tenure —for example, by raising the minimum educational requirement or by reflecting new institutional priorities in recruitment. Such changes are no doubt essential to the improvement of higher education. But individual jeopardy, through their application to those already on probationary appointment, should be held to a minimum.

24. The commission recommends that each institution develop and systematically use a plan for communicating its personnel policies to its faculty and give special attention to new appointees. The terms and conditions of service should be clearly spelled out. The institution's formal policy statement should be provided in convenient form and responsible officers should be assigned to insure that it is distributed and understood. For each new appointee, the specific criteria that will be used in evaluating performance during the probationary period, and the procedures by which these will be applied, should be explained in writing. The communication should make as clear as possible what the chances for award of tenure are, and how far they depend upon the specialized needs of departments, available funding, institutional policy on the proportion of tenured faculty, etc.

In the commission's judgment, if an institution changes its criteria for tenure, it should insure that probationary faculty appointed prior to the change should be given an opportunity to qualify under the new standards.

Explicit Judgment in Decisions. Those who are granted tenure must be assumed to have what William Van Alstyne has referred to as a "rebuttable presumption" of fitness. The decision to award tenure asserts that the individual, having satisfied institutional and professional standards, is presumed qualified to be a permanent member of the faculty until retirement. This presumption is rebuttable only for specified cause through appropriate due-process procedures.

The crucial element in the entire tenure process is the decision to award it. Tenure is often defended precisely on the ground that it forces institutions to make hard personnel decisions, whereas a contract system could easily lead to postponement of decision and finally to no decision at all. The success or failure of a tenure plan hence depends more upon the quality of the tenure decisions than upon anything else. The decision must rest upon sound criteria, genuinely reflecting institutional purpose and priorities. It must come after a continuous evaluation process, during which the probationary candidate is regularly informed and counseled about his performance and his prospects. The decision must make explicit use of all relevant information, including students' views of the teacher's effectiveness. The decision should be part of a sound and affirmative faculty development plan, in which the faculty member is assisted in realizing his potentialities. The decision must be open to inspection through procedures which will assure that adequate consideration has been given to all relevant factors in the case and that the decision was not arbitrary or capricious and did not violate academic freedom or constitutional rights.

Above all, the decision to award tenure must be a *decision*. It must be a formal, explicit judgment, in which responsible professionals affirm, after the most careful deliberation on available facts and probabilities for the future, that the individual under consideration should indeed be a permanent member of the institution's faculty.

In the commission's judgment, one of the most pervasive and most serious weaknesses in the tenure system at present is the failure of institutions to base the award of tenure on an explicit judgment— their failure genuinely to decide. In all too many institutions, tenure is achieved by default, through the mere passage of time. Tenure is automatic in many institutions after a given number of years of service. In many states, in fact, higher education statutes—often modeled, it would seem, upon statutes devised for the lower schools—mandate tenure after a specified period of service. It is sometimes argued, of course, that the renewal of term appointments past a stated time, whereupon tenure becomes automatic, is a kind of decision. But it lacks the positive and explicit character that sound decisions on permanent service should have. Tenure statutes should not take the form "If a faculty member shall be appointed for a seventh (or xth) year of service in this institution, he shall be deemed to have tenure" but rather "No faculty member shall be appointed beyond his sixth (or yth) year of service in this institution unless a formal recommendation for the award of tenure, in accordance with such and such criteria and procedures, shall have been submitted and approved by the governing board." The distinction is fundamental. If institutional regulations took the latter form, automatic tenure would be impossible and the rationale of the tenure process would be reaffirmed.

There is good reason for the general agreement in the academic community—an agreement embodied in the tenure standards of the 1940 statement—that the probationary period should be of limited duration. It should be long enough to permit careful consideration of the faculty member's qualifications. But it should not be so long as to postpone unduly the faculty member's enjoyment of the full benefits of permanent status, keeping him in jeopardy of termination into middle life. And it should not be so long as to erode the tenure principle by greatly increasing the numbers who do not have its protection. The seven-year rule of the 1940 statement should be interpreted as in essence saying to institutions "You must make a final tenure decision by the end of the faculty member's sixth year of service. If you do not, the penalty is that he will acquire tenure just as if you had decided to award it to him." If the initial selection of faculty members were perfect, if every new appointee had precisely the qualifications needed by the institution for the long term, and if the institution's needs did not change during the probationary period, then the penalty would be meaningless. But in that case there would be no need for a probationary period at all. Tenure could and should, on these assumptions, be granted instantly, upon appointment. But these assumptions are never true, no matter how carefully the initial appointments are made. In the real world, a probationary period is necessary, and tenured status must rest upon explicit judgment.

25. *The commission recommends that the award of tenure always be based on an explicit judgment of qualifications, resulting from continuous evaluation of the faculty member during the probationary period, in the light of the institution's stated criteria.*

The commission urges that tenure never be acquired by default, through the mere passage of time in probationary service.

Initial Appointment. The effectiveness of any personnel policy obviously depends in large measure on the care taken in initial appointments. Institutions vary greatly in the procedures used to ensure that those appointed are most likely to be able to contribute to the institution's program. Since institutions differ enormously in their attractiveness to applicants, in the resources available to identify promising prospects, and in their internal arrangements for monitoring the appointment process, these differences probably will continue to be great. But improvement can be made. Institutions can be more selective and attempt from the outset to achieve a better fit between the individual and the needs of the institution. Since the effectiveness of the subsequent steps in the tenure chain depends so heavily upon the care taken in the initial step, each institution should review its practices and devote special attention to their improvement.

26. *The commission recommends that each institution develop procedures to ensure the most careful screening and judgment of the*

prospective faculty member's qualifications before he or she is initially appointed to probationary status.

Monitoring Departmental Recommendations. Characteristically, the department initiates recommendations for appointments, reappointments, and award or denial of tenure. This is the proper basic locus of responsibility because it is in the department that the most reliable judgment of professional competence can be made.

But reliance on departmental judgment, while necessary and on the whole effective, entails serious risks, which should be minimized through deliberate institutional policy. Weak departments tend to become still weaker through weak appointments. Strong departments sometimes endanger their strength and balance by an excessive number of appointments in restricted areas of study. In-breeding is a danger. Fashions seize disciplines and produce imitative appointments, which may damage the institution when the fashion has passed. The recommendations of small departments can be compromised by the narrowness of their professional base. Cliques and coteries can influence departmental recommendations, and strong individuals sometimes wield disproportionate influence in departmental councils. Stated institutional policies can easily be sabotaged or replaced by informal policies more to a department's liking—especially in such sensitive and controversial matters as the recruitment and retention of women and members of minority groups.

For reasons such as these—and any experienced faculty member or administrator can readily supply others—regular and reliable arrangements must be made to monitor the recommendations of departments and to secure their reconsideration and revision if they are found defective in policy, procedure, or substance.

Since institutions vary widely in size and complexity of organization, no single arrangement for reviewing departmental personnel recommendations can be given preference. Whatever the specific plan (complex universities will no doubt require a review step at the school or college level and another at the university level; in smaller institutions a single review mechanism at the institution-wide level will probably suffice), the review procedure should embody at least three principles: (1) it should involve faculty members from outside the department and should not be merely an administrative review; (2) it should be designed to ensure reasonable conformity with general institutional policies and procedures, within whatever limits of variation the institution has decided to permit; (3) while not usurping the department's responsibility for professional judgment, it should monitor that judgment in terms of broad professional standards; (4) it should review, on a regular or selective basis, recommendations for nonreappointment or denial of tenure as well as recommendations for reappointment and award of tenure.

27. *The commission recommends that each institution develop reliable procedures for review of departmental personnel recommendations above the department level. These should involve faculty from outside the department concerned and should be designed to ensure adherence to institutional procedures and criteria and to prevent departmental in-breeding, doctrinal conformity, or the spread of mediocrity.*

Length of Probationary Period. This report has already noted the great variation among institutions in the maximum length of the probationary period permitted before a tenure decision must be made. The maximum period permitted under AAUP guidelines is seven years. Allowing for a full year's notice in the event of an unfavorable decision, this means an effective probationary period of six years; and since the procedures for consideration, recommendation, and review require in the normal case several months, the period from initial appointment to the beginning of the final decision process may well amount to only a little more than five years. But only a minority of institutions (37.6 percent: 25.8 percent of the public and 48 percent of the private institutions) have in fact established a seven-year maximum for probationary service. The median maximum for all institutions is six years, which means an effective probation of four years or a little more. At the other end of the scale, 18 percent of all institutions set the maximum probationary period at three years or less; 28 percent, at four years or less. For these institutions the effective probationary period is extremely short. And all of this assumes that the maximum allowable period is actually used. We know, of course, that many personnel decisions, either to reappoint or not to reappoint, are made before the maximum period has elapsed.

There are manifest advantages in not prolonging the probationary period unduly. Some of these no doubt influenced the reduction in the AAUP's 1940 statement to a seven-year maximum from the ten years recommended in its 1915 declaration. If the decision on tenure is to be unfavorable, it is in the interest of the individual to find a new post as early as possible and of the institution to replace him with someone whose chances of permanent appointment will be greater. Seven years, on top of the normal time spent in graduate study, is a long period of uncertainty, usually bringing the faculty member to his early or middle thirties before he has established himself in an institution. And from a merely operational point of view, it becomes more difficult to make negative decisions the longer a teacher in probationary status has served on a faculty and has become a part of the institution and the community.

On the other hand, the tenure system depends in a fundamental way on the effectiveness of the probationary period—in helping the younger faculty member to develop his abilities as teacher and scholar and in conducing to reliable judgment about his future growth and contribution to the institution. A system of "instant" or "automatic" tenure, which eliminates or routinizes the judgmental process, is not a tenure plan in the sense in which we use the term and recommend its continuation. The probationary period must be long enough for its value as central to the tenure process to be fully realized.

In the judgment of the commission, the probationary period used in many institutions is much too short. Even if initial appointment procedures were more careful than in fact they are in many institutions, even if arrangements for counseling and assisting new faculty in their professional development were more effective, even if criteria for reappointment and institutional needs and priorities for the future were more fully harmonized, a period of one, two, or three years of probation is too brief. The award of tenure is not only a major commitment of future resources, vital as this is. It is a decision about the future quality, content, and direction of the institution's educational program, and it therefore must be taken with extreme seriousness.

The commission believes, therefore, that institutional policies should deliberately encourage the use of longer probationary periods, except in individual cases where it is early apparent that there has been a mismatch between the individual and the institution. Specifically, the current standard of seven years as the maximum period of probationary service should stand, but institutions now setting a maximum at two, three, or four years should reconsider their policies.

It is sometimes argued that probationary service approaching the seven-year limit may be needed in institutions whose programs stress scholarship and research and the supervision of graduate and professional students, but not in institutions primarily concerned with undergraduate teaching. In the former, it is said, more time must be allowed for the completion of significant scholarly projects, especially when these projects are undertaken by a new faculty member, who is at the same time getting up new courses, establishing a family, and the like. Teaching (which sometimes sounds in such discussions like "mere" teaching), this argument runs, can be assessed on a regular basis, since it is continual not intermittent, and waits not upon inspiration, equipment, or the backlogs of professional journals. And teaching ability, it is implied, is inherently easier to appraise than scholarly or research ability, and for this reason, too, an abbreviated probationary period of two or three years should suffice.

The commission vigorously rejects this line of argument and the assumptions both of fact and of value on which it rests.

The cultivation of scholarship and research capacity represents the core of graduate training in the United States. Concerning a new faculty member's competencies, the one area upon which evidence is available from the outset—in his dissertation and in the judgment of his professors—is his scholarly and research ability. Whether the teacher can develop from this point remains to be determined, and a probationary period of adequate length must be provided to give him a chance to show that he can.

But with respect to the individual's teaching ability nothing much will be known. Under prevailing graduate school practices, he will have had no formal instruction in the art of teaching. He may have had some limited experience as a teaching assistant, but usually without serious supervision or assistance, and typically in courses he will not be called upon to teach again. He will start from scratch in his new institution. He will be responsible for his own courses; his abilities will need to be developed in courses and other professional assignments of different types, of varying degrees of difficulty, and at different levels. The purpose of the probationary period is not merely to arrive at some rough judgment of how competent a teacher he is now, but to provide for a more sophisticated program of development and growth, from which can flow a responsible prediction of what kind of teacher he is likely to become.

Teaching is not easier to assess than scholarship or research. If anything, it is more difficult. We are far from approaching the consensus about the modes of effective teaching that we have achieved with respect to excellence in scholarship. Institutions are only beginning to work toward ways to emphasize teaching and to evaluate it reliably. There are inherent problems: access to the classroom, the relativity of method to audience and objective, the volatility and evanescence of the teaching situation, the importance of experiment and risk-taking, the significance of individual style. The serious use of student evaluations is only in its infancy. Both in the short run and the long, teaching is difficult to evaluate. Perhaps the common assumption that it is easy is related to the comparatively low importance which teaching assumes, for the reasons we have stated, in the current personnel practice of many institutions.

For all of these reasons the commission favors the use of longer rather than shorter probationary periods, even in institutions whose commitment is primarily or exclusively to undergraduate teaching. We believe that the maximum period ought not to be less than five years. Assuming a year's notice in the event of a negative decision, that would permit between three and four years of development and appraisal, surely the minimum for so critical a part of an effective faculty program.

The commission realizes that some institutions operate under state tenure laws which mandate shorter probationary periods, after which tenure is automatically conferred. The commission urges institutions and state education agencies to work for the revision of such statutes to permit more adequate probationary periods; until they are revised, we suggest that institutions use the limited time available in the most intensive and imaginative manner.

There will be special problems, during the coming decade of transition, in using the probationary period more fully and effectively. Unfairness may occur if junior faculty, for whom alternative posts will be increasingly hard to find, are reappointed for longer periods, without careful counseling as to their progress and chances, only to be replaced with less expensive beginning teachers. Institutions may be tempted to hold on as long as possible to excellent younger faculty, recruited at pains during the expansionist years, while knowing that straitened circumstances make tenure unlikely. Special problems will arise from the effort to expand the representation of women and members of minority groups. Each institution will have to cope with such problems in the light of its own circumstances. The commission is convinced that special efforts are justified in order to ensure the renewed effectiveness of the probationary period.

28. The commission recommends retention of the seven-year period as the maximum for probationary service, and recommends that institutions, as a matter of policy, use probationary periods of not less than five years.

Credit for Prior Service. There is wide variation, as we have already seen, in institutional policy with respect to allowing credit for prior service in another institution to reduce the total period of probationary service. A little over half of all institutions allow no credit for prior service. This group includes most of the two-year colleges (70 percent of the public, 74 percent of the private) and most of the public four-year colleges (70 percent). On the other hand, about two thirds of the universities and 60 percent of the private four-year colleges do allow credit, usually up to three years. The 1940 statement of principles provides that the maximum probationary period may be extended beyond seven years if a teacher has served "a term of probationary service of more than three years in one or more institutions" and if there is written agreement that his appointment in a new institution will run for not more than four years.

In the judgment of the commission, credit for prior service, if given, should be controlled, within these general guidelines, by a careful assessment of the nature of the prior service, of its relevance to the institution's own program, and of its quality. This is consistent with the commission's general view that if tenure is to be renewed and strengthened, the probationary period must be administered with a new seriousness.

29. The commission recommends that each institution develop an explicit policy as to the nature and amount of prior service in other institutions that may be credited to the fulfillment of the probationary qualification. The amount of time credited should in each instance be determined by the specific relevance of the prior service to the institu-

tion's own needs and criteria. Evidence as to the quality of the prior service should be secured from the institutions in which the individual served.

Giving Reasons for Nonreappointment. A basic issue in many recent court cases has been the refusal of an institution to give the faculty member a written statement of the reasons for a decision not to renew a term appointment or not to grant tenure. Two such cases were decided by the Supreme Court in June 1972. In the Roth case (Board of Regents of State Colleges et al. *v.* Roth) the court decided that the faculty member, whose one-year contract in a public institution was not renewed, had no due-process right under the Fourteenth Amendment to a statement of reasons or a hearing on the nonrenewal, since there was no evidence that his nonreappointment involved either a denial of liberty or a deprivation of a property right. In the Sindermann case (Perry et al. *v.* Sindermann) the court ruled that the state college system in which Sindermann had been employed for ten years, though it had no formal tenure policy, had by long-standing practice created a de facto tenure program. Sindermann's length of service, the court held, entitled him to an opportunity to demonstrate that he had a claim to continued employment and, if he substantiated that claim, to a hearing at which he could be informed of the reasons for his non-retention and could challenge their sufficiency—the case having become, at that point, essentially equivalent to a dismissal case under a formal tenure policy.

The implications of these Supreme Court decisions are discussed in Chapter Four. For our present purposes it is sufficient to note that public institutions are not obligated, as a matter of constitutional due process, to provide a statement of reasons for nonrenewal of faculty contracts, unless the faculty member can establish either that he has been deprived of his liberty (for instance, by some aspect of the case that would stigmatize him or foreclose other opportunities for employment) or that he has been deprived of a "property" interest in continued employment (for instance, through the acquisition of tenure, de facto or otherwise, under the policies and practices of the institution).

But whatever may be the legal obligations of the institution under constitutional standards, the question of good academic personnel policy remains. This distinction was explicitly recognized by

Justice Stewart in the majority opinion in the Roth case: "Our analysis of the respondent's [Roth's] constitutional rights in this case in no way indicates a view that an opportunity for a hearing or a statement of reasons for nonretention would, or would not, be appropriate or wise in public colleges and universities. For it is a written Constitution that we apply. Our role is confined to interpretation of that Constitution."

Currently, institutions differ widely in their policies. In the spring of 1972, respondents sampled in the Higher Education Panel survey were asked: "Does your institution give formal written reasons to the faculty member concerned for nonrenewal of contracts (probationary or recurring term appointments) or for denial of tenure?" Table 1 shows the various replies.

Table 1. INSTITUTIONAL POLICIES ON GIVING REASONS FOR NONREAPPOINTMENTS (PERCENTAGE DISTRIBUTIONS)

	Universities		Four-Year Colleges	
Provide Reasons	Public	Private	Public	Private
Never	13.3%	19.4%	26.9%	14.5%
Sometimes	50.8	61.3	34.9	46.9
Always	35.9	19.4	38.2	38.5

	Two-Year Colleges		All Institutions		
Provide Reasons	Public	Private	Public	Private	Total
Never	14.0%	.0%	17.5%	12.0%	14.7%
Sometimes	18.0	58.8	26.0	50.0	38.0
Always	68.1	41.2	56.6	38.1	47.3

Public institutions, probably because of their greater exposure to legal action, provide reasons more frequently than do private institutions; but only a small proportion in each of the categories never provide reasons.

The complexity of the issue is illustrated by the change between 1964 and 1971 in the position of the AAUP. In 1964 one of the association's advisory letters concluded:

*What appears reasonable to those responsible for the decision
may not appear reasonable to the faculty member concerned, for
there are often grounds for a decision that are either very difficult
to discuss frankly or which the faculty member cannot appreciate
(very often, of course, they do not reflect adversely on him). As
a result, if an institution is compelled to state its reasons, it may
find that is raising more problems than it has solved; it may
grasp at the inconsequential or the unfounded simply to lend
support to its decision, or it may place itself in the position of
granting tenure by default.[10]*

In its 1971 Statement on Procedural Standards in the Renewal or
Nonrenewal of Faculty Appointments, the AAUP advocated the
provision of reasons in writing if the faculty member requests them.[11]
The shift in the AAUP's position seems to have been prompted by
recognition of the increasing preference for quasi-judicial procedures.
If reasons need not be given, arbitrary decisions are more easily con-
cealed, and perfunctory or inadequate consideration of a faculty
member's qualifications may more frequently occur.

The commission believes that if the institution's criteria for
reappointment and for award of tenure are clearly set forth, and if the
probationary period is conducted in an open, positive, and helpful
manner, as our other recommendations contemplate, the interests of
both the institution and the faculty member will be best served if
reasons for nonrenewal or denial of tenure are always supplied if
requested.

*30. The commission recommends that the probationary faculty
member who is not recommended for reappointment or for award of
tenure should always be given an explanation of the action in an
informal conference with the department chairman, and, if he requests
it, should be given a statement of reasons in writing.[12]*

[10] *AAUP Bulletin,* Spring 1964, p. 85.

[11] The AAUP statement is printed in *AAUP Bulletin,* 1971, 57, 206–210.
See also the commentary on the AAUP statement, while it was under consideration, by a special AAC committee appointed to review the statement (Association of American Colleges, Spring 1971, mimeograph, 13 pages).

[12] Suggested guidelines for good institutional practice in supplying reasons in nonrenewal cases are developed by W. T. Furniss in "Giving Reasons for
Nonrenewal of Faculty Contracts," *Educational Record,* 1971, *52,* 328–37.

"Permissible Reasons" for Nonreappointment. It is essential
that institutions, faculty, student, and the general public understand
the important distinction between *dismissal* and *nonreappointment* or
nonrenewal (see Glossary). Unfortunately, these two terms are too
frequently used as synonyms. Dismissal is the termination of service
before the end of a term contract or during a tenure appointment but
before retirement or termination for physical disability or financial
exigency. Nonreappointment or nonrenewal, by contrast, is the decision
not to offer a further contract of employment, or not to award tenure.
Reference is often made to those whose probationary contracts are not
renewed as having been "dismissed." The distinction is of immense
importance, and it must be preserved if sound personnel practices are
to have any prospect of success.

Dismissal, whether during a term or a tenured appointment,
is a grave action, which should be undertaken only for cause, with full
procedural safeguards, and with the burden of proof resting on the
institution to demonstrate before proper tribunals that dismissal is
warranted.

Nonreappointment or nonrenewal is certainly a serious matter,
both for the individual and for the institution, and should be sur-
rounded with carefully devised procedures through which the institution's criteria for reappointment and award of tenure can be fairly
administered. But the decision not to reappoint or not to grant tenure
is not a form of dismissal. Nonreappointment is a regular and indispensable feature of any tenure system that includes a selection process
resting on probationary service. Only if probationary periods are truly
probationary, only if some are selected for continued service and others
are not, will tenure have any significance as the principle for assembling
the faculty best suited to the institution's present and future needs.

Nonreappointment, therefore, must conform to different standards from those for dismissal. Nonreappointment does not involve
bringing charges or showing "cause" why the individual's service should
be terminated. It involves the application of relevant criteria, through
a process subject to disclosure, leading to a judgment that it is not
desirable for the institution to offer another term appointment or to
confer academic tenure. The individual must of course have available
a settled procedure under which he can show cause that the decision
is arbitrary or capricious or that it violates his academic freedom or

his constitutional rights. The burden of proof is upon him, but if he develops a prima facie case the institution must come forward with an appropriate showing that the reasons were not in fact violative of academic freedom or constitutional rights, nor arbitrary or capricious.

"Permissible reasons," therefore, and not "cause" provide the standard by which decisions not to reappoint or to award tenure should be evaluated.

31. In the commission's judgment, permissible reasons for non-renewal of term appointments and for decisions not to award tenure must meet the following tests:

(1) They must not violate the faculty member's academic freedom or punish him for exercising his academic freedom, either in the performance of his duties or outside the institution.

(2) They must not violate the faculty member's constitutional rights or punish him for exercising them.

(3) They must not be arbitrary or capricious.

(4) They must represent the deliberate exercise of professional judgment in the particular institutional circumstances.

The commission believes that permissible reasons for non-renewal or nonappointment to tenure include but are not limited to the following: (1) unsatisfactory performance or lack of progress in meeting the institution's stated criteria for reappointment or award of tenure; (2) performance and qualification which although satisfactory will not enable the institution to achieve its educational objectives and standards; (3) full staffing at the tenure level in the areas of the candidate's principal competence or specialty; (4) changes in the institution's academic program; (5) budgetary constraints which make it impossible or imprudent to renew the appointment or to increase the tenure staff.

Supplemental Information. Good personnel decisions require good information. Decisions will more likely be based on pertinent information, rather than hunch, impression, or hearsay, when institutional regulations prescribe the criteria for reappointment and the award of tenure and the documentation to be provided in applying the criteria. Where a carefully planned program of faculty development is in effect, colleagues, chairmen, and administrative officers will have systematic opportunities to observe and record, and their observations will come to constitute a dependable body of relevant information for future decisions.

But in the nature of things information is never complete, and in personnel decisions, which involve many intangibles that will be interpreted and assessed by different individuals in different ways, every effort should be made to see that those responsible for making judgments and recommendations have all the information they can get from every appropriate source. We have already referred to the valuable opinions of students and to the views of other probationary faculty members. The commission believes that the individual under consideration can provide useful information and should as a matter of regular practice be encouraged to do so. A fuller explanation of his scholarship, an indication of future research plans, a discussion of his teaching, a reply to questions from members of the department who know him less well, a projection of his future aspirations in teaching—these or other topics may well help the department or its personnel committee make a sounder decision.

Whether the contribution of the individual concerned is made in person or in writing or both will be a matter of local practice, although the procedure should be as informal and collegial as the occasion will allow. What is crucial, however, is that the opportunity to present evidence or information which he thinks may be helpful must be given in good time, during the process of consideration, and well before a decision has in fact or in effect been made. Only then will the procedure be useful, and seen as a manifestation of the good faith of the faculty.

32. The commission recommends that each institution develop procedures under which a probationary faculty member being considered for reappointment or for tenure will be given an opportunity, well in advance of the final decision, to present to the departmental committee charged with making the recommendation any evidence bearing on the question that he believes may be relevant and helpful to his case.

Appeal Procedures. In the Higher Education Panel survey of institutional tenure practices in the spring of 1972, most institutions reported that they had procedures under which a faculty member whose contract was not renewed or who was denied tenure could appeal the decision. Eighty-six percent of all institutions so reported. Of all institutions with tenure practices, 87 percent said that they had appeal procedures, ranging from a high of 95 percent of the private two-year colleges to a low of 81 percent of the private four-year colleges. But only 19 percent of all institutions using contract rather than tenure plans had procedures for appeal, including only 7 percent of the public institutions (all two-year colleges) in this category.

The survey questionnaire did not specify what sort of procedure should underlie a "yes" answer. It is reasonable to suppose that the appeal procedures currently in use range all the way from a full opportunity for submission of evidence and a hearing before an appropriate faculty body to the mere opportunity of writing a letter of complaint to an administrative officer or to the governing board. The encouraging availability of appeal procedures in tenure-granting institutions may be more apparent than real.

In the commission's judgment, such appeal procedures should be universal.

33. The commission recommends that each institution should develop clear procedures under which a faculty member who, by an otherwise final decision, is denied reappointment or tenure can secure an impartial review of the decision if he believes that it results from improper procedure, or rests on grounds which violate academic freedom or constitutional rights, or is substantively arbitrary or capricious. In such appeal procedures, the burden of proof should be on the faculty member.

"Cause." Although a tenure appointment is expected to be continuous until retirement, barring termination for disability, it has always been recognized that a tenure appointment (or the appointment of a nontenured member) can be terminated for good cause under proper procedures. The crucial problems have always been to develop procedures to ensure that dismissal actions would be conducted with full observance of academic due process, and to define the "cause" for which dismissal would be appropriate in an institution of higher education.

On the procedural question much work has been done. In particular, the Statement on Procedural Standards in Faculty Dismissal Proceedings, endorsed by the Association of American Colleges and the American Association of University Professors in 1958, has had wide influence in guiding institutional practice. Many institutions, using the 1958 statement as a guide, have developed internal procedures of the kind recommended by this commission.

With respect to the definition of "cause" as the basis for dismissal actions, less work has been done. There is no broad consensus within the profession as to what should constitute cause for dismissal. Perhaps the very absence of general agreement has contributed to the rarity of formal dismissal proceedings in higher education.

The difficulty is understandable. A definition of "cause" clear enough to provide a basis for fair proceedings and yet capable of commanding the broad assent of the academic community, both in what it includes and in what it excludes, is inherently difficult to construct. Given the great diversity of views about the nature of higher education and the role of faculties, general agreement may indeed be impossible to secure. And given the traditional diversity of institutional objectives and commitments—a diversity that should be encouraged rather than reduced—individual institutions obviously should have the major responsibility for formulating their own definitions of adequate cause for dismissal.

It is no doubt largely for this last reason that the AAUP has refrained from developing a definition of cause and has concentrated on the procedural side of the problem. The framers of the 1915 declaration, addressing themselves to the question of "cause," laid it down that "In every institution the grounds which will be regarded as justifying the dismissal of members of the faculty should be formulated with reasonable definiteness." They would not, however, "attempt to enumerate the legitimate grounds for dismissal, believing . . . that individual institutions should take the initiative in this."[13] The 1940 Statement of Principles on Academic Freedom and Tenure refers to incompetence and moral turpitude in the discussion of termination for cause, but in a procedural context and without elaboration. Again, in the AAC-AAUP 1958 Statement on Procedural Standards in Faculty Dismissal Proceedings the problem of defining "cause" is identified but not dealt with:

One persistent source of difficulty is the definition of adequate cause for the dismissal of a faculty member. Despite the 1940

[13] *Academic Freedom and Tenure*, p. 175.

*Statement of Principles on Academic Freedom and Tenure and
subsequent attempts to build upon it, considerable ambiguity and
misunderstanding persist throughout higher education, especially
in the respective conceptions of governing boards, administrative
officers, and faculties concerning this matter. The present statement assumes that individual institutions will have formulated
their own definitions of adequate cause for dismissal, bearing in
mind the 1940 statement and standards which have developed
in the experience of academic institutions.*[14]

This is a very large assumption, for which there is little warrant
in general institutional practice. B. N. Shaw, for example, in his recent
study of tenure practices in state universities and land-grant colleges,
reports that only about half of the eighty institutions surveyed provided
specific criteria for the interpretation of "cause."[15] Some twenty-five
distinct criteria, were employed by the institutions which provided
them. A like variety was reported in 1959 by Byse and Joughin, who
concluded that "the criteria for dismissal are too often unnecessarily
vague."[16]

The commission believes that the higher education community
should work toward a broadly acceptable definition of adequate cause
for dismissal. While institutional independence in this matter must
be preserved, general standards must be sought if the higher education
community is to achieve a broad unity of sentiment concerning the
essentials of faculty and institutional responsibility upon which the
academic enterprise must rest. Exclusive concern for procedure, combined with the assumption that institutions can and will elaborate
their own substantive standards, can lead only to a continuation of
present misunderstanding and confusion. In the absence of general
standards—or even of criteria by which particular standards can be
assessed—there is the ever present possibility of that we will again see
the kind of case that disfigured the academic community during the
McCarthy period, or that the courts will be left to determine institutional policy in higher education, or that, on the contrary, institutions
will enunciate elaborate and detailed codes of behavior.

[14] *AAUP Policy Documents and Reports* (1971 ed.), p. 5.
[15] Pp. 62–65.
[16] Pp. 44–49.

However difficult the task of developing more generally acceptable standards of cause for dismissal, the commission believes that the attempt must be made and calls upon professional associations and institutions to work together to that end. The commission's recommendation is intended to promote further discussion of this difficult problem.

34. The commission believes that "adequate cause" in faculty dismissal proceedings should be restricted to (a) demonstrated incompetence or dishonesty in teaching or research, (b) substantial and manifest neglect of duty, and (c) personal conduct which substantially impairs the individual's fulfillment of his institutional responsibilities. The burden of proof in establishing cause for dismissal rests upon the institution.

Sanctions Short of Dismissal. Traditionally, faculty personnel policies in American higher education have been developed on the theory that dismissal from the institution is the only sanction for which explicit provision need be made. The rigorous and elaborate procedures to assure fairness through academic due process have been largely shaped by awareness of the severity and permanence of an unfavorable outcome of dismissal proceedings. The procedures, and actions taken under them, have been of an "all-or-nothing" sort: either the accused faculty member must be found guilty and subject to dismissal or he is innocent and escapes other penalty. Given the result contemplated, such procedural strictness is clearly necessary. The AAUP's 1968 Recommended Institutional Regulations on Academic Freedom and Tenure recognized the possibility of lesser sanctions. That is, in certain cases cause for dismissal may have been established, but a hearing committee—after considering all the circumstances—might recommend an academic penalty less than dismissal. Such lesser sanctions have been used—sometimes as a result of a regular hearing in which dismissal was originally contemplated, sometimes informally—through administrative action and usually without the safeguards of academic due process.

In the effort to assure the continuing accountability of the faculty, it is manifestly insufficient to have a disciplinary system which assumes that only those offenses which warrant dismissal should be considered seriously. Faculty members are from time to time guilty of offenses of lesser gravity. There should be a way of recognizing these and imposing appropriate sanctions. And it is equally insufficient to make do only with disciplinary procedures designed for capital offenses. Simpler procedures—though assuring due process in the particular context—are obviously required for offenses for which sanctions short of dismissal are contemplated.

But the problem is complicated. A special AAUP joint subcommittee—reporting in 1971 on its charge to consider the question of sanctions short of dismissal, "in order to provide a more versatile body of academic sanctions"—provided an illustrative list of such sanctions but could not recommend a single intermediate procedure, short of the elaborate formal procedure for dismissal, appropriate for all lesser offenses. On the other hand, the subcommittee recoiled from recommending an array of distinct procedures, subtly differentiated, for use in different sorts of cases.

The subcommittee listed the following lesser sanctions as suggestions: (1) oral reprimand, (2) written reprimand, (3) a recorded reprimand, (4) restitution (for instance, payment for damage done to individuals or to the institution), (5) loss of prospective benefits for a stated period (for instance, suspension of "regular" or "merit" increase in salary or suspension of promotion eligibility), (6) a fine, (7) reduction in salary for a stated period, (8) suspension from service for a stated period, without other prejudice.

As to the procedural problem, the subcommittee, after setting forth a number of pertinent considerations to be used in exploring alternatives, called upon the AAUP to review institutional arrangements that are beginning to appear and to give publicity to those it finds worthy of emulation. The subcommittee cautioned that not all lesser cases should be treated in the same manner as dismissal cases, "especially as this may mean on the one hand that many just grievances may simply go unredressed because of the discouragement that the elaborateness of dismissal procedures imposes upon the aggrieved party and upon the institution, and as it may mean on the other hand that the institution is frankly encouraged to seek more devious and subliminal ways of disciplining its faculty."[17] This commission agrees.

35. The commission recommends that each institution develop and adopt an enumeration of sanctions short of dismissal that may be

[17] *AAUP Bulletin,* December 1971, pp. 524–27.

applied in cases of demonstrated irresponsibility or professional misconduct for which some penalty short of dismissal should be imposed. These sanctions and the due-process procedures for complaint, hearing, judgment, and appeal should be developed initially by joint faculty-administrative action.

Standards of Notice. Adequate notice of nonreappointment should be given, and the amount of notice should be proportioned to length of service in the institution. The commission believes that the standards developed by the AAUP and now widely observed are fair to both the individual and the institution.

36. The commission recommends that all institutions adopt the following standards for notice of nonreappointment: at least three months before the date of termination of an initial one-year contract; at least six months before the date of termination of an initial two-year contract or of a second one-year contract; at least twelve months before the date of termination of a contract after two or more years of service in the institution.

Special Problems

A number of special problems, several of them of great urgency and long-term significance, require attention in many institutions as part of the effort to strengthen faculty personnel policy.

Eligibility for Tenure. The question of eligibility for tenure is a matter of concern on most campuses. Originally designed to assure the protection of academic freedom of teachers and scholars, tenure has become also a valued mark of status, normally conferring a wide range of other benefits, both material and intangible. Various groups of professionals who serve in nonteaching posts but whose work is closely related to the teaching process of the institution (for instance, professional librarians, counseling staff, and full-time research staff) have put forward claims to eligibility for tenure. Institutional policy with respect to eligibility for tenure for such nonteaching personnel varies widely across the country. No doubt it should and will continue to vary.

The commission makes no categoric recommendation on this matter. But it believes that institutions should develop explicit policies on eligibility for tenure and should develop and enforce standards to ensure that the concept of tenure is not weakened if tenure is to be extended. The safeguards of academic freedom should of course be

explicitly extended to all officers of the institution, whether or not they
enjoy faculty status and tenure. The commission believes that tenure
standards should not be lowered to permit the inclusion of nonteaching
personnel, though specific criteria for tenure will necessarily vary for
different professional groups. Standards for professional qualifications,
length of probationary service, and other key requirements for academic
tenure should be broadly equivalent among all personnel categories.
The commission believes that if members of the professional nonteaching staff are to enjoy the benefits of academic tenure, they should
accept its responsibilities as well. Institutional arrangements should
therefore be made under which they can serve, on an equal footing with
teaching faculty, in institutional governance, on review panels, hearing
boards, and the like. If it is not feasible to develop such equivalent
standards and principles of participation, the professional groups in
question should have their own more appropriate forms of continuing
service appointments.

    *37. The commission recommends that if nonteaching profes-
sional personnel are made eligible for academic tenure, the institution
should develop for these groups tenure standards equivalent in rigor
to those applicable to the teaching faculty.*

    Part-Time Service. It has long been standard academic prac-
tice to restrict eligibility for tenure to those appointed to full-time
service in the institution and to count only full-time service toward the
fulfillment of the institution's probationary requirement. This practice
derives fundamentally from the theory of the profession—that only the
regular faculty, by virtue of their full commitment to professional service in an institution, can make a valid claim to the unique privileges
and responsibilities associated with academic tenure. Part-time service
has always been more or less impromptu and ad hoc, related more to
temporary or emergency needs, or to the desire to provide apprentice
training to graduate students, than to permanent institutional requirements or long-term individual interests. To be sure, part-time service
by practicing professionals has always characterized professional schools
—notably, medicine, architecture, and law; but special arrangements
have grown up to handle such arrangements, designed to assure appropriate recognition and participation for the part-time faculty while
at the same time according fundamental responsibility to those who

have made a complete commitment to the institution and to academic life.

In recent years this traditional practice has been called into question. In particular, the restriction of tenure positions (or of probationary service prior to tenure) to those who can accept full-time service is alleged to operate as a serious obstacle to the pursuit of academic careers by women. Many women, it is said, desire to engage on a continuing basis in the academic profession for which they have been trained, but to do so in combination with marriage and family responsibilities. They wish to be considered for regular membership in the faculty, to accept the full range of responsibilities of such membership, to do so on a long-term basis, not casually; but they wish to participate on a reduced scale appropriate to their family responsibilities. It has been proposed, therefore, that academic tenure and the qualification procedures related to it be made more flexible, so as to permit part-time service, under appropriate circumstances, to count toward the award of tenure, and to permit tenure positions to be held on a part-time as well as on a full-time basis. Several institutions (for instance, Princeton and Columbia) have already modified their tenure regulations in this way.

This problem, like most of the others relating to tenure, is complex and difficult. In a good many institutions, of course, part-time faculty are seldom employed, and then usually in an adjunct status because of the value to the institution of the expertise arising from their normal professional occupation. Here difficulties may be minimal; and it may be relatively easy to create, more or less *de novo*, a limited number of tenure positions in which academic professionals can be appointed to serve part time on a long-term basis. But in other institutions—such as large public and private universities located in urban areas which have traditionally employed part-time faculty in large numbers—it may be extremely difficult to determine with any degree of fairness which part-time faculty members might be eligible for consideration under new tenure guidelines. Some collective bargaining contracts, it should be noted, already provide for handling opportunities for part-time service on a seniority basis. Here, then, the problem would be that of defining a new category of part-time appointees in accordance with new criteria.

Changes that may occur in the situations of those who at first find full-time service impossible will also present problems. Would a part-time tenure position be convertible into a full-time tenure position if the faculty member should find it possible to change? If so, a clear definition of the conditions under which such shifts would be allowed will need to be developed. If not, this fact and its consequences must be made clear and agreed to from the outset.

There are also such questions as equity in salary, fringe benefits, and teaching load to be reckoned with, and the need to hold any part-time tenure appointments to a number consistent with the stability and influence in institutional governance of the full-time faculty.

A number of institutions have begun experimenting with new methods of dealing with the problem of part-time faculty. At Columbia University part-time career appointments with tenure are made to faculty members eligible for promotion to all ranks to enable them to care for their children. Princeton University extends part-time appointments with tenure for personal reasons and as an additional way of bringing distinction to the university which may not be possible through full-time appointments only. Wesleyan University has been discussing a plan that would distinguish temporary from regular part-time faculty members and prorate salaries and fringe benefits accordingly.

On balance, the commission views tenure for *regular* part-time faculty members as desirable. It can enhance institutional and personal flexibility by allowing faculty members to ease into retirement or to complete important research projects or administrative assignments, and by allowing for institutional expansion or reduction in given disciplines. Part-time appointments can serve to increase flexibility during the probationary period by allowing faculty members to undertake a less stringent workload during the critical years of child rearing or for other personal reasons. Finally, part-time appointments with tenure can assure the institution of an experienced and professionally committed part-time faculty while assuring job continuity to the part-time faculty member. Nevertheless, criteria for the award of tenure and promotion should be uniform for all appointees in a given discipline, including those with reduced assignments; reduced workloads, however, should be considered on a proportional basis perhaps over a longer period of time. Shifts from part-time to full-time status and the reverse would, of course, depend on the availability of appropriate positions in line with the future plans of the institution.

38. *The commission recommends that institutions consider modifying their tenure arrangements in order to permit part-time faculty service under appropriate conditions to be credited toward the award of tenure, and to permit tenure positions to be held by faculty members who for family or other appropriate reasons cannot serve on a full-time basis.*

Administrative Office. It has long been standard practice to appoint department chairmen from the ranks of the faculty. Deans and administrative officers at the vice-presidential level commonly hold faculty appointments, usually with tenure, in the department of their discipline. The question arises as to the relation of academic tenure and administrative office. Should tenure be granted in administrative posts? That is, should department chairmen or deans or provosts have tenure in those offices as well as (or instead of) in their capacities as professors of this or that; or should they acquire tenure even in the absence of any colorable ground for their holding tenure as a professor? If a regular faculty member with tenure is appointed to a chairmanship or deanship or other administrative office, should his tenure as professor continue? Or should it cease when he takes an administrative office? Or should it continue only if his administrative responsibilities are less than full time, permitting him to continue some teaching and scholarship?

If the faculty member's tenure continues while he occupies an administrative post, should it continue indefinitely or for a limited period? What arrangements, if any, need to be made to enable the administrator whose tenure in a department has continued during his administrative service to prepare to resume his full faculty role?

Policy and practice on all these matters vary greatly among institutions. Often there is no settled policy, and many variations in practice exist within a single institution. The commission does not believe that there are simple answers to these questions, but it does believe that certain principles of sound institutional policy can be stated.

Administrative positions in which the responsibility is for academic questions and which involve dealings with the faculty on professional matters—chairmanships, deanships, academic vice-presidencies—ought as a general rule to be filled by persons with extensive faculty experience, who have or receive regular faculty tenure in the institution or for whom the cognizant faculty is prepared to recommend tenure if they are appointed from outside. If such persons are to be encouraged to accept administrative responsibilities, retention of tenure will normally seem to them a prerequisite, given the vicissitudes of administrative office and the fact that it customarily means setting aside for a time the teaching and scholarship which attracted them to the profession in the first place.

On the other hand, the commission is convinced that administrative positions at the level of chairman and above should not carry tenure as such. The basic rationale for tenure is in its contribution to the academic freedom of the teacher and scholar; the significance of tenure will be attenuated and perhaps at length lost if it extended to positions in which academic freedom, strictly construed, is not central to the function being performed. Deans and vice-presidents are fundamentally agents of administration, however important it may be that they should view their work in a broad faculty perspective. The principal administrator and the several faculties must have latitude in making changes from time to time; and if tenure were conferred in administrative office, the probable result would be recurrent administrative crisis or permanent administrative impaction. Department chairmen are at once the representatives of their colleagues and of the administration; it is desirable that chairmen serve for limited, if renewable, terms, and that they not come to think of themselves as permanently separated from their colleagues.

But if faculty members should retain their tenure while serving in administrative positions, and if tenure should not be awarded for administrative service as such, means must be found to ensure that when the administrator returns to full-time service he will be able to function effectively on the terms which led to the original bestowal of tenure. Examples abound in which the length or the completeness of immersion in administrative duties has rendered the faculty member quite unfit to return to regular faculty service: he has not been able to keep up with his field, his teaching skills have grown rusty, he has lost touch with his colleagues and the new directions of the department. When he returns to his department, he may crowd out younger faculty of great promise. The commission believes that this problem can best be handled by setting a limit on the length of full-time administrative service during which faculty tenure can be retained, unless the administrator continues his professional activities in teaching and scholarship in a significant way. Further, the commission believes that institutions should make special arrangements to assist faculty to keep current in their fields while serving in administrative posts and to help them make the transition to full-time faculty service. Among the methods worthy of consideration are periodic brief leaves for professional development and refreshment during administrative service; arrangements to permit or encourage administrators to continue some teaching and scholarly activity; leaves of absence prior to return to faculty service.

39. The commission recommends that institutions not grant tenure in administrative posts of department chairman and above.

The commission recommends that faculty members serving full time in administrative positions retain their faculty tenure up to a stated maximum period (say ten years) and that exceptions be conditional upon the maintenance while serving as administrators of a significant involvement in teaching and scholarship.

The commission further recommends that institutions develop special arrangements to enable faculty serving in administrative roles to keep current and active in their professional fields and to facilitate their return to full-time faculty service.

Early Retirement. Age of retirement and ways to permit or encourage retirement before the mandatory age is reached are currently subjects of lively interest. Early retirement has several potential benefits for the institution or individual faculty members:

1. Reduction in the number of those currently on tenure would open up tenure positions to which a larger number of young faculty members could be appointed than would otherwise be possible, if the institution's tenure strength must be stabilized at about its present level.

2. Reduction in the number on tenure through early retirement is a less painful way of dealing with grave financial exigency than involuntary separation.

3. Even where financial problems are not so grave as to require reductions in faculty size, early retirement may help relieve a budgetary squeeze by permitting the replacement of relatively high-salaried tenure faculty with younger faculty at lower salaries.

4. Early retirement may be a way of separating from the faculty those whose contributions have become less significant and valuable over the years.

5. Early retirement may be a means of enabling an institution to shift tenure positions, at a time when tenure strength cannot for budgetary reasons be increased, from fields in which there is declining interest to fields in which the institution wants to expand its commitment.

6. Early retirement may meet the desires of the faculty member who is tired, bored, out of sympathy with changed conditions in academic life, or who wants to take up a new career, pursue a hobby, or whatever.

Countervailing tendencies in American life and in the academic profession are at work here. Retirement at earlier ages appears to be on the increase generally and to be the declared objective of increasing numbers of labor organizations and other employee associations and groups. Arrangements to permit early retirement have become a subject of vigorous bargaining between employers and unions, and there is every reason to suppose that this trend will continue. Evidently Americans in ever growing numbers wish to shorten the period of their employment and lengthen the retirement years, or even undertake new careers in their late fifties or early sixties.

On the other hand, academicians have traditionally sought to prolong the period of employment. Many institutions set the retirement age at seventy; some even later. Many retired professors have continued to teach, to write, and to carry on their research for years after formal retirement; not a few institutions have year after year supplemented their regular faculty with professors who had retired elsewhere; and some institutions have used a late retirement age, or the absence of a mandatory age, as a powerful recruiting device. No doubt these traditions and habits owe much to the desire, in a profession that until recently has not been well paid and has not enjoyed very generous fringe-benefit programs, to maximize retirement annuities by prolonging the period of individual and institutional contribution. But this is not the whole story. Most professors, unlike many who are pressing for early retirement, enjoy their work and would like to continue as long as they are physically able. For them, early retirement, however appealing it may be to increasing numbers of Americans, is not inherently attractive.

The question of lowering the retirement age or encouraging early retirement in higher education, therefore, cannot be approached in simple confidence that it is the wave of the future in a leisure society. And quite apart from these basic problems of professional tradition and psychological orientation, the financial question is crucial. Early retirement, even where it is desired by the faculty member and in the interest of the institution, is not feasible unless it can be made economically attractive. Only a few faculty members are likely to command outside resources large enough to permit them to consider early retirement if it involves a reduction in the income they can expect to the date of regular retirement or in the income from retirement annuities or pension plans after normal retirement. Any serious consideration of early retirement, therefore, must be based on an analysis of ways in which supplemental benefits can be provided.

TIAA-CREF, in response to the growing interest in early retirement, published a bulletin on *Provisions for Early Retirement* in April 1972. The bulletin analyzes several early-retirement plans already in effect and provides valuable information on important aspects of early retirement. The bulletin concludes with a list of the steps any institution might take in exploring an early retirement program:

Determining an appropriate level of early-retirement benefits that will be financially feasible for the institution and the individual.

Deciding whether the supplementary benefits are to be available at the option of the staff member or the institution.

Deciding whether the program is to be established for a limited period of time or made a permanent part of the institution's retirement plan.

Estimating the cost-benefit results of the program for the foreseeable future.

40. The commission recommends that institutions develop attractive options for early retirement or reduced service that will enable those who wish to do so to leave tenured positions before the mandatory age.

The commission recommends that TIAA-CREF continue its exploration of methods of funding institutional early-retirement options and make the results of its studies widely available to institutions. Similar efforts should be undertaken by those responsible for state and other retirement programs.

Financial Exigency. It is not necessary here to rehearse the grave financial plight in which many colleges and universities now find themselves. Many institutions have been forced to reduce their programs, to curtail or eliminate the appointment of new staff members, and to refuse reappointment to nontenured faculty. Beyond this, some institutions have had to make reductions in staff by canceling term contracts before their stated date and by terminating tenure appointments. Forecasts of future budget problems suggest that many more institutions will face these problems during the next few years.

Financial exigency or changes in academic program have always been recognized as grounds for termination of tenure appointments. The AAC-AAUP 1940 statement stipulates only that "termination of a continuous appointment because of financial exigency should be demonstrably *bona fide*." Recently, more detailed policy guidelines and procedural standards have been enunciated by the Association of American Colleges and the American Association of University Professors.[18] The commission commends them to the attention of all institutions.

A number of problems require special attention in handling staff reductions as a result of financial exigency.

Since staff reductions are usually associated with changes in the academic program, the broad policy question of where program curtailment or program termination is to be made deeply affects the interests of students, whose future plans and the quality of whose

[18] Association of American Colleges, *Statement on Financial Exigency and Staff Reduction,* November 8, 1971. American Association of University Professors, "Recommended Institutional Regulations on Academic Freedom and Tenure," *AAUP Bulletin,* 1968, 54, 448–452, esp. section 4(c); "The Role of the Faculty in Budgetary and Salary Matters," *AAUP Bulletin,* 1972, 58, 170–172, esp. 171; *On Institutional Problems Resulting from Financial Exigency: Some Operating Guidelines,* November, 1971. See also Association of State Colleges and Universities, *Memo: To the President,* February 25, 1972, p. 2. For a general discussion see J. W. Gillis, "Academic Staff Reductions in Response to Financial Exigency," *Liberal Education,* 1971, 57, 364–377.

education may be substantially modified. Institutions obliged to consider program reductions for financial reasons should therefore set up procedures for informing students of specific program changes, their timing, and their consequences not only for the faculty involved but for present and future students.

There may be a temptation to use financial exigency as an opportunity to eliminate from the faculty a member who is allegedly incompetent, troublesome, uncooperative, conservative, or radical. Procedures for dealing with financial exigency should be designed for scrupulous avoidance of any taint of suspicion that they are being so used. If incompetence or irresponsibility is in question, proceedings should be undertaken with full due-process guarantees under recognized procedures and standards for dismissal or other disciplinary action.

Although there is general agreement that in staff reductions the interests of the tenured faculty should normally predominate over the interests of those who are on term appointments, sometimes the quality of the educational program may be seriously compromised if that principle is automatically applied. Circumstances can be envisaged in which it may be necessary to terminate a tenure appointment rather than a nontenured one. Problems of this sort can be handled equitably and in the best interests of the institution as a whole only if faculty play a key role in decisions about the institution's response to fiscal crisis, and only in an atmosphere in which there is no suspicion that the management of budget problems is being used to mask an attack upon the principle of tenure.

The handling of staff reduction may also raise difficulties in connection with the institution's efforts to increase representation on its faculty of women and members of minority groups. As the AAC statement says, "Strict adherence to preferential retention of tenured faculty members or strict recognition of seniority, for example, may result in disparate rates of reduction for women or members of ethnic or racial minorities and thus jeopardize recent progress toward fairer representation of these groups in the academic community. Staff-reduction decisions may also raise problems in relation to laws and regulations governing discrimination" (p. 4).

41. The commission recommends that each institution develop, in consultation with representatives of its faculty and student body, guidelines and procedures with respect to reduction of personnel to be used after it has been found necessary to reduce the size of the faculty because of financial exigency or changes in the academic program.

Disability. 42. The commission recommends that each institution develop standards under which disability of a faculty member can be determined, and procedures that will protect both the institution and the faculty member in cases where disability is claimed as a ground for dismissal, modification of assignment or salary, or early retirement. The commission urges institutions which do not now have long-term disability-insurance plans to adopt them promptly.

"*Soft*" *Money.* During the great period of college and university expansion in the 1950s and 1960s, when immense amounts of new money were pumped into higher education from all sources, but especially from the federal government, many institutions adopted personnel practices which plague them now that the springs of support are drying up. Institutions used grant funds from government agencies, foundations, and other sources to establish new faculty positions and to defray faculty salaries, in whole or in part. This was done not only with the permission of the granting agency but often, especially in the creation of new positions, as a condition of the grant, the objective of the agency or foundation being to expand a field of study, introduce a new program, secure geographical spread in graduate training, or meet higher manpower objectives. From the institution's point of view, this practice permitted program development and sometimes improvement of quality at a far more rapid rate than would have been possible even under the generally expansionist budgets of the time. And though it was clearly understood on all sides that the grants were temporary, experience suggested that renewals or new program support would continue to pour from the cornucopia; the prevailing euphoria induced visions of endlessly increasing support.

But there is no free lunch. Federal programs were cut back, foundation largesse diminished, and the present period of financial stringency began. Positions created on soft money had to be eliminated or absorbed into the regular budget. Where these were tenure positions, they could not easily be eliminated; and falling back on regular sources of funding placed severe strains on the budget and often distorted the overall program by forcing the shift of funds from other units. Nor was the problem, of course, confined merely to the funding of faculty salaries from temporary sources. Institutions that applied strict rules against the creation of positions funded with short-term money found themselves in a similar bind because the support for a regularly funded position—assistants, equipment, computer service—was often provided from short-term grants, which the institution had later to fund from the regular budget. Other institutions, which permitted term appointments but not tenure positions to be based on grant or contract money, found that they had to promote more of their probationary faculty than normally in order to keep them and fulfill the original purpose of the grant.

Institutions which had this kind of experience have no doubt developed policies to prevent its recurrence. But academic memory is short, and similar temptations may again occur. Legislators, agency officers, and foundation officials have a large responsibility to help assure that their grant programs do not put institutions in the position of living so far beyond their means that the fundamentals of sound staff planning are compromised. Institutions themselves, of course, must take care to ensure that short-term opportunities, however attractive, are compatible with realistic long-term planning. The principle of tenure ought not to be gambled away in the competition for temporary funds.

43. The commission recommends that institutions prohibit, as a matter of policy, the establishment of tenure positions supported in whole or in part by funds available to the institution on a short-term basis, such as research grants and contracts or foundation-sponsored projects, unless continuing support for such positions can be clearly identified in the regular budget of the institution.

Collective Bargaining. The rapid growth of collective bargaining in higher education raises the question of the relation of collective bargaining to tenure and other faculty personnel matters. This question is explored in some detail in Chapter Five. Since collective bargaining in an academic setting is in its infancy, faculties, administrations, governing boards, and national bargaining organizations must consider carefully the options open to them. Whatever resemblances academic institutions may have to the kinds of organizations in which collective bargaining has developed in this country, there are profound differences, often overlooked. The concept of tenure is one of these. Another is the remarkable diffusion of authority throughout the institution. The availability of tested standards and procedures for handling personnel questions is still another. Another is the presence in the academic institution of several distinct constituencies, each having a deep stake in the outcome of decisions—including students, whose interests have come in recent years to necessitate more formal modes of participation. This feature of the academy stands in sharp contrast to the simple two-party interest pattern of labor and management, for which most collective bargaining laws and practices are designed. Yet another difference is the fact that the norm or ideal in academic personnel decisions is a deliberative, not an adversary, posture; adversary relations in the academy represent a breakdown in the system.

Discovery or invention of ways to adapt collective bargaining to use in higher education will test educational statesmanship in the coming years. The commission believes that academic freedom and tenure are so central to the entire academic enterprise that they should not be exposed to the exigencies of the collective bargaining process but should continue to be supported through tested academic procedures.

44. The commission recommends that collective bargaining in colleges and universities not extend to academic freedom and tenure and related faculty personnel matters, and that grievances involving issues of freedom and tenure be referred to academic procedures outside the collective bargaining process.

Needed Information and Research

In view of the fundamental importance of the subject, it is astonishing how little reliable information is available about personnel practices in American institutions of higher education. Information is not compiled on a consistent basis that would permit comparisons or reliable projections of trends to be made. Many institutions do not know how many of their own faculty hold tenure appointments, how old they are, at what rate they will retire. Consequently, institutions that wish to undertake a review of their own policies and staffing plans must do so without information about comparable institutions or about investigations and experiments going on elsewhere. Duplication of effort is the order of the day. Coordinating boards and legislatures, when making decisions about broad personnel questions, must proceed largely in the dark. Topics that are the staple of debate and controversy—such as "accountability" and "innovation"—have seldom been subjected to serious analysis.

For no aspect of higher education is Allan Cartter's dictum more distressingly accurate than for faculty personnel matters: "Traditionally, educators have done less questioning about themselves and the processes of which they are an integral part than they have about the world outside the university."[19]

The commission is convinced that substantial improvement of faculty personnel policies, including tenure, will be facilitated if relevant information, systematically collected and reported, is available to all institutions on a regular basis and if research efforts are intensified.

Current and reliable information is needed about tenure policies and practices in American institutions. Studies such as the one reported in Chapter Six should be expanded and conducted annually in order to provide current information to institutions and to lay the basis for long-range research.

45. The commission recommends that the American Council on Education, in collaboration with other educational associations, provide a clearinghouse for information about faculty personnel practice in higher education, maintaining a current file on institutional tenure policies and practices, and publicizing and making available to interested institutions the results of reviews and developments relating to tenure throughout the country.

The commission further recommends that the Office of Research of the American Council on Education develop an annual inventory on tenure and related matters in American higher education and publish the results on a regular basis. The inventory might take the form of an expansion of the survey reported in Chapter Six.

The commission also recommends that the ACE Office of Research administer on a periodic basis—say, every four or five years— a faculty questionnaire of the type used in the 1969 survey of college and university faculty (see Chapter Seven), publishing the results in a form that will be useful to institutions in their staff planning and to researchers on faculty personnel problems.

Research is needed on the alternatives to tenure and their

[19] "Graduate Education and Research in the Decades Ahead," in *Campus 1980* (New York: Delacorte, 1968), pp. 274–275.

educational effectiveness. Experiments with alternatives to tenure will no doubt continue. Among the questions that need to be answered about alternative personnel plans are these: Which problems allegedly arising from tenure do these alternatives really solve? Do institutions with contract systems have more accountability, less "deadwood," more flexibility, more dedication to teaching, and more responsiveness to students? Is academic freedom as secure? What are the relative costs and benefits, not only in budgetary but in educational terms? Similar institutions, one with a tenure plan and one without, could be compared for quality of program and performance. In short, basic research is sorely needed in this area.

46. The commission recommends that institutions which are currently experimenting with alternatives to traditional tenure arrangements undertake, as soon as they have had sufficient experience with these arrangements to warrant a judgment, to invite evaluations of the experiments by appropriate national professional groups (preferably by evaluation teams representing several organizations) and that the results of such evaluations be made available for the information and guidance of other institutions.

Further research is needed on teaching effectiveness and methods for evaluating it. Commendable efforts in this direction have been undertaken by the AAUP and the AAC in their joint Project to Improve College Teaching, and by the Center for Research and Development in Higher Education at the University of California, Berkeley. But much more needs to be done, particularly in connection with differences among disciplines, levels of instruction, and types of institutions.

47. The commission recommends that professional associations and research centers continue and expand their efforts to develop more sophisticated conceptions of teaching effectiveness and more reliable methods of evaluating teaching, and to disseminate the results of these studies to interested institutions.

✻◗✻◗✻◗✻◗✻◗ **III** ◗✻◗✻◗✻◗✻◗✻

Academic Tenure
in America:
A Historical Essay

Walter P. Metzger

◗✻◗✻◗✻◗✻◗✻◗✻◗✻◗✻◗✻◗✻◗✻◗✻◗✻◗✻◗✻◗

The current debate over academic tenure calls into question everything about it except its age. Among the usages of our universities, tenure is commonly regarded as a latecomer, probably not older than the Great Depression, certainly not older than Civil Service laws. No doubt, the former did teach professors to hedge against the hazards of the labor market, and the latter did spread the gospel of job security far and wide. But we drastically foreshorten the story when we take yesterday and the day before as starting points. In all the ages of academic man—the age of the master, the age of the employee, the age of the professional—the desire to protect the academic office has run strong. In each age, some kind of tenure was established—tenure as privilege, tenure as time, tenure as judiciality. A long looking back seems much in order, and not merely to enlarge today's debate. An academic who traces the history of academic tenure recapitulates the evolution of his species and comes into more knowing terms with himself.

Tenure as Privilege: The Era of the Master

From the time it emerged in the high middle ages to the time it was reshaped by the Reformation, teaching in a *studium generale* or university was a highly privileged occupation. In a turbulent and sometimes violent age, rulers of church and state took special pains to ensure the safety of the scholar's person.[1] As early as 1158, the Emperor Frederick Barbarossa issued an edict promising scholars in his domains safe conduct in their journeys, protection from attack upon their domiciles, and compensation for unlawful injury (the famous *Authentica Habita*).[2] With this as precedent and example, the sovereigns in other lands followed suit, and for centuries the royal institution joined with the far-reaching Roman Papacy to shield university scholars from their would-be plunderers and assailants—the country brigands and the city mobs.[3]

Not only the physical security but the material comfort of scholars became an object of high-placed solicitude in the middle ages. As long as they had the power to be bountiful, popes gave preference to clerical academics in filling ecclesiastical benefices, often by choosing them from lists drawn up by these very supplicants; in addition, as a special indulgence, scholars could hold these offices for lengthy periods

---

[1] Unless otherwise indicated, the word *scholar* is here used to refer to any resident of the university and not exclusively to students, which is the meaning the word gradually acquired.

[2] H. Koeppler, "Frederick Barbarossa and the Schools of Bologna: Some Remarks on the 'Authentica Habita'," *English Historical Review*, 1939, *54*, 606–607.

[3] This section draws heavily upon P. Kibre, *Scholarly Privilege in the Middle Ages* (Cambridge, 1962).

in absentia and still enjoy their fruits.[4] Student fees (charged despite papal insistence on *gratis* education for the poor), institutional salaries (in some places), stipends from endowments (in other places) made up the rest of the academic income, which might seldom have been extravagant but which was probably seldom scant.[5] To these direct emoluments, monarchs and municipalities appended a variety of what we would now call fringe benefits. It became customary for those ascending the French and English thrones to reaffirm, in solemn ceremony, the immemorial right of scholars not to serve in the army or pay taxes—rights which kings pinched for men and money could hardly have acknowledged without pain. It became customary, too, for city councils, despite perennial tensions between town and gown, to offer or renew the offer of material concessions to residing scholars: freedom from local tolls and duties (provided they did not traffic on their own account), provision of good housing at fair prices (sometimes by commandeering houses if such were not available on the market), protection against overpriced or spoiled commodities, even relief from disturbing noises and distressing smells.[6] Thanks to such patronage and preferment, the lot of the academic in the middle ages can be said to have been remarkably safeguarded, disburdened, well-provided, even salubrious.

But these and other external favors, much as they were cherished by their recipients, did not constitute the whole, or even the most essential, part of the medieval *privilegia scholastica*. The inescapable lesson of experience was that favors beneficently granted could be capriciously retracted, that protections provided by the Crown or Curia could be nullified by functionaries closer by (indeed, one reason scholarly rights were repeatedly acknowledged was that they were repeatedly infringed). Armed with a formidable collective pride that

---

[4] H. Rashdall, *Universities of Europe in the Middle Ages,* new edition edited by F. M. Powicke and A. B. Emden (1936), Vol. 1, p. 537n. This monumental work, superseded by later scholarship in some details, still places all historians of the university heavily in its debt.

[5] G. Post, "Masters' Salaries and Student-Fees in the Medieval Universities," *Speculum,* 1932, 7, 182–198.

[6] For a convenient summary of scholarly privileges, see Kibre, pp. 325–330. Also L. Thorndike, *University Records and Life in the Middle Ages* (New York, 1944), passim.

chafed at an insecure dependence, medieval scholars were not content simply to seek access to the seats of power; they also sought *immunity* from the reach of power and a corporate *autonomy* that would empower them to assist and defend themselves. The principal immunity they sought was to be exempt from the jurisdiction of temporal (and often ecclesiastical) tribunals in criminal and civil legal actions. The key to the autonomy they sought was to gain through the device of incorporation (variously termed *communitas, collegium, societas, consortium*) the right to elect their own officers and representatives, to sue and be sued as a single juristic person, and—above all—to enact the rules and regulations to which they and those who dealt with them had to conform. The constitutional history of the medieval university is in large part a recital of the vicissitudes—and of the considerable fulfillment—of these two distinct yet allied ambitions. It is largely to them that we refer when, in awarding degrees, we pay our ritual respects to the "privileges and immunities thereunto pertaining." And it is largely from them that we derive, albeit only in root, the modern concept of academic tenure.

Needless to say, to attempt to recount this constitutional history in full detail would be an unmanageable undertaking, given the number of medieval universities (seventy-nine by the end of the fifteenth century), the variety of institutional types (two, plus diverse admixtures), the span of time to be encompassed (four centuries, at a conservative reckoning), and the spatial limitations of this essay. To brave this complexity and flux, it is necessary to concentrate on one type alone (the magisterial university, from which the universities of this country have descended), to draw illustrations from only certain sites (the University of Paris, the universal mother, and the universities of Oxford and Cambridge, our direct forebears) and to derive only the most general conclusions from this welter of reduced, but still immense, experience.

It is evident, first, that the privileges sought by self-assertive scholars were not exclusively academic. The Northern universities were ecclesiastical foundations under apostolic authority. Virtually all the *magistri* (and a good many of the more advanced *scholares*) were clerks in holy or minor orders. While it is true that these universities were more than seminaries and that a certain number of masters and students were only nominally clerks, committed to the observance of celibacy but not to careers within the Church, it is undeniable that an air of sacerdotal sanctity hung over the academy and its members and secured to them a number of special privileges. Between the legal immunity of scholars and the canonical benefit of clergy there was plainly an intimate connection, as there was between the success of the university in resisting the reach of the civil magistrate and the success of the Roman Church in resisting the dictates of lay authority.[7] In addition, as the etymology of the word suggests, a university denoted a guild, or rather a congeries of guilds, organized ethnically into "nations," by habitat and endowment into "colleges," by field and degree-granting power into "faculties."[8] That members of a particular occupation should be allowed to organize themselves into societies for mutual aid and self-protection was not advanced as an academic peculiarity: it was an idea imbedded in an associative form that spread through Europe in the middle ages and that encompassed a burgeoning variety of professions, crafts, and trades.[9] Finally, the marked migratory proclivities of students (and, to a lesser degree, of masters) had the effect of creating swarms of aliens who would alight on hostile, often zenophobic, towns. In similar circumstances, colonies of foreign merchants pressed for extraterritorial rights and privileges; not surprisingly, associations of foreign scholars did the same. The *civis in civitate* that the university came to represent was thus one of many formations designed to offset the disabilities of outsideness in a provincialized world.[10]

    [7] E. G. Roelker, *Principles of Privilege According to the Code of Canon Law,* Canon Law Studies (Catholic University, 1926), passim.
    [8] Only later did the word *university* imply some kind of universality, either in comprehensiveness of curriculum or in cosmopolitanism of attendants. At the start a *universitas* was simply any aggregate of persons granted a legal corporate existence. Rashdall, Vol. 1, pp. 5–6.
    [9] H. Pirenne, *A History of Europe,* translated by B. Miall (New York, 1938), pp. 382–390.
    [10] In the Italian city-republic of Bologna, it was the association of foreign students that forced the host community to accept its own rector as the judical authority in actions involving students, even where local citizens were parties to the suit. This, plus the fact that the first professors were Bolognese citizens who sought to exclude all but their fellow citizens from the privileges of the doctorate, provided the stimulus for the creation of a student-dominated university, one of the archetypes in the middle ages. But even in the master-controlled

And yet, despite these overlaps, it would be a mistake to conclude that the privileges sought by medieval scholars were simply the
composite reflections of the statuses they shared with other groups. For
the fact of the matter was that members of the medieval university
were not priests immersed in the cure of souls, illiterate craftsmen
joined together, bands of commercial travelers; they were, and were
treated as, men of learning or as the disciples of men of learning at a
time when learning was a precious light. For what they received or
took by way of privilege, they gave back much of high contemporary
value: the tenets of religious faith—clarified, systematized, and
cleansed of error; careful renderings of the canon and civil law, on
which spiritual and temporal administration alike depended; the tools
of dialectic logic, the foremost utensils of the scholastic mind, honed
by ceaseless practice in disputation; the re-found thoughts of the Arabs,
the Jews, the Hellenes, immense accretions to the Christian store,
which might have been lost but for academic bibliophiles or suppressed
but for academic synthesizers.[11] Nor did they, in performing these
feats for mind and culture, slight the needs of the mundane world.
Great faculties became great counsellors: the Faculty of Theology of
the University of Paris became the leading arbiter of doctrinal issues
before the Church. Great universities became great diplomatists: it fell
to Paris in the fourteenth century to lead the pan-European effort to
resolve the Great Schism in the Papacy.[12] And not only at the pinnacle
was the world's work done: every university returned to society a supreme utility—cadres of educated persons to man important secular
and religious posts. Later, these dividends would be depreciated by
humanistic critics, empirical methodologists, religious reformers. But
in the golden season of the *studium,* its remittances were unquestionably reckoned great and good. Not for nothing did popes call the University of Paris "wisdom's workshop" and French kings adopt it as
their "eldest daughter" and official rhetoricians salute it "as the foun-
tainhead of the stream of knowledge that waters the whole Christian
world." And not for nothing did regional rulers woo away scholars

university, the quest for artificial citizenship did much to instigate and nourish
the corporate academic life.
    [11] See C. H. Haskins, *The Rise of Universities* (Cornell, 1923).
    [12] Rashdall, Vol. 1, p. 573.

from their neighbors and tremble when their own university threatened to suspend its operations or close its doors.

It was, indeed, this sense of exceptionality that led the masters of Paris, in the first century of their chartered existence, to distinguish an academic vocation from one that was broadly and simply clerical. Two conflicts with the local hierarchy—one over external licensure, the other over diocesan discipline—served to heighten that distinction. In the middle ages, the Church had charge of the credential (the *licentia docendi*) that entitled holders of degrees to give "ordinary" academic lectures. Where the prelate vested with authority to give or withhold these needed passports was closely identified with the university (as he was at Oxford and Cambridge), the system of ecclesiastical gatekeeping did not raise magisterial tempers. But at the University of Paris, where the licensor was the chancellor of the Cathedral Church of Notre Dame, a church official subordinate to the local primate, this matter caused very hot disputes. To the masters of the Faculty of Arts, the most numerous and most combative of the tetralogy of faculties, external control of access imperiled internal control at every vital point. By requiring candidates for the license to swear allegiance to himself, the chancellor raised for them the specter of a faculty weakened by foreign loyalties; by reserving the right to revoke a license, he appeared to assert that he could displace a master after he had been duly incepted; by awarding the licensing to whom he pleased, he seemed to hold the academic status cheap (one faculty remonstrance accused him of issuing licenses to his own relatives, to women, even to actors). The struggle of the Paris masters against this church official went on for almost the whole of the thirteenth century. Tied in with conflicts with secular authority as well, it was marked by several cessations of lectures, one wholesale though temporary dispersion, and many fervent appeals to Rome, which in the end were to prove decisive. From this struggle, which was the earliest and surely one of the most tumultuous in the annals of faculty self-assertion, the masters emerged on the whole victorious. By papal decree, the chancellor was compelled to award the *licentia docendi* only to persons certified by the faculty; the oath of obedience was to be sworn not to him but to the university; the power of revocation fell into deseutude and became obsolete. Never again, while the era of the master lasted, would

external authority interpose itself so blatantly into the process of qualification, thereafter deemed a faculty preserve.[13]

The battle against diocesan discipline was more sporadically
waged and less decisively concluded. The city of Paris was the see of
a powerful bishop who had the power to try clerical offenders under
canon law and the will at times to punish them unsparingly. Given a
choice between lay and episcopal justice, the cleric scholars of Paris
might seek the latter as a safer harbor; moreover, they might avail
themselves of the authority of the episcopate in their own theological
disputes. Still they resented the haughtiness and stringency of this local
potentate and worked to reduce his power over them, largely by expanding the authority of competing courts—the court of the con-
servator apostolic (the local protector of papal interests) and the
court of the academic rector (the representative of the university as
a whole). The records of this jurisdictional conflict offer instructive
reading to anyone interested in the development of a self-conscious
academic class. In 1219, after appeal by the university to the Holy
See, the Bishop of Paris was forbidden to excommunicate a master or
a student without express permission from the pope himself. (Here
one observes the faculty playing off the distant against the nearby
hierarch.) Similarly in 1361, after appeal by the university to the King
of France, the bishop was compelled to release a university scholar
whom he had imprisoned on a charge of heresy. (Here one observes
the faculty's tactic of forming advantageous alliances, even with the
state against the church.) Again, in 1376, an official of the bishop,
who had refused to release a scholar accused of major crimes to the
rector's court, was excommunicated by the university for breaking the
vows he had taken as an erstwhile member of it. (Here one observes
a host of things, including the sweep of the academic claim to judicial
competence, the persistence of the academic claim to loyalty, and the
dimensions of academic gall.)[14] But what is perhaps most revealing
about these cases is the distinction between inside and outside that the
masters went to endless pains to draw even within the confines of the

[13] Kibre, pp. 121–131; Rashdall, Vol. 1, pp. 304–312; Vol. 3, pp 81–87,
93–100.
[14] Kibre, pp. 88, 150–151, 180–181.

holy church. Always ready to rise in defense of cleric privilege when the lay provost and his henchmen committed sacrilegious arrests and seizures, the clerks of the faculties of Paris did not show much priestly submissiveness when they thought that their own superiors mistreated them, except to make reverent (and quite political) genuflexion to the pope.

It is from this intermingling of shared and special privileges that we may draw our first approximation of what tenure meant in the middle ages. Since the word applied to this setting is an anachronism, it is necessary first to disengage it from its modern associations. Tenure in magisterial universities was not an attribute of occupancy of office, with set emoluments and prescribed functions, but an attribute of admission to a *corpus,* possessed of a legal personality and (in part through delegation, in part through usurpation) of considerable governmental power, of a kind of mini-sovereignty. Admission to this body was accomplished not through a contract of employment but through the crossing of certain qualificatory thresholds—the earning of degrees, the exhibition of certain prowesses, the acquisition of a license—over which the masters took command. Continuation as a member depended not on the performance of specific duties (one could remain a master in good standing even if one did not teach) but on adherence to collegial comities. And expulsion from this body could be directly effected not by an outside agency but only by the body itself. At bottom, tenure as privilege was a declaration of opposition to any academic sanction from any nonacademic source.

But tenure, as we know it today, does not simply build battlements against external dangers; it also fortifies the individual against menacing forces from within. On this score, the world of the master may be said to offer only a few foretokens of the modern form. Not only the Franciscans and Dominicans, whose regimens were dictated by their respective orders, but every member of a faculty lived under common rules to which he took compelling vows. To be admitted to the *consortio magistrorum* was to submit to a rulership of peers, a rulership stiffened by a siege mentality, a taste for detailed regulation, and a subscription to received religious truth. Hardly a facet of academic life was left uncovered by written ordinance, and no ordinance was ever written that did not specify the penalty for its breach. Vio-

lation of the statutes respecting costume, class attendance, the pace
and order of lectures was usually punishable by fines or suspension;
failure to protect the secrets of the corporation, refusal to join in a
cessation or strike, or stubborn adherence to fallacious dogma could
incur the penalty of expulsion.[15]

This is not to say that sanctions were imposed arbitrarily. Academic due process is not an invention but a rediscovery of the modern
university. Both at Paris and at Oxford, provision was made for a
formal hearing of charges against scholars and for the appeal of adverse decisions from the court of trial to the entire congregation.[16] Nor
is this to say that drastic punishments—most notably expulsion, which
was deemed a horrendous penalty—were inflicted lightly. Sometimes,
in cases involving religious error, a hierarchy of censures would be
concocted (ranging from merely "bad-sounding" and "ridiculous" to
the ultimate "heretical") in order to allow for gradations of sin and
limit the use of the harshest sanction.[17] Nor, again, is this to say that
peer pressures were so overbearing that no one was ever able to resist
them (as we may infer from such famous defiances as those by William
of Ockham, Marsilius of Padua, Nicole Oresme, John Buridan, and
Nicholas of Autrecourt).[18] Finally, this is not to say that one master
was as likely as another to feel the scourge of peer disapproval. As is
perhaps the case today with respect to junior faculty it was the novice
theologian—not the man of established reputation—who most often
came under hostile scrutiny from his fellows. Still, a good deal of personal independence was sacrificed on the altar of collective power.
A society so autocratically religious and at the same time so demo-
cratically governed could offer its members margins for maneuver but
could not permit them to flout its will. The nonconforming academic
could pit one authority against another (for the church did not
always speak consistently), could distinguish philosophy from theology

---

[15] H. Denifle and A. Chatelain, *Chartularium Universitatis Parisiensis*
(1897), Vol. 1, pp. 277–279, 538–539, 589–590.

[16] Rashdall, Vol. 3, p. 137.

[17] M. M. McLaughlin, "Intellectual Freedom and Its Limitation in the
University of Paris in the Thirteenth and Fourteenth Centuries," unpublished
doctoral dissertation (Columbia University, 1954), p. 270.

[18] W. L. Wakefield and A. P. Evans, *Heresies of the High Middle Ages*
(New York, 1969).

and call the former a freer zone ˈ(for the university embraced both kinds of knowledge), could convert indictments into opportunities to expound and prosyletize his ideas. But he could not assert that he was immune to the group's disfavor, either by virtue of a right to freedom, or by virtue of a right to privacy.[19] One of the latent functions of modern tenure is to limit the tyranny of colleagueships. This was not the function of medieval tenure, nor could it be of any system that allowed academics in combination to be their brothers' keepers—and by implication their forsakers too.

Two further differences bear noting. In the chronicles of old Oxford and Paris, the act of removing a master is commonly referred to as a privation (*privatio*), sometimes as a banishment (*exilium*), but not as a discharge or dismissal. This terminology at once reminds us that a master was not an employee of the university but one of its corporate directors: not having been hired he could not be fired, though he could be blackballed and expelled. However, even in Italy and Northern Germany, where the master was appointed to office and paid a yearly salary, his removal would go by these awesome names. Plainly, to be excluded from the fellowship meant something more than disemployment. To be sure, it could entail the loss of a valued benefice, of a "living" in the ecclesiastical sense. But it did not necessarily preclude a living in the broader sense, for this society had more than one cranny hospitable to learned talents, and a person ejected from the university, provided he bore no worse stigmata, could find a niche in the *studium* of his abbey (thus, John-Peter Oliveri) or even a place in the Roman court (thus, Siger de Brabant).[20] But *privatio* brought other misfortunes, not so easy to repair: it entailed the loss of academic privileges, first and foremost; it added to this the pain of ostracism, solemnly pronounced; it could mean suspension of degrees or blockage of study toward more advanced ones; finally, where perjury or infidelity was the cause, it could result in excommunication and bring about that most acute exclusion—from the sacraments of the Church. Matching the extensiveness of the sanction was the far-reach-

---

[19] Another group likely to be penalized for divergent viewpoints were the mendicant friars, whose academic status was assailable because their academic fealties were held in doubt. Rashdall, Vol. 1, pp. 344–396.

[20] McLaughlin, pp. 130, 344–349.

ing ambit of offenses to which it could be legitimately applied. The medieval university did not distinguish between academic and civil misconduct, between professional and public crimes. This was most patently the case at Oxford, where the Court of the Chancellor of the University dealt out punishments for any misdeed, criminal or civil, spiritual or academic, committed by an academic member, unless it was a capital crime. But this was also essentially true at Paris, where there was a greater division of judicial labor, but no agreement on where the lines were to be drawn. The medieval punishment of privation went with a world that had not yet learned to think in monetary terms about employment, in secular terms about professing, and in segmental terms about the moral life.

Nor had it learned to assign different formal rights to different elements in the university. To one who has been familiarized to the distinction between *Lehrfreiheit* and *Lernfreiheit,* between procedures appropriate to dismissal and procedures appropriate to disenrollment, the medieval failure to differentiate between the judicial rights of faculty and students may seem, to say the least, quite strange. Yet it is a fact that in the medieval university (commonly referred to, incidentally, as the *universitas magistrorum et scholarium*), students no less than faculties were the addressees of its chartered privileges: both had access to its tribunals; both were involved in bishop-rector tugs of war; both could be deprived. In part, this lack of differentiation may be explained by the criss-crossing of statuses (with a shifting and rotating regency, students studying for advanced degrees could be tyro masters, while veteran masters sometimes did not teach at all); in part, it may be explained by the uniformity of statuses (the sharing by masters and students of a common clericality). These would seem sufficient explanations but for the fact that the university's jurisdiction included all sorts of groups besides—papermakers, vendors, booksellers; students *in perpetuo* and students in name only and students who had long since become alumni; the servitors and retainers of scholars; at Oxford and Cambridge, almost the entire town. In some degree, it would appear, the lack of differentiation must be laid to the expansionary impulse inherent in privilege itself. Modern tenure specifies, eliminates; medieval privilege generalizes, includes.

It is as difficult to say just when the era of the master ended as to supply a date for the expiration of the middle ages. Trends hostile to an academic system based on privilege had been gathering strength even in its heyday; specific features of that system have survived until modern times. Still, the history of institutions, while it shuns the flawless age and the complete debacle, does sometimes tell of a decisive moment, of an event that divides the flowing chronicle into a period of vitality however tenuous and a period of dissolution however slow. For the medieval university, the Protestant Reformation was that kind of partitioning event. It did not strike the first blows against faculty immunity and autonomy. Half a century before, when the king of France set up the Parlement of Paris as the supreme tribunal of the university and forbade resort to cessations, the major weapon in the masters' armory, he had served notice that the days of double justice were numbered and that the law of the state would be supreme.[21] Long before Luther wrote his manifesto, the universities of central Europe had given signs that they were heading toward a new era of state dependence when they developed a permanent and increasingly secular professoriate, paid by town and ducal funds.[22] But the Protestant Reformation did strike the blows that killed. The destruction of papal supremacy upset the equipoise between *sacerdotium* and *imperium*, on which the power of the *studium* had been based. The confiscation of church properties and endowments made burghers and princes more than ever the crucial financiers of universities. The nationalizing of the church put an end to the ecumenicism of the academy, so that even the University of Paris, Catholic and ultramontane in policy, became Gallican in membership and sway.[23] In raising the level of subversive currents, the Reformation served almost to obliterate the distinction between inside and outside, the old line of tenurial defense. The Augsburg formula of religious compromise, *cuius regio, eius religio*, became a formula of academic domination, *cuius regio, eius universitas*, the confessional preference of the prince supplanting the collegial standard by which the fitness of professors had been judged. The presumption that a political unit could not comprehend within itself two forms of political belief and worship led to the ex-

[21] Kibre, pp. 221–226.
[22] J. M. Fletcher, "Wealth and Poverty in the Medieval German Universities" in J. R. Hale and others, *Europe in the Late Middle Ages* (London, 1965), pp. 410–436.
[23] S. d'Irsay, *Histoire des universités* (Paris, 1932), Vol. 1, pp. 191–222.

pulsion of Catholics from Tubingen in 1535, of Lutherans from Leipzig in 1539, of Protestant suspects from Vienna. The proliferation of religious sects, each conceiving itself a priesthood of believers and many seeking to become the established church, led to tergiversations such as occurred at Marburg, where Lutherans were installed in the sixteenth century only to be replaced by Calvinists in the next. The link between treason and heresy broke the older chains of academic feality: witness Protestant Königsburg, where the faculty took its oath of loyalty not to the university but to the Prussian duke.[24] The blows were heavy and of many sorts.

After the seventeenth century the universities of central Europe began to lose their sectarian and despotic character. The founding of nonconfessional universities like Halle (1694)' and Gottingen (1732) were indications that the passions of religion, and even the politics of religion, were subsiding. The reawakening of speculative philosophy in the eighteenth century served to shift the locus of authority in religious matters from church and state to individual, where it was seated on the throne of conscience. In the early nineteenth century the introduction of science into the curriculum brought in tow the ideology of research, which argued that the knower needed self-direction and lauded new knowledge as a social good. The result was that a certain measure of the old autonomy and even a semblance of the old immunity regained institutional form. In separate faculties and in a common senate, continental professors in the nineteenth century exercised large powers of administration: they set educational standards, awarded academic degrees, extended the *venia legendi* (offspring of the *licentia docendi*) to novices desiring to teach. They elected their own officials, including the rector, who presided over all the faculties; they formed a quasijudicial court to hear cases involving student discipline; they enjoyed the right to appoint instructors and to nominate candidates for chairs. Finally, they were presumed to hold office *durante vita,* barring serious offense. To foreign visitors, this system appeared to have all the essential attributes of the medieval *consortio magistrorum,* and not a few of these visitors, impressed with its smooth workings and high results, carried home with them the happy tidings that they

[24] F. Paulsen, *The German Universities, Their Character and Historical Development* (New York, 1895), pp. 1–37.

had seen the past and knew it worked. But in fact, the system that emerged in central Europe was not a replica of the old order; it was an alliance between state and corporation in which the state was the dominant force. The universities of Germany, for example, did not have the power of the purse: they could not function without state appropriations, could not create a new chair without securing state approval, could not erect a building or endow a scholarship without gaining ministerial consent. Faculty cooptation was under one great critical constraint: the minister of education did not have to, and more than occasionally did not, accept faculty suggestions for high appointments. For all their vaunted freedom, professors were obliged not to subscribe to subversive doctrines. In the codifications of this partnership, an element of contradiction always entered. Thus, the Prussian Land Code of 1794 declared the universities to be both privileged bodies and public institutions, while the Prussian Constitution of 1850, after guaranteeing academic freedom, told academics that they first had to prove to official powers their moral and scientific worth.[25] This contradiction reveals what the master in these regions had become: a member of the higher civil service, accorded unusual prestige and scope.

Children of the Protestant Reformation, the American colleges founded in the seventeenth and eighteenth centuries were heirs to the tradition of the mastership and contributors to the dialytic process that broke that tradition down. Significantly, however, the line of descent did not go directly from the continent of Europe to North America; it traveled to the English islands before it took the transatlantic hop. At least in its early phase, the history of tenure of this country was to be shaped by the angularity of this descent.

Like their sister universities across the Channel, Oxford and Cambridge, with their ecclesiastic ties and cleric memberships, were much buffeted by the events of the Reformation. In some ways, they suffered harsher blows. Alone among sovereigns who opposed the pope, Henry VIII constituted himself a pope and invented a state religion even as he declared one. Moreover, each of his close successors

<hr/>

[25] E. Spranger, *Wilhelm von Humboldt* (Berlin, 1910); J. Ben-David, *The Scientist's Role in Society* (New York, 1971), pp. 112–135.

brought a different church polity and prescriptive canon and thus
created new articles to be sworn to, new sets of forced choices to be
confronted, and new batches of academics to be expelled.[26] To assure
compliance with the orthodoxy of the moment, as well as to conform
instruction to royal taste, the Tudor and Stuart monarchs converted
the instrument of visitation, heretofore used to arbitrate disputes, into
a royal commission with injunctive power to impose new oaths, de-
tect recusants, and rewrite statutes.[27] Royal visitations were ad hoc
affairs; royal patronage was used for similar purposes with regularity.
Taking over the dispensing powers of the pope, to which they added
their own practiced skill in bestowing spoils, the English kings in the
sixteenth and early seventeenth centuries managed to secure the appointment of their favorites to once-guarded academic posts. With
regard to the independence of the universities, it little mattered that
certain happy reforms, like the encouragement of the study of Greek,
were accomplished by royal command; or that considerable generosity,
as evidenced in the creation of regius professorships, was extended at
royal behest; or even that the magisterial corporations, stripped of
their papal charters, were placed on a new legal footing by royal acts.
Even bounty could produce dependence, as the masters must have
noted when, after being restored to their powers in the early part of
the reign of Queen Elizabeth, they were largely stripped of them by
constitutional changes at the end. By the time the first Stuart gained
the throne, it was clear that the English universities had devolved into
royal institutions, though it remained to be decided by revolutions
whether or which royalty would wield the rod.

　　If anything, the academic policies of the English kings were
even more Erastian, their spoilations of academic offices even more
incessant, their assaults on academic autonomy even more far-reaching
than anything accomplished by the Valois or Hapsburgs or by the
princelets of the German states. Yet the teachers of Oxford and Cam-

---

[26] This section draws heavily upon C. W. Mallett, *A History of the
University of Oxford* (London, 1924–1927), three volumes; J. B. Mullinger, *The
University of Cambridge* (Cambridge, 1873–1911), three volumes; M. H. Curtis,
Oxford and Cambridge in Transition, 1558–1642 (Oxford, 1959); H. C. Porter,
Reformation and Reaction in Tudor Cambridge (Cambridge, 1958).

[27] Curtis, pp. 17–30.

bridge held to their corporate traditions more successfully than did their foreign counterparts. Fatefully for these universities and for the American colonial schools they sired, something else transpired in this period: the triumph of tutorial pedagogy and the college way. From as far back as the thirteenth century, Oxford and Cambridge had distinguished themselves from Paris by the wealth and importance of their colleges. At first, these institutions (following the lead set by Merton College, Oxford, founded in 1264) were simply societies supported by endowments for the purpose of assisting scholars embarked on an advanced (usually divinity) degree. The important peculiarity of this arrangement was that the beneficiaries, called fellows, were not just pensioners aided by a charitable trust; they were members of the corporation formed to administer the moneys and were thus entitled to lay down by-laws and coopt successors within the terms of the founding deed. A second stage of development was reached (marked by the founding of New College, Oxford, in 1379) when senior fellows began to take responsibility for the conduct and instruction of their younger colleagues. For this purpose, college "tutors" were drawn from the existing body and paid for their services from college funds; the mode of instruction was intimate; the regimen and the abode were shared. Until the last decades of the fifteenth century, the colleges did little more than prepare young scholars for the rigors of the regular work in course, whose ultimate goal and capstone glory remained the theological degree. With the start of the Reformation, they went further—they absorbed the teaching and administrative functions of the university. Encouraged by the Tudor interest in the *litterae humanores* and by the opening of state positions that beckoned to broadly educated men, the sons of the well-born and the wealthy began to flock to the Oxbridge colleges, where they could study Art for its own sake, savor new languages and philosophies, and live in sumptuous surroundings that agreed with their habits or their hopes.[28] A clientage that could afford to pay for the full cost of its education (a rarity then as it is now)' was induced by the colleges to do so, with the result that both the coffers of these establishments and the pockets of the tutors were more amply filled. Happily, the financial threats posed by

[28] J. H. Hexter, "The Education of the Aristocracy in the Renaissance," *Journal of Modern Philosophy,* 1950, 22, 9.

royal anticlericalism and cupidity did not materialize: the colleges were allowed to keep their church lands, which formed the major part of their endowments, and were exempted from the annates and other tributes that had been diverted to Windsor from Rome.[29] Along with changes in the statutes that transferred governmental powers from the regent masters to the heads of colleges (variously called masters, wardens, principals and—prophetic term!—presidents) and that required students to study under tutors (once useful, now indispensable), the prosperous condition of the colleges gave assurance that they could live with rampaging monarchs and ride out the Reformation storms.

In the tutor-fellow, the master lived—or was reborn. There were, of course, some important differences between them. The fellow resided with students; the master lived apart. The fellow taught only undergraduates; the master could be associated with higher faculties. The fellow depended heavily on private benefactions; the master depended heavily on livings in the Church. The fellow, therefore, was fastened to the inscribed desires of the benefactor: he had to satisfy the terms of the bequest to gain admission; he had to avoid violating those terms to stay in place. If the founder or donor chose to reserve certain fellowships for inhabitants of a specific region or to his own kin and if he chose to void the fellowship when the holder entered into marriage or received other means of support, his wish would carry from the grave. The master, by and large, was free from such testamentary controls. But the similarities between them overwhelm their differences. Both were members of self-governing corporations. Both gained privileges from that membership and not from the performance of a special function: just as there were nonregent masters, so there were non-teaching fellows whose corporate citizenship nonetheless remained intact. And both (the fellow less consistently) enjoyed unlimited tenure unless deprived. With some exceptions, the Oxbridge colleges did not explicitly limit fellowships to a fixed term of years. From the complaints of academic critics that beneficed clergymen were retaining fellowships rather than yielding them to the young and poor, it may be inferred that, assuming good behavior (that is, the continuing tolerance of peers), and no doctrinal misadventure or royal disfavor, these

---

[29] Mallett, pp. 74ff.

holdings were tenable for life. And such was the open vista of the medieval master too.

Tenure as Time: The Age of the Employee

In 1650, a small college that had existed for some years near the Charles River outside Boston was granted a corporate charter by the General Court of the colony of Massachusetts Bay. To further the "goode work" that had been begun and to educate the young "in knowledge and godliness," the twin ends of Puritan pedagogy, the charter created a self-perpetuating corporation that was to be the legal personification of the college—the possessor of its properties, the elector of its officers, the source of its internal laws. This body politique was to consist of the president, the treasurer, and five fellows—the latter designated in the charter as the five current tutors of the college, the whole instructorial staff. The document was not without traces of ambiguity, or perhaps one should say evidences of double-mindedness. It retained the Board of Overseers, the body of ministers and magistrates that had up to then governed the institution; all orders and by-laws of the corporation had to gain its consent before they took effect. It neglected to say whether college tutors (up to the stipulated number) were fellows of the corporation *ex officio* or whether they had merely been so nominated at the outset, the future to be determined by open choice; it neglected to say whether fellows of the corporation had to be college tutors or even college residents. Two boundaries were therefore left unclarified: that between the inner and outer powers and that between the governing and teaching roles. But as a treatise on the nature of the academic status and on the prerogatives that were its due, the charter was precise and legible enough. Written at the urging of President Henry Dunster, formerly of Magdalene College, and reflecting the views of many an English schoolmate who had joined him in the great migration to these shores, the charter can be read as an argument for the academic world they had left behind. By demoting the external Board of Overseers, it in effect contended that its domination was insulting to men in a learned calling and anomalous in institutions of college grade. By naming tutors to the corporation, it in effect asserted that academics were autonomous as of right and should be incarnated as such in law. By exempting the members of the college

from corporate and personal taxes up to a specified limit and from
military exercises and the civil watch, it revived a very old and very
hallowed memory. In a word, the aim of the charter of Harvard College was to fashion one Cambridge after another, to import a tradition
by legal act.[30]

This aim was unfulfilled. Hardly had the document been
sealed when Harvard began to retreat from the chartered vision. First
of all, it was poor—so poor that it could not pay enough to keep its
tutors very long or maintain their complement at full strength. Within
a few months, most of the tutors designated as fellows slipped away
from the college; of their successors, few stayed more than a few years
before moving on, usually to pulpit destinations; throughout the seventeenth century, there were never more than three tutors (and therefore never more than three tutor-fellows) on the scene. High turnover
and depleted ranks produced a surplus of openings on the corporation,
a problem that had to be resolved by the appointment of nonteaching
and nonresident fellows, often former tutors who had graduated to a
nearby parish and were tendered the honor without pay. But even
where the two statuses were conjoined, as they were in the case of every
tutor appointed for the first five decades, the power and prestige of the
double office were less than the charter writers must have sought.
Drawn from the latest crop of college graduates, aspiring to careers
outside the walls, the tutor was no match for the president in years,
experience, weight, or dignity, and thus no reminder to that *primus*
that he was meant to govern *inter pares*. From the beginning, writes
the leading historian of Harvard College, "the president treated the
tutors as senior students helping him in discipline and instruction."
The college as a simulated family—the father rearing younger children
with the aid of a retinue of older sons—arose very early as a central
image.[31] The president, moreover, was the only member of the corporation who held a seat on the Board of Overseers, where (the charter
notwithstanding)` for many years the main powers stayed. Reflecting
the authority of the distant Crown, the creedal anxieties of the local
church, and the fiscal concerns of the assembly, which allocated money

[30] S. E. Morison, *Harvard in the Seventeenth Century* (Cambridge,
1936), Vol. 1, pp. 3–25.
[31] Morison, Vol. 1, p. 15.

to the college, this body of high state and church officials was of no mind to yield control over the institution to a fluctuating group of unseasoned teachers, nor did the latter have the stature to insist they do so. For the first fifty years or so, the overseers chose the president and tutors and set their salaries, thereby infixing the belief that a lay grasp of competence and finances is essential to the sound running of a college. Not until 1707, when the reorganized corporation began restricting its fellowships to senior tutors (and appointing the rest without further portfolio) did the overseers begin to relax their power; and not until 1780, when the republicanized corporation became entirely lay, did the overseers tend to become a vestigial body. But by that time the external board was deferring very largely to a mirror image of itself.[32]

The same theme, with local variations, was played out in Anglican Virginia, in the second college chartered in the colonies. Like Harvard, William and Mary was founded on an autonomous ideal and saddled with a two-headed government. A charter awarded by the English king in 1693 gave over creation of this namesake college to a group of provincial dignitaries who, once their generative task was done, were to transfer the property of the institution to the current president and masters, organized into a "body politic and incorporate."[33] Since the original board was to continue as the "sole and undoubted visitors and governors," it was not clear what powers were to accompany the conveyance of possessions, but the statute passing title in 1729 did state that the external body was not to "suffer themselves to be troubled, except in matters of great moment, where there is some difficulty to be got over," and this language could be fairly interpreted as assigning the "visitors" only arbitral powers. The influence of Oxford was supremely evident here, not only in the use of names like *visitor* and *master* and in the granting of a charter royal but also in the provision for an academic chancellor (a position usually filled by the bishop of London), in the representation of the college in the House of

[32] S. E. Morison, *Three Centuries of Harvard, 1636–1936* (Cambridge, 1936), pp. 153–160.

[33] J. E. Kirkpatrick, "The Constitutional Development of the College of William and Mary," *William and Mary Quarterly*, second series, April 1926, 6, 95–108.

Burgesses, and—a more regrettable emulation—in the required oath
of subscription to the Thirty-Nine Articles of the English Church.

For several decades, the president and masters—most of whom
were ordained ministers trained at Oxford—ran the college without
interference and, judging from the distinction of its alumni, with
considerable success. But British forms and American realities could
not long accommodate one another. In the 1750s and 1760s, a series
of disputes between laymen and clerics in the colony embroiled the
visitors and the faculty of the college, and the political differences thus
engendered soon gained a constitutional cast. The visitors, acting on
the theory that they had merely delegated powers to the faculty that
they were at liberty to recall, proceeded to forbid the masters from
marrying, from residing outside the college, and from taking pastor-
ates; when opposition to this and other intrusions mounted, they dismissed half the teaching force out of hand. True to their Oxonian
descent, and with more *amour-propre* than the Harvard tutors mus-
tered, the president and masters of the college gave a stout reply: "We
are humbly of the opinion that . . . (while we have been represented
as being) in the same situation with His Majesty's ministers, who are
dismissable at pleasure, the two cases are widely different. Those
gentlemen are the servants of the king. . . . We presume that we are
not the servants of the visitors; we have a charter to incorporate us
into a regular society, which we never heard the former ever had."[34]
"We have a charter to incorporate us" was a powerful and sometimes
winning cry only as long as the faculty could appeal to the Privy
Council or the bishop, no friends of the assertive Virginia gentry; on
this appeal, two professors and some faculty powers were restored. But
the Revolution was close at hand; after it was over, neither king nor
episcopacy remained; without these props, the ideal of faculty autonomy had no staff to lean on. In 1790, the Reverend John Bracken
brought suit against the visitors of the college for having deprived him
of his professorship without a trial and thus of his rights as a member
of the corporation. The argument of the lay board's attorney, John
Marshall, that "the will of the visitors is decisive," prevailed in the
court of the new state of Virginia.[35]

[34] "Journal of the President and Masters of William and Mary College,
May 4, 1768," *William and Mary Quarterly,* second series, 1897, *5,* 83.

[35] Bracken *v.* Visitors of William and Mary College, 3 Call 574.

Yale and Princeton, third and fourth in charter order, brought the laicizing tendency to its climax by relieving it of the burden of ambiguity. Yale, founded in 1701, began with one governing board composed of nonacademic trustees and vested with undivided powers. Princeton, founded in 1746, had the distinction of being the first college in the colonies to be placed in lay hands by royal authority. Thereafter, the form was set, and academic charter writing, at least in this respect, ceased to be an innovative occupation. In the medieval university, inside confronted outside; in the American college, outside was ensconced within.

Why did lay control triumph so decisively—and so distinctively —in America? The foregoing would suggest that the absence of a scholarly class—a common lack in young colonial societies—made the machinery of scholarly control unworkable. No doubt to some extent it did; yet when a more mature professoriate was imported (as it was by William and Mary and would be by other colleges) the outcome was very much the same. It has been argued that lay control of colleges was but a short step from lay control of churches, which was the heart of Congregational polity, and that the lay form of academic governance was reasoned by this analogy. This is eminently plausible, but it must also be said that results were not ultimately different when Anglicans and Presbyterians, with different polities, set about establishing colleges. It has been argued, too, that the sectarian inspiration of the early colleges naturally promoted cleric guardianship and an extraparietal urge to pry and that this undermined faculty autonomy. This seems eminently to have been the case at Yale, which was founded to offset Harvard's latitudinarianism and which lay under a board composed of ministers; yet multidenominational colleges like Columbia and Pennsylvania, not to mention the secular institutions that were to arise in later days, did not revert to faculty control. Fully to explain the event, it would be better to start with a broader picture. The shift to lay control in America, it should not be forgotten, coincided with a drastic diminution of faculty privileges everywhere, not excluding model England. The Harvard overseers did not set precedents when they took over, nor did the William and Mary visitors break new ground: incursions into academe by state and church officials, visitations that became invasions, had been the order of the day—and of the century. What *can* be attributed to America is the inability of aca-

demics to recover the corporate power they had lost. And this may be
attributed not only to a host of native factors—meager resources,
Puritan ecclesiasticism, the leveling thrust of a raw society—but to the
kind of institution that was imported—a college, not a university or a
college nesting in a university; a private college, not an instrument of
the state, capable of reaching a *modus vivendi* with it; a residential
college which had the look, if not the aspiration, of a common school.

In the retreat from borrowed canons, a milestone was reached
when the early colleges began to formulate tenure policies. Indeed, the
appearance of those policies was a clear sign that teaching and governing had been dissociated, or were well on their way to becoming so.
One of the consequences of that dissociation was that the relationship
between faculty and corporation became contractual (that is to say,
bilateral, and founded on the promised exchange of valued objects);
one of the concomitants of a contractual relationship is that it focuses
attention on its duration. In a collegial or consociative relationship
(one that is multilateral, unspecific, founded on adherence to common
norms) time is not a critical dimension. Generally, such a relationship
is formed on the presupposition that it will last, and it is either explicitly fixed *durante vita* or—which has much the same effect—it is
given no temporal definition (thus, the Harvard charter said nothing
about the duration of the corporate fellowship and thereby implied
that it was unlimited). But time and timing are of the essence in a
promissory bond between two parties, especially when the promise involves an exchange of a salary for a service and when one of the parties
is a fiduciary, pledging resources he does not own in return for a service secured for others. It then becomes necessary to consider how long
each party will have hold of the exchangeable commodity, at what
intervals the transfers will take place, and whether and with how much
notice the agreement can be terminated before it has run its course.
Long before it was formalized by written instruments and deemed
correctible by legal action, this relationship gave rise to that kind of
regulation we have labeled *tenure as time.*

To trace the early development of this kind of tenure, we return to Harvard, not because its history is in all ways typical, but
because its records are good and its acts precursive. At Harvard, an
early challenge was posed to the enduring fellowship which, since it

was hyphenated with the tutorship, worked with a two-in-one effect. Shifts in seventeenth-century English politics, by causing the revocation of the Harvard charter, gave college leaders an opportunity to rethink the advisability of lifetime tenure in both positions. In 1696, the provincial council drafted a new charter that would have limited the term of fellows to ten years; in 1697, President Increase Mather proposed to limit the term to seven; in 1700, the provincial legislature amended this proposal by including tutors in the seven-year limit—each with the option of renewal.[36] After this, the attack on the lifetime fellowship abated. None of the proposed new charters was adopted; in 1707, the old charter was restored; in time the evolution of the corporation of teachers into a lay board of trustees quenched the impulse toward reform at the upper tier. Tenure of the tutor, however, continued to present an enticing target. In 1716, the corporation passed the rule that "all tutors, now or hereafter chosen," shall hold their positions for no longer than three years, "except continued by a new election."[37] Looking back on this event, which marked the first time an American college established term appointments, a later president of Harvard undertook to disclose its rationale. "The corporation," wrote Josiah Quincy, in his antebellum history of Harvard, "began to perceive the inconvenience [of appointing] very young men without limitation of time, who, if they possessed good talents would speedily be induced to resign and [who] if they did not possess the ability to become eminent in a profession, would be fixed on the college for life."[38] This contribution to antitenure ideology—an ideology that would never want for adherents and contributors—could have been more succinctly worded: "Those who can't preach, teach." The modern aphorism to the same effect would be: "Those who are good have no need for tenure; those who have need for tenure are no good."

But the facts of the historic case were a bit more complicated. It may be doubted that the corporation in 1716 was much concerned about the perversities of self-selection arising from unlimited appointments: lengthy incumbencies still were rare; the one longevous tutor on the faculty, Henry Flynt, was still young and much esteemed; the

---

[36] Morison, *Harvard in the Seventeenth Century*, Vol. 2, pp. 511, 513.
[37] J. Quincy, *History of Harvard University* (Cambridge, 1840), Vol. 1, p. 281.
[38] Quincy, Vol. 1, p. 282.

more urgent problem of the moment was to create a more stable faculty, not a more plastic or rotative one. Moreover, under the charter,
the corporation had the power to remove a tutor; what it did not
have, prior to the rule, was the power to remove him without a show
of cause, since the overseers had to give assent and could be appealed
to for a hearing. The "inconvenience" was thus not caused by endur-
ingness as such, but by the difficulties and embarrassments involved in
putting judgment to a formal test. It is noteworthy, too, that the first
tutor appointed under the new rules and the first to feel its sting was not
a "very young" man at all, but a person of some age and experience,
a former rather than prospective minister, against whom the complaint
of incompetence was never raised. But this tutor, Nicholas Sever,
happened to be the ally of the high Calvinist faction of the Board of
Overseers, a faction strongly at odds with the liberal president, John
Leverett; moreover, a year before Sever's appointment was allowed to
lapse, the tutor had led a campaign to seat himself and other tutors on
the corporation, a campaign which, if successful, would have displaced
the president's religious friends. One cannot now say with certainty
why Leverett did not renew Sever's appointment; the genius of the
limited appointment is that, without affirmative renewal, it ends not
with a bang but with a hush. Still, it is a reasonable guess that the
president acted, or failed to act, because he did not wish to have a
refractory subordinate rise to the status of a combative equal. If this
was so, it would not be for the last time that contentiousness in academia would be nonrenewed. The still open question is why the three-
year rule was adopted in the first place since this was done some years
before the tutor's plot unfolded. Again, it is difficult to speculate about
motives from a far remove. But a later statement of administrative
policy offers a suggestive clue. According to the first codified statutes of
the college, the purpose of a limited appointment (when tied to the
option of renewal) was "to excite tutors from time to time to greater
care and fidelity in their work."[39] Not just the possibility of a smooth
removal, but the chance to exercise greater discipline on the remainder
was the boon this system offered. The implicit argument was that in-
security could be used as a spur to greater effort; the still deeper argument was that faculty members were a work force to be exerted by

[39] Quincy, Vol. 1, p. 282.

economic threats. Harvard, as we shall see in a moment, did not extend this rule to all its faculty, and the consequences of its not doing so were vast. But these words may be used, as well as any others, to mark the interment of the academic master and the rise of the academic employee.

It took some years before the board and the corporation would see eye to eye on the desirability of term appointments. Suspecting that the three-year rule was designed to protect the Leverett faction on the corporation—that is, to withhold fellowships, not weed instructorships —the board refused to ratify it or permit it to apply to Sever, who stayed a Harvard tutor for six more years, three of them concurrently as fellow. Gradually, however, the clouds of religious controversy thinned out sufficiently to reveal to both governing bodies their common administrative ground, and, in 1734, they agreed to a three-year term for tutors. The rule, however, did not apply retroactively, so that when one previously engaged tutor (and fellow), Henry Flynt, showed an alarming intention to live forever, and when another tutor fellow, Thomas Prince, showed an alarming inability to abstain from drink, neither could be easily gotten rid of. Prince was dismissed on charges in 1742. Flynt stayed on until 1759, when, at the age of seventy-nine and after fifty-six years of service, he acceded to mortality. That long stint might have convinced the corporation that a retirement pension would be helpful, but much more than a century would have to pass before this would be seen as an answer to superannuation. Instead, the corporation took another step toward the temporalizing of appointments: in 1860, it limited not only the time of each tutorial appointment but the time each teacher could spend within that rank, the maximum number of years being set at eight.[40] The evident purpose of this rule was to prevent incumbencies from being lengthened by reappointments given out of neglect or sympathy; it was intended to defeat the impulsions of kindness in the serious business of evaluating personnel. Much later, a time limit on temporary service would be seen as serving another function—of providing a period of probation in which the novice would gain the benefit of an internship and the institution the benefit of a second look before making a permanent commitment. But the probationary purpose of such a rule would not be

---

[40] Quincy, Vol. 2, pp. 82–84.

glimpsed until a faculty consisting of a handful grew into a more considerable company, stratified into higher and lower ranks. Except for the office of the president, there was no rank higher than tutor at Harvard until the third decade of the eighteenth century. Then, in slow order, Harvard began to set up endowed chairs, to whose incumbents it gave the proud title of professor. In 1721, it received a money gift from an English Baptist merchant to set up the Hollis Professorship of Divinity; seven years later, it received another gift from that same source to support the Hollis Professorship of Mathematics and Natural Philosophy; thirty-six years later, with the help of a college alumnus turned Maecenas, it set up the third of these high offices—the Hancock Professorship in Oriental Languages.[41] As much as the magniloquent title of these positions, their assured (if never quite adequate) support and their specialized (if still roomy) commands lent them a loftiness and dignity that the post of tutor could not claim. Selected with care and ceremony, the professor stood in sharp contrast to his plainer work fellow—mature where the other was often callow; prominent or at least promising in a discipline where the other ran the gamut of subjects with obscure effect; allowed to marry and live off campus, where the other still abided by the cleric rule of celibacy and the life immured. The sharpness of this contrast led to a distinction in the conditions of their employ.[42] Though the bequests relating to professorships did not specifically prohibit term appointments, it appears that all who were appointed to these offices served without limit of time. For what it signified and what it foretold, their exemption from the three-year rule was most significant. First it showed some understanding of the converse of the Quincy apothegm: namely, that for men of quality and self-consequence, it is *infra dignitate* to be compelled to pass repeated muster. Limited appointments therefore might be self-defeating, in that they were as likely to repel the worthy candidate as to eject the weak incumbent.[43] Second, the exemption

[41] Morison, *Three Centuries*, pp. 66–69, 108.

[42] Conceivably, the line of influence ran the other way, the appearance of the disciplinary professor depreciating the value of the college mentor and strengthening the move to abridge his term.

[43] Recruitment of academic talent, both at home and abroad, was made more difficult when the institution proposed to offer term appointments. Thus Thomas Jefferson wrote to Nathaniel Bowditch, whom he was trying to lure to

may well have reflected a certain institutional prudence. The preliminaries to the appointment of Edward Wigglesworth as the first Hollis Professor of Divinity were marred by an inquisition into his religious beliefs, the distortion of the terms of the bequest to make it conform to New England orthodoxy, and a great deal of intramural tension. The election of Isaac Greenwood to the first Hollis scientific chair was precipitated by word that the English donor was thinking of nominating a Baptist, a prospect that struck terror in the hearts of those who would sectarianize even mathematics. It is hard to believe that these preelection difficulties did not induce postelection restraints, that the desire to keep the peace did not affect the decision to forego controls. Third, the question had to be faced: would Harvard continue to be a college with a tutorial faculty and a few conspicuous professors or would it be a university with a large professorial corps? By 1820, the two dozen professors on the faculty, many supported by university funds, and the somewhat smaller group of tutors and instructors supplied the answer. Having offered undated appointments to professors when they were a rarity, Harvard continued the practice when they became abundant. Not alone among universities, but with the high visibility of success, it advertised the close connection between institutional eminence and ambition and a sizeable teaching force appointed—as it was termed—"indefinitely."

There are some indications that Harvard began at this point to apply the rule that became breezily known as "up or out." The out was dictated by the limit on time spent in temporary service; the up was made possible by the creation of a structure of ranks. Such evidence as is available to us suggests that other institutions of higher learning, as they developed more complex tables of organization, also began to use their lower ranks as proving grounds. But it would appear

---

the University of Virginia: "Our society is neither scientific nor splendid, but independent, hospitable, correct, and neighborly. But the professors of themselves compose a scientific society. They will be removable only by a vote of two-thirds of the visitors, and when you are told that the visitors are Mr. Madison, President Monroe, and myself, all known to you by character, Senator Cabell, General Cocke, Mr. Watson, gentlemen of distinguished worth and information, you will be se..sible ʰ at the tenure is in fact for life." October 26, 1826. In P. A. Bruce, *History of the University of Virginia, 1819–1919* (New York, 1950), Vol. 3, pp. 98–99.

that they did not set a limit on the total years of trial: they allowed the up but did not enforce the out. The effect was to create a two-track system, in which the nonpromoted teacher, reappointed time and again, kept pace in compiling years of service with his higher ranking colleagues. The virtue of a two-track system was that it did not necessarily fling anyone off the road. But, unlike the single track that led to an inescapable fork, it offered the nonpromoted teacher no surcease from the pain of temporariness, and no certainty as to when, if ever, he would gain relief. Not until well into the twentieth century would academics vote decisively against the two-track system and for a version of the system of up or out.

During the nineteenth century, the chief competitor of "indefinite tenure," whether of the up-or-out or double-track variety, was the austere system of appointing all faculty members for a year, vacating their positions at the end of term, and reappointing only those among the previous incumbents who could pass a *de novo* test. Most common in state-supported institutions, the Draconian use of the term appointment was justified by governing boards on the grounds that they were given yearly appropriations by the legislature and that they lacked the authority and the wherewithal to commit themselves for a longer period of time. But this vascular closing and opening of positions was not demanded by the periodicity of appropriations: governing boards could and did make indefinite appointments with the proviso that the continuation of the contract would depend on the adequacy of support. When they chose to terminate appointments at the end of each budget year, they were yielding not to necessity but to desire. Such a procedure appealed to the state official who believed that the practices of the public school were applicable as well to the university, to the regent arriving from the world of business who looked on professors as hired hands, to the lawyer who sought the safest way to avoid a possible suit for breach of contract, to the spoilsman with an eye out for friends. And it occasionally appealed to a president who wanted to improve the faculty or cleanse it of discordant groups. But, in the latter part of the nineteenth century, most often it was the presidents who led the opposition to this policy. Many of them perceived that annual reappraisals brought on annual sieges of springtime nervousness that imperilled the efficiency of the faculty; many were aware that in purges they themselves were purgable; and some regarded commercial comparisons as a very philistine mistake. As a rule, they preferred contracts of varying fixed durations for faculty members in lower ranks and indefinite appointments for the rest.[44]

The trend between 1860 and 1914 was clearly—though not universally—away from the astringent mode. At the University of Wisconsin, the Board of Regents, acting on by-laws that required professors to be elected by ballot at each annual meeting, twice (1858, 1867) swept the faculty clean, then adopted a more passive policy of declaring the "terms of office of every officer of the university" to be continued "at pleasure, unless otherwise expressly provided."[45] In 1867, the Board of Trustees of Cornell University were urged by President Andrew Dickson White to scrutinize the work of all professors at the end of each academic year and to remove any who received an adverse vote. A year later, the board endorsed an ambiguous but obviously less activistic policy of offering yearly contracts that would be renewed unless it was displeased. In 1881, hearing intimations that the faculty was irreligious, the board considered asking for the resignation of the entire body but settled for the forced resignation of one professor; in the 1890s, a new president, through various dicta, assured the faculty that it was not everlastingly on trial before the board; in 1914, Cornell reported that, though its appointments were technically for one year, "it is the established policy of the university that a man once installed continues indefinitely."[46] A survey of forty-three land-grant colleges in 1914 revealed that while most institutions were supremely vague about the terms and conditions of employment, only two appointed teachers strictly annually.[47] In 1910, a survey of the twenty-two major universities that made up the prestigious Association of American Universities disclosed that none made all the faculty run the gauntlet of annual reappraisal, though for the most part those in the rank of instructor were appointed for one year.[48]

[44] E. D. Sanderson, "Definiteness of Appointment and Tenure," *Science,* June 19, 1914, *39,* 895.

[45] M. Curti and V. L. Carstenson, *The University of Wisconsin* (Madison, 1948), Vol. 1, pp. 107–108, 173–177, 233.

[46] M. Bishop, *A History of Cornell* (Ithaca, 1962), pp. 76–77, 86, 237. Sanderson, p. 894.

[47] Sanderson, p. 895.

[48] C. R. Van Hise, "The Appointment and Tenure of University Pro-

But what guarantees against removal (it became increasingly pertinent to ask) did indefinite tenure provide? What restraints did it impose on the discretion of governing boards? would be another form of that same question. Schematically, the possible answers could have been arranged in a series of diminishing assurances. At the top of the column, an indefinite appointment would be defined as that which makes the recipient absolutely unremovable, save by death or by retirement. This would have been a logical, but entirely phantastical, upper limit: though the words *permanent* and *indefinite* were often used interchangeably, there was nothing in academic traditions or even in glittering European examples to warrant the expectation of an ironclad, lifetime guarantee. However, it would not have been fanciful or unprecedented to have held that the recipient of an indefinite appointment was unremovable except for grave dereliction—gross neglect of duty, physical or mental incapacitation, serious moral lapse. This had been, more or less, the ground for corporate removals; this was what the German professoriate meant by tenure; this was what an American professor, often promoted in rank as he gained this status, might have been led to expect. At a significantly lower level, indefinite tenure might merely assure the recipient that he would keep his place as long as he remained proficient. This was a long descent from the assurance of level two, for it would have permitted dismissal on the strength of a revised administrative judgment rather than on the basis of a specified professional offense. But it still could have offered something valuable: the presumption that, until proven otherwise, the tenure holder *was* proficient. Both at level two (*presumptive permanence*) and at level three (*presumptive competence*), the body seeking to dismiss, not the person desiring to remain, would bear the onus of justification. If therefore followed that, before dismissal could take place under either of these standards, a charge would have to be formed, its accuracy would have to be assayed, and its gravity would have to be weighed on scales balanced in the teacher's favor. At level four, all presumptions favorable to the teacher would disappear, and all that would be assured to him would be the right to be dismissed for cause, for some definite and indicated reason. This would imply much less

fessors," *Journal of Proceedings* (Association of American Universities), November 1910, *12*, 58–59.

judiciality, for nothing would have to be ascertained except whether the reason stated conformed to prescriptions of the rules or statutes. At level five, even this meager procedural guarantee would vanish. A person on indefinite appointment would be subject to dismissal at any time by the will of the governing authority. No probative process would be needed, for pure volition requires no test and no defending; the teacher involved might be listened to, but this would be a hearing in the physiological rather than juridic sense. Level five would be the ground floor of assurance; but there might be even below it one or two subbasements. At each level, notice of an impending termination might be assured if only to extend to the indefinite appointee the same warning that is given to the term appointee from the beginning of his appointment. At each level, the board vote effecting a dismissal might have to be reached by more than a mere majority—this to avert a hasty or ill-judged removal. At the very depths, then, indefinite tenure would not forbid even a closely decided and unwarned dismissal. At that level, the difference in assurances between definite and indefinite appointments would shrink to merely this: the former would, and the latter would not, predict the date of its termination.

Which of these levels of assurance best describes the operative meaning of indefinite tenure in this period? The candid historian will confess that his most easily available sources—charters, by-laws, dismissal cases, legal cases, comments by academic spokesmen—do not lead him toward confident answers. The seminal documents of a university set very broad parameters within which a variety of policies —and customs that do the work of policies—can be fitted at different times. Dismissal cases give a distorted picture of the tenured life: first, because they deal with the outbreaks of conflict and thus omit the normal pattern of compromise and concession; second, because they deal with the records of conflict and thus miss the vaster universe of spoken and *sub rosa* strife. Legal cases misdescribe reality in these ways too and are further marred by the caprices of litigation. Official statements are official statements—that is, they are subject to the discounts that must be applied to the words of institutional men when they are on guard. Still, the historian must make the best of such materials as he has and may make better use of them if he knows and reveals their limits. The following—which should be read in the light of this *caveat*

—are some of the conclusions about the assurances of indefinite tenure
to which these materials point:

1. From the late colonial period on, as charter traces of the
mastership were erased, the protective potency of indefinite tenure
declined. In their first proceedings (1701), the trustees of Yale employed a Latin formula that had been traditionally used to denote
presumptive permanence (and that was later to be used in the Federal
Constitution to describe the character of federal judicial tenure): the
rector and masters, they agreed, "shall continue in office *Quamdiu
Bene Se Gesserint*"—during good behavior.[49] In 1745, at the height of
the religious controversy set off by the Great Awakening, Yale secured
a second charter which gave the board broader discretionary powers,
the better to combat theological sin. Dismissal was now effectible for
cause, and cause was defined as "*any* misdemeanor, unfaithfulness, default, or incapacity"—an extremely broad, though not infinite, standard
of *grounded discontinuance*.[50] At Harvard, the first professorial bequests
tended to favor *presumptive permanence,* one donor describing the
grounds for termination as "want of ability to execute the trust or
misbehavior in the office or immoral and scandalous behavior out of
it."[51] Like Yale, Harvard in due time relinquished this emphasis on
misbehavior and this test of flagrancy. Soon after the Civil War, the
rule was that all professors "appointed without express limitation of
time" could be dismissed for "inadequate performance of duty and
misconduct."[52]

Still, Yale and Harvard did set standards for their boards to
follow. At Columbia (née King's) College, charter revision had a
more powerful downward thrust. The first charter of that institution
(1754) left open to mutual agreement whether the faculty would hold
office "during good behavior" or at the "will" of the governors. Later

[49] F. B. Dexter (Ed.), *Documentary History of Yale University* (New
Haven, 1916), pp. 28–29. The rule also required a two-thirds vote by the whole
board of trustees to remove the rector or a master.

[50] E. C. Elliott and M. M. Chambers, *Charters and Basic Laws of
Selected American Colleges and Universities* (1970), p. 591. Here the numerical
obstacle was removed from the path of the board.

[51] See Quincy, Appendices, Vols. 1 and 2.

[52] H. Hawkins, *Between Harvard and America* (forthcoming), pp. 25–
26.

charters (1784, 1787) provided that professors and tutors could be removed if they were "incompetent" or if they "abused their trust" but that removal could ensue only "after a full hearing."[53] In 1810, the New York legislature—in a new charter—provided that teachers were to hold their office "at the pleasure of the trustees"; it dropped the definition of "cause" as well as the requirement of a hearing.[54] The standard of *durante bene placito,* unattended by any substantive "ifs" or procedural "buts," appeared to catch just that sense of legal responsibility and subjective competency that the draftsmen of private charters had been searching for. In any case, it became a formula they became increasingly disposed to use. In the public sector, the same formula was given a slightly different intonation: "removal whenever in the judgment of the board the interest of the college require it." Together, the (pre-Freudian!) pleasure principle and its *pro bono publico* equivalent carried this message to governing boards: as far as the charters were concerned, they were now at liberty to discharge professors in any manner or on any grounds they wished.[55]

2. During the nineteenth century, predeterminative hearings in dismissal cases (by the board or an administrative body) fell out of fashion. Indeed, they may never have been warmly embraced. The hearing that preceded the removal of Thomas Prince from Harvard in the eighteenth century (see above) may strike the modern reviewer as an example of scrupulous behavior, but it surely struck the Harvard community as an extremely painful ordeal. The embarrassments caused by the public charge (drunkenness, from which branched such subsidiary accusations as "rude and ridiculous gestures," calling a colleague a "puppy," laughing in church); the constitutional problems created by the demands of fairness (the corporation had to yield jurisdiction to the rival overseers because its own members were among the complainants); the awful tedium of a lengthy trial (six months,

---

[53] "Minutes of the Governors of the College of the Province of New York, 1755–1768," in J. B. Pine (Ed.), *Charters, Acts of the Legislature: Official Documents and Records* (New York, 1920), pp. 45–49.

[54] Elliott and Chambers, p. 152.

[55] The pleasure principle could be read into charters and by-laws that did not actually enscribe it. See *Joint Corporation-Overseers of Harvard, Report of 1856* (Cambridge, 1856), p. 10.

twelve sessions, a plethora of legal nicety) could hardly have encouraged anyone to seek a rapid repetition of the experience.[56] In any event, with the exception of a preceding case, the dismissal of Isaac Greenwood (again!) on a charge of drunkenness, Harvard did not repeat the experience, which may bespeak a subsequent wisdom in appointments, a subsequent increase in temperance or—as some evidence would suggest—a subsequent adroitness in removing unwanted members without going to such pains.[57] In the second half of the nineteenth century, the predismissal trial became an explicit target of administrators. They seemed pointless to President William Rainey Harper of the University of Chicago, who believed that a professor should leave his post "when, in the opinion of those in authority, he has been guilty of immorality or when for any reason he has proved himself to be incompetent."[58] They seemed inequitable to President Nicholas Murray Butler of Columbia, who equated the right of an institution to dismiss a teacher without bringing charges against him with the right of a teacher to quit his institution without impugning it.[59] Indeed, hearings prior to dismissal were not customarily accorded. An examination of 122 institutional histories covering the period from 1860 to 1914 reveals that of sixty-eight dismissals and four near dismissals, only six were preceded by a hearing. Without provision for hearings, professors could feel personally secure. Certainly lengthy terms were common, and outright dismissals rare. But without provision for hearings, indefinite tenure offered very little protection to professors who fell from grace. There could be tenure as a reasonable expectation and tenure as a retrospective fact; but there could not be tenure as a fully acknowledged right.

3. Professors were at liberty to challenge administrative acts in court. There, by successful suit, they could have improved the guarantees of indefiniteness. Since the legal status of academic tenure is the

[56] Quincy, Vol. 2, pp. 28–34.

[57] Hawkins, pp. 25–26.

[58] "The President's Report: Administration," University of Chicago Decennial Publications, first series, Vol. 1 (Chicago, 1903). Reprinted in R. Hofstadter and W. Smith, American Higher Education: A Documentary History, Vol. 2 (Chicago, 1961), pp. 782–783.

[59] N. M. Butler, "Government and Administration," in Scholarship and Service (New York, 1921), pp. 163–171.

subject of the companion to this essay, it will not be closely examined here. But a few comments on the ability of professors in this period to use legal processes to advantage are needed to fill out this sketch.

The most striking characteristic of legal actions brought in this area before the Civil War is their paucity. Part of the explanation is demographic: an exceedingly small population at risk produces a yet smaller population of victims. Part of the explanation may also lie in the lack of a promising legal theory on which hopes for judicial redress could be based. The courts relegated one such theory to the pigeonhole of fallen causes when they refused to accept the argument that professors had a freehold in their offices from which they could not be deprived without a formal hearing and a show of cause.[60] In one leading case, judges showed themselves unwilling to try the facts of a dismissal case anew and thus exhibited a judicial modesty that would later harden into principle and make boards almost invulnerable to the second guess.[61] The most logical line of attack for professors under private boards (the overwhelming majority before the Civil War) was to allege that their dismissal violated the terms of their employment contracts and to seek judicial remedy for the breach. But if the large discretion reserved to such boards in private charters did not make this approach seem uninviting, the known reluctance of the courts to decree specific performance of employment contracts (that is, to order reinstatement)' may well have had this effect. Even so, it does not seem that such opportunities as were available were fully seized. In *Murdoch,* the Supreme Judicial Court of Massachusetts, while it deferred to the findings of the governing board under one main charge, held that three other charges against the professor did not justify dismissal and thus opened the door to future challenges of the substantive criteria for termination. Contractual exegesis might still have formed the basis for suits requesting money damages, and one wonders why it was not resorted to more frequently, especially since, in the later period and in the face of a more cautious drafting of promissory language,

---

[60] The argument was put forward by the plaintiff in the Bracken case, cited above. It was advanced by Daniel Webster and ignored by Chief Justice John Marshall speaking for the majority of the Supreme Court in Trustees of Dartmouth College *v.* Woodward, 4 Wheaton 625–654 (1819).

[61] *James Murdoch, Appellant from a Decree of the Visitors of the Theological Institution of Phillips Academy in Andover,* 24 Mass. Reports 303 (1828).

professors did resort to it in great numbers. Our assumption is that
one of the main reasons for early inactivity lies in another cause—in the
weakness of the litigatory spirit due, in very large part, to the prevailing ethos of resignation.

In the colonial and antebellum colleges, ligatures between faculty and administration (and to some extent with the board as well)
were established by a shared religious purpose, a common didactic
function, a similar intellectual background, and continuous face-to-face
address. As long as a common culture allayed the discrepancies of
power, the disciplinary exercise of power, while it might be internally
resisted, was likely to have too much legitimacy to be blatantly opposed. And a high degree of personal closeness, even in contractual relationships, was likely to discourage jousts at law. When the president
declared a member of this intimate group *non grata* and called the
sentimental compact dead, that member might feel cruelly wounded,
but he was barred by the character of that association to seek to impose himself by legal fiat and encouraged by the pain of that disfavor
to depart. It was when this *gemeinschaft* toppled, as it did in the latter
part of the nineteenth century, that the ethos of resignation lost some
of this underpinning of consent. Many factors contributed to this result.
The laicizing of the presidency, which accompanied the unfrocking of
the faculty, destroyed the primitive cohesiveness that was the gift of a
religious aim. The president abandoned teaching and research to concentrate on administration: the cleavage of the academy into two
vocations ended the harmony of a shared routine. Moreover, as professors gained scholarly prestige and saw themselves as the heart of the
university, the specialist in nothing but administration ran the risk of
being looked upon by the faculty as a man with unmerited power, as
someone organizationally powerful but academically second class. Still
another factor sapped the old relationship: the growth of an administrative apparatus. Like their counterparts in government and business, the presidents of academic institutions coped with the complexities of expansion by adopting a more complex mode of management.
The late 1880s and 1890s saw the introduction of bureaucratic methods
into places that had been governed *en famille:* the transfer of administrative burdens from the president to a registrar and comptroller; the
delegation of executive duties to a graded lieutenancy of deans; and
the prolific use of written records. At the same time, the governing

boards, faced with issues too complex to be handled by intermittent scrutiny, relied more and more on their presidential deputy and became both less intrusive in routine matters and less open to faculty points of view. With that much delegitimation of authority, the stage was set for legal actions when dismissals were announced.

Moreover, with the rise of public higher education, especially after it reached its proliferant land-grant phase, new opportunities were opened to test the legality of dismissals. Though denial of employment by a public agency was not yet thought to raise a federal constitutional question, the creation of governing boards by public law gave the state courts responsibility to review their actions to see that they remained within the scope of law and to declare them *ultra vires* when they transgressed. The hope of public academic teachers that they would benefit from judicial control of official action received some early encouragement. In 1874, the regents of Kansas State College dismissed one Professor B. F. Mudge without giving him three months' notice as required by the institution's by-laws. In awarding the professor recovery of three months' salary, Judge Valentine of the Supreme Court of Kansas took cognizance of the regential claim that the provision for notice in the by-laws clashed with the statute that reposed absolute discretion in the governors and was therefore null and void. The judge declared that adherence to the by-law would not constitute an illegal abdication of authority:

> *The power reposed in the board of regents is very extensive.*
> *. . . [But] there is no express limitation upon the power of the board to make a contract to employ a president or a professor or a teacher for any period of time, and we know of no implied limitation that would prevent the board from employing . . . a president or a professor or a teacher for three months or for even a longer period, provided it were not unreasonably long, . . . especially so, when the board reserves the right to discharge such president, professor, or teacher at any time for misconduct.*[62]

The judge not only saw no legal impediment to term appointments of moderate duration and with adequate safeguards, but believed that

[62] Board of Regents of the Kansas State Agricultural College *v.* B. F. Mudge, 21 Kansas Reports 223 (1878).

such appointments were in the best interest of the institution: "No man of spirit or self-respect and of capability would want to hold office unless he felt that he was reasonably certain to hold the same for a reasonable period of time. The shorter and more precarious the tenure of office, the less attractive, important, and valuable it would be."[63] But even if the board did not agree, it had made a promise to stay its hand for the notice period, and the judge was old-fashioned enough to think that a promise should be kept: "While the legislature unquestionably intended to confer upon the board of regents extensive powers, yet it did not intend to confer upon them the irresponsible power of trifling with other men's rights with impunity; and making the regents responsible for their acts does not in the least abridge their powers. It only tends to make them more cautious and circumspect in the exercise of them."[64]

Anyone who thought that this reasoning would prevail by its moral and legal obviousness (a board that could not make a valid contract for three months could not make one for an hour—or a millisecond; a board that could renege on one promise could do so with impunity on others) was in for a rude awakening. In 1899, treating a fact situation almost identical to that of *Mudge,* an Arizona state court took a position diametrically opposed to that of the Kansas court. It held that the statute giving the University of Arizona regents power to remove any employee "when in their judgment the interests of the university required it" laid a positive obligation on the board not to bind itself for three months, for then, said the court, giving vent to its own temporal anxieties, it could do so for "six months . . . or a year, which would be in direct violation of the interests of the institution as the legislature has created it."[65] With few exceptions, this general argument came to be the law.[66] Not only the promise of termination notice but the promise of appointment for a stated term was rendered legally unenforceable by this kind of statutory construction. If the court recog-

[63] Board of Regents . . . , at 229.
[64] Board of Regents . . . , at 230.
[65] William Stowe Devol *v.* The Board of Regents of the University of Arizona, 6 Arizona Reports 259.
[66] See State Board of Agriculture *v.* Meyers, 20 Colorado App. 139 (1904).

nized tenure as time, the only time it recognized was the instant present.

It followed that if a notice requirement offended an *ad libitum* statute, a due process requirement, which imposed more than a scintilla of restraint upon the board, would be doomed as well. In 1894, a Wisconsin state court ruled that the plenary powers granted the Board of Regents of the Wisconsin normal schools absolved it of any obligation to offer teachers a predismissal hearing. This was judged to be correct both as policy and as law: "This power is wisely given to the board. . . . The trial of a teacher in a normal school on charges of misconduct, with its delays and publicity and the excitement it would produce and the feelings it would engender, would be very injurious to the school."[67] Nor, barring fraud or bad faith, were the grounds of a dismissal action deemed fit subjects for judicial investigation. At the same time that they gave free rein to governing boards, the courts kept a tight leash on themselves. "Is the Board of Regents to do as it pleases, without control, erroneous as its action may be?" asked a West Virginia court. "Yes, so far as the courts are concerned."[68]

As far as the courts were concerned, the boards of private institutions were equally unanswerable for error (which was as much as to say, for malice, meanness, ignorance, and all the other besetting sins to which all human beings are heir). In the private sector, the right to arbitrariness could not be deduced from constitutional or statutory language. But other strained constructions were equal to the task. In People ex rel Kelsey *v.* New York Medical School (1898), a New York state appellate court was presented with a case in which a private board acted under one section of its by-laws that allowed it to dismiss a professor summarily and ignored another section which required it to hold a hearing. A lower court had held that the two sections had to be read together and that the board could dismiss "at pleasure" only by recourse to judicial process. The appellate court disagreed. It saw the rules as presenting the board with alternatives: removal at pleasure, a mode to be reserved for the teacher innocent of any wrongdoing but "with temperamental qualities which render association with

[67] Gillan *v.* Board of Regents of Normal Schools, 88 Wisconsin 7.

[68] Hartigan *v.* Board of Regents of West Virginia University, 49 West Virginia Reports 14 (1901).

him disagreeable," and removal upon charges with attendant publicity, a mode designed to punish the miscreant who would have escaped too lightly if he had been silently removed.[69] That a board presented with these alternatives might choose to dispatch the teacher against whom they could not build a substantial case, that charges are not meant to punish guilt but ascertain it, that penalties result from disemployment even when it is accomplished *sub silentio* seem not to have occurred to these learned judges. They even went as far as to imply that contracts lacking the "pleasure principle" would be legally unenforceable. For without this, they argued, the contract would lack required mutuality: "The professor may leave at his pleasure; the board may terminate his professorship at its pleasure. If the realtor's view be correct, the 'pleasure' is his and his alone. It would follow that he has an appointment which constitutes a unilateral contract of retention for life or during good behavior; in other words, a contract which he alone can specifically enforce and which is dependent upon his individual will."[70]

Of all the arguments used in this period against legal tenure, the doctrine of mutuality most clearly illustrated the remoteness of legal casuistry from the realities of social life. It would take some time before the courts would recognize that contractual promises may be mutual without being coextensive and before administrators would admit that the institution and the teacher bargain too asymmetrically to be required to comport themselves as equals in the ways they break their ties.[71]

At the close of the period we have been discussing, indefiniteness as an attribute of an appointment deserved its name in more ways than one. This is not to say that it was devoid of meaning, that tenure as time was the merest myth. The successful fight against academic hirings of the start-and-stop variety, the development of an internal "feeder" system and the adumbrations of a probationary period, the link between relaxed controls and professorial distinction—these were

[69] People of the State of New York ex rel. Charles B. Kelsey *v.* New York Post Graduate Medical School and Hospital, 29 Appellate Division 244 (1898).

[70] People . . . , at 248.

[71] See the argument in C. Byse and L. Joughin, *Tenure in American Higher Education: Plans, Practices and the Law* (Ithaca, N.Y.: Cornell University Press, 1959), pp. 92–93.

not trivial accomplishments. But indefinite tenure was not a bulwark; it was sometimes too nebulous to be a trench. In law, it had little sense or consequence: not only were all appointments in a legal sense temporary, they were (in the dominant view) instantly extinguishable. In practice, it meant what academics thought it meant, which could be much or little. Some institutions handed it out as a reward and as one of the perquisites of promotion, but some gave it to every faculty member or to faculty members in every rank. Some teachers doubtless read it as a statement of intention to retain and were content with a gentleman's understanding; others may well have been concerned about the lack of a procedural distinction between a nonrenewal and a dismissal or the lack of clear understanding of what could and what could not be defined as "adequate cause." In this, as in all academic matters, much depended on the people and the place. What could be said about indefinite tenure was that it did not do much to improve either.

Tenure as Judiciality: The Age of the Professional

In the spring of 1913, a letter signed by eighteen full professors on the faculty of the Johns Hopkins University was sent to their colleagues of equal rank at nine other leading universities, urging them to join in the formation of a national association of professors. The letter stated that the scholarly and scientific interests of academics were served by the disciplinary societies but that their institutional and societal interests, which were equally pressing and important, were not being adequately cared for; that, as members of a profession "essential to the well-being of society," professors had reason to be concerned about its "efficiency, public influence, and good repute"; that a professional organization was needed to support those interests through "collective action" and to give "authoritative expression" to those concerns. On the whole, the high-placed recipients of this letter responded favorably. Committees of eminent professors advanced the project; six hundred "distinguished specialists" accepted an invitation to become charter members; in January 1913, at a convention of academic luminaries, the American Association of University Professors was born.

In listing activities for the association, the Johns Hopkins call had given prominent mention to two. It proposed that the new professional body undertake "the gradual formulation of general principles respecting the tenure of the professional office and the legitimate ground for the dismissal of professors" and that it establish "a representative judicial committee to investigate and report in cases in which freedom is alleged to have been interfered with by the administrative authorities of any university or in which serious and unwarranted injury to the professional standing and opportunities of any professor is declared to have occurred."[72] The first proposal looked forward to tenure rules that would be shaped to the interest of professors rather than to the interest of lay controllers and that would be standardized for the entire nation rather than left to each campus ward. The second proposal, remarkable for its audacity, urged the organized professors to set themselves up as the judges of administrative conduct in all those tangled and bristling affairs that end in academic dismissals. But it was in the joining of these two proposals that their historic significance can be said to lie. For many years, professors had evidenced concern about their security of tenure. And for many years—intensely since the controversy over evolution in the 1870s—professors had sought "academic freedom"—immunity from institutional sanctions in matters of expression and belief. What was so unusual and worthy of mark was the marriage of these two concerns in one professional plan of action.

Of the many proposals put before the Association, these had least relevance to the circumstances of their sponsors. The Johns Hopkins University had never wavered to any alarming degree from its original adherence to *Lehrfreiheit*. It had a system of indefinite tenure in which the trustees formally reserved the right to remove anyone who, in their opinion, was guilty of misbehavior or inefficiency: a system about as threatening—or innocuous—as Harvard's. The eighteen signers of the call—among whom could be counted nine editors of scientific journals, five directors and deans, three occupants of special chairs—had no particular reason to be concerned about "the legitimate ground for dismissal" or their own "professional standing." It would appear, then, that those who were least in need of tenure reform and an academic constable were the first in the founding group to propose them. In explaining this seeming incongruity, something must be conceded to the force of altruism and more to a rule of composition—eighteen may endorse a document, but only one is likely to compose it. The man who framed the Hopkins letter was the philoso-

---

[72] The Johns Hopkins "Call," Lovejoy Papers, AAUP.

pher Arthur Oncken Lovejoy. In many respects, Lovejoy was indistinguishable from his fellows. Like them, he stood high in his university and in his discipline: in 1910, at the age of thirty-seven, he had been called to Hopkins as full professor; with his major contributions to philosophy still ahead of him, he had already achieved national prominence as a critic of philosophic schools. If he exhibited a streak of independence—a migrant who had left the pack, he had gone to France not Germany for advanced instruction and had returned without the conventional Ph.D.—he also conformed to the Calvinistic ethic that infused an academic breed—he regarded his occupation as a calling, he lived by a sober genteel code, and he imparted, in an age of progressive causes, a great deal of reformistic energy to the conquest of a variety of social sins.

In one respect, however, Lovejoy was distinctive: he had been involved in the foremost academic freedom case of his generation, the dismissal of Professor Edward A. Ross from Stanford in 1900. Others in the Hopkins group had felt the tremors of this case at its far periphery, but only Lovejoy, who had been a young associate professor on the Stanford faculty at that time and had resigned in protest against the action, had stood at the very epicenter, where fixed relations trembled and every fissure posed a moral choice. That experience had implanted in him the conviction that modern professors faced a subtle peril—attacks on their academic freedom that were officially disguised as something else. He had perceived that the victim of a masked removal was poorly equipped for vindication: he could not get a pre-dismissal hearing because the institution did not grant a hearing; he could not have a review in court because the courts would not review. Believing that the academic right to dissent could not be safeguarded in this country while curtailments of it masqueraded under other names, he had envisioned two practical solutions: first, to turn the dismissal process into a judicial process that would forestall improper removals or clearly identify them when they came; second, and until the latter could be accomplished, to make the investigation of suspect dismissals a prime professional obligation and to conduct this investigation in a severely professional way. These ideas had simmered in his mind for more than a decade; finally, in the Hopkins letter, they germinated into a concrete plan.

The Ross case brought into illustrative combination four of the major tendencies that ushered in the age of the professional: the appearance of the political activist on the faculty; the growth of ideological conflict between academic social scientists and trustees of wealth; the emergence of an "academic freedom public" with high acoustical sensitivity to complaint; the inclusion of this public into the administrators' significant world. All through the decade of the nineties, one or another of these tendencies had revealed itself in specific incidents; their simultaneous manifestation—which portentously arrived with the new century—was the noteworthy aspect of this case.[73]

The first tendency was personified by Ross, a member of a group of "new" economists who challenged the laissez-faire orthodoxy of their elders and sought to influence public policy. More outspoken than most members of this group, Ross had campaigned vigorously in public forums for free silver, a ban on Oriental immigration, municipal ownership of utilities, and public scrutiny of the Southern Pacific Railroad. Jane Lathrop Stanford, widow of a California rail baron and sole trustee of Stanford University, quickly got wind of these opinions, conceived them to be in error and likely to compromise "her" university, and demanded that Ross be dismissed. If this confusion of patronage and proprietorship was more flagrant here than in other places supported by the vastly rich, and if the petticoat instigation of the incident gave it a flavor incomparably its own, the analogy between academic and commercial employment and the shift in the academic freedom storm center from the classroom to the arena beyond the walls were not atypical in this period. Nor was the response of the Stanford president, David Starr Jordan, who was, above all things, aware of how deeply the institution had been mortgaged to the continuing generosity of its benefactress. Torn between the desire to protect the position of a professor and to protect the fortunes of the institution, Jordan first tried to temper and circumvent and then reluctantly capitulated to the founder's will. Holding the individual

[73] For the pertinent evidence in the Ross case, see O. L. Elliott, *Stanford University: The First Twenty-Five Years* (Stanford, 1937), pp. 251–308. Elliott had been serving on the Stanford faculty at the time and had taken the side of the administration. His history, written many years later, though still sympathetic to the administration, makes unquestionably clear the ideological basis of Ross's removal.

expendable for the larger good of the organization, Jordan induced Ross to resign.

Of an academic generation that would not suffer abuse in silence, Ross gave his side of the story to the press.[74] At once, journalists of the populist persuasion, quick to condemn the tycoon Medicis, seized upon the incident as a parable of the fate of liberal professors in institutions dominated by the moneyed class. In this quarter, concern for academic freedom was a satellite concern of politics: purges of conservative professors in certain populist institutions had not aroused this group to similar indignation.[75] But there was another public to whom academic freedom was a fixed necessity and its denial, under any auspices, intolerable. To the community of social scientists, recently organized by specialty, an ideological dismissal was triply evil: it injured a disciplinary colleague; it announced that the specialty was a branch of lay morality rather than a full-fledged science; it cast doubt on the honesty and independence of those who gave the trustees no offense. The presence of a professional community defending academic freedom by way of defending its own scientific status was a new and important factor no ambitious president could ignore. Had he sought to match the least of his peers or had he sought to please a limited constituency, Jordan might have made no bones about the grounds of the dismissal. But as head of a university that called itself "the Harvard of the West" and that needed distinguished scholars to support its boast, Jordan could not admit, once the issue got abroad, that Ross had been deposed for his opinions and that at Stanford social scientists had to watch their step. Instead, he let it be known that Ross had been deposed for his own shortcomings; that the head and fount of his offending had been his "slangy and scurrilous" way of speaking and not the substance of what he said; that he had worse but unmentionable faults which the long-suffering administration

[74] Stanford was in some ways a throwback to the familial college where faculty occupied a post as a child might a seat at the parent's table, just as long as the head of the household wished. These symbols were potent enough to cause Ross to resign when he lost favor; not strong enough to keep him from making a public outcry after he left the fold.

[75] See R. Hoftstader and W. P. Metzger, *The Development of Academic Freedom* (New York, 1955), pp. 423–425.

could no longer bear. Angry at what he regarded as Ross's betrayal of his confidence, Jordan probably believed these allegations; but, sincere or not, he was giving testimony to the rule that when discharged professors do not hold their tongues, when a professional community exists to hear them, and when that community is important to the president, artlessness becomes a defect in administrators and candor will be in short supply.

The Ross case, like many *causes célèbres,* began with a conflict of testimony and revealed a serious social lack. What Ross had presented to the public as a crystalline case of repression was transformed by the president's retort into an untransparent case of motives. If Jordan's version was correct, it would exonerate him, the founder, and the institution. If his version was false, it would crown the first offense with a second offense of defamation. Much hinged on the question of motives—the probity of a president, the reputation of a scholar, the prestige of a university, and, by extension, the right of professors everywhere to speak without penalty on public issues. But no social institution then existed that was equal to the demands of such a question. The courts were not likely to be of help: Ross had waived whatever contractual claims he might have had when he resigned; Jordan had spoken with sufficient care to avoid a libel or slander suit; the "why" of an academic dismissal had almost ceased to be justiciable; besides all this, the cryptic elements were social and psychological, and courts deal with cases, not disputes. None of the other inquisitional resources of society were suitable to the task: ecclesiastical tribunals, once a significant probing agency, had no place in this secular setting; state departments of education could not reach a private institution; legislative committees of investigation were not yet tooled to such inquiries and might in any case do more to politicize the issue than to supply the quietus of proof. Most important, the self-examining powers of the university proved inoperative. Ross could not ask the governing board to review his case because his chief antagonist *was* the governing board. He could not hope for an authentic verdict from the faculty because the faculty, which had not been consulted in the beginning, had been compelled, after the event, to pledge its loyalty to the president or risk reprisals. At that, one faculty member was dismissed for defending Ross, and seven more resigned. But conscientious gestures were not substitutes for a test of truth.

In December 1900, the members of the American Economic Association voted at their annual meeting to investigate the dismissal of Ross. It cannot be said that they deliberately set out to supply a missing institution. Their aim was more modest and more immediate: to rehabilitate the reputation of a colleague so that he might get a decent job. Nevertheless, their tactics accomplished the broader purpose. Rather than circulate a supportive petition (which they had done in 1897 when another member, the bimetallist E. Benjamin Andrews, had been discharged), they decided to take an agnostic posture until they themselves had found the facts. In the association were a number of economists who shared Ross's views on public issues and a few who had also paid for them. But Richard T. Ely, the president and a member of the left-wing faction, filled the committee of inquiry with conservatives—for Ross's sake, so that the report could not be discounted as a product of partisan affection; for the group's sake, so as not to let an unprecedented venture into a charged situation deepen its own ideological rifts. Thus, with short-term objectives in mind and with organizational politics an important factor, the economists fashioned an instrument of which the academic world was much in need: a professional board of inquiry, activated by a personal complaint but acting on behalf of a lofty principle, demonstrating professional esprit but avowedly neutral to the opposing parties, dealing with the complexities of motive but wedded to the supremacy of fact. And the report was as empirical and sedate as the economics of the men who wrote it. Without concluding on Mrs. Stanford's culpability, which the uncooperative president would not disclose, it demonstrated with telling documents that the charges against Ross had no foundation, while his charges against the university were plausible on their face. As well he might, Ross regarded this report as the cause of his professional redemption, the stroke that turned him from a doubtful figure into a man with a heroic past.[76]

But postmortem investigations by allied professors, however carefully conducted, could not supply the whole answer to the problem. For one thing, without legal power to subpoena witnesses or

[76] "The Dismissal of Professor Ross," *Report of a Committee of Economists* (1901); E. A. Ross, *Seventy Years of It* (New York, 1936), p. 85; A. W. Coats, "The First Two Decades of the American Economic Associations," *The American Economic Review*, September 1960, 50, 556–574.

search the files, these investigators had to rely on a degree of administrative openness which, if it had been present in the first place, might have made their entry into the case superfluous. Further, as outsiders, they ran the risk of arousing parochial resentments that could hamper their inquiry. As it happened, the economists never did succeed in conquering the reserve of the Stanford president, and while their unsuccess could be laid in part to their technique—they did not visit the campus but relied entirely on postal interrogation—the chances were that even a more refined procedure would not have cut the Jordian knot. For another thing, a postliminary inquiry came too late to avert the action, perhaps too late to undo its effects. Ross, for instance, was never restored to his post at Stanford; he did secure an excellent position at Wisconsin, but so happy a sequel could not be assured to professors of lesser stature or to those not so blessed with important friends. The lessons imparted by Ross's failure to gain reinstatement were that once a teacher is wrongfully dismissed, he dies in the minds of the misdoers and that not even a vindicating report can perform the miracle of resurrection. Plainly, the best time to discover whether the ulterior ground of a dismissal agreed with the insinuated or stated ground was *before* the dismissal was enacted and gained the solidity of an accomplished fact. Above all, it was understood that this way of getting at the covered truth was too expensive of volunteered time, too exhaustive of disciplinary energies, to be used whenever there was need for it. Even when cap-and-gown inquiries became routinized by the AAUP, they had to be employed selectively, given the high ratio of complaints to the available answering means.

It was in this context that a further solution was put forward by certain prominent members of the profession: let the local faculty be involved in all decisions looking toward dismissal; let it be involved before such decisions become irreversible; let it be involved in a judicial manner—as evaluators of alleged offenses, as triers of disputed facts. From their point of view, this proposal was but a logical extension of two tendencies already at work in campus governance, especially at the major universities: the growing participation of the faculty in the recruitment and selection of its own members and the growth of formal faculty-administration consultation in many areas of academic life. The first tendency was reinforced by trustee forbearance (in 1910, all but one of the twenty-two leading universities in America reported that their governing boards simply ratified the president's nominees for faculty positions)`, by the shrinking of presidential competence (no longer able to locate likely candidates by turning to the church or to a social circle, they came to rely on specialists to recruit other specialists), and by the breaking down of faculties into departments (a process, largely completed in major universities by 1900, which installed professors as resident agents of their disciplines and as assessors of the qualities of their own kind.)[77] The second tendency was a bureaucratic response to the problem of bureaucratic disconnectedness. Between 1883 and 1909, thirty-eight of the largest institutions of higher learning, including all the major ones, set up committees to join administrators and faculty members in the work of allocating scholarships, designing new curricula, defining educational goals. Joint boards to oversee whole divisions (for example, at Harvard and Wisconsin) and universitywide faculty senates chaired by members of the administration (for example, at Chicago and Michigan)` were other fruits of this synergetic tendency.[78] To certain professional spokesmen, it seemed but a short next step to involve the faculty formally in the dismissal process. Looking outside the academy, they found a supportive (though inapt)` parallel in the delicensing procedures of law and medicine. Though, unlike these entrepreneurial professions, the closer institutionalized professions did not offer confirming examples, they could argue that school teachers and civil servants did not enter the dismissal process because they played no role in the appointment process and that industrial scientists and salaried engineers did not judge the rightness of a prospective discharge because they did not customarily share any of the prerogatives of management. And, in the back or front of their minds, they beheld the German university and its presumed hegemony of peers.

In championing predismissal trials by local faculties, spokes-

---

[77] See A. T. Hadley, "Academic Freedom in Theory and Practice," *Atlantic Monthly*, March 1903, *91*, 342; "Report of Committee T on the Place and Function of Faculties in University Government and Administration," AAUP *Bulletin*, March 1920, *6*, 39–47.

[78] J. K. Munford, "Committees in Higher Education: A Study of the Evolution and Function of Faculty-Administration Committees in Thirty Eight Colleges and Universities, 1870–1915," unpublished doctoral dissertation (Stanford University, 1949).

men for the profession took pains to argue that they would not shelter the professor against the institutional sanctions he deserved. Before an audience of presidents, John Dewey maintained that they would facilitate the removal of incompetents by bringing into play the resources of highly critical connoisseurs.[79] Lovejoy made the point that a university peremptory within its borders was likely to be in bad repute beyond. "Every dismissal now, whether justified or unjustified, is likely to be the occasion for a hue and cry about the violation of academic freedom." In his view, a faculty hearing was an indispensable method of generating information that would spare the unoffending institution, even as it would the innocent professor, the injury of a false report.[80]

The idea was very coldly received by the leading presidents of universities. Addressing a conference of trustees in 1905, President Andrew S. Draper of the University of Illinois flatly asserted that the task of judging the faculty was no part of the functions of the faculty but remained an administrative responsibility that would not be relinquished and would not be shared.[81] No friend of working partnerships at any level ("The business of university faculties is teaching. It is not legislation and it is not administration"), Draper might have been thought to speak for the more Napoleonic segment of his fraternity. But President Charles R. Van Hise of the University of Wisconsin, who collaborated with the faculty on many matters and who consulted it informally on dismissals, was also opposed to letting it sit in formal judgment on its own. His reason—which endless reiteration would turn into a platitude—was that professors were likely to protect professors and ignore the interests of students and the public.[82] At this moment, there might well have been a particular reason for fearing that faculties would judge by the errant principle of "my coprofessional right or wrong." About this time a number of publicists and professors were attempting to revitalize a cause that had been dormant

[79] J. Dewey, "Faculty Share in University Control," *Journal of the Proceedings and Addresses* (Association of American Universities), 1915, *15*, 31.

[80] A. O. Lovejoy, "Comments on Faculty Share in University Control," *Journal of the Proceedings and Addresses* (Association of American Universities), 1915, *15*, 37–38.

[81] A. S. Draper, "The University President," *Atlantic Monthly*, 1906, *97*, 35–39.

[82] Van Hise, pp. 61–62; Curti and Cartsensen, Vol. 2, pp. 43, 55–56.

since the early nineteenth century—the cause of outright faculty control. Headed by an irrepressible factotum of academic reform, the
Columbia psychologist J. McKeen Cattell, given to raucous antiad-
ministration rhetoric, desiring fundamental changes in the charters,
this movement was not identical with the movement to empanel
faculties in dismissal cases, which was led by less bellicose personalities
and sought specific change within existing forms. Nevertheless, both
movements did draw refreshment from a common source—the inordinate restiveness of American academics in this period—and both did
serve as tributaries to the complex current that would lead to the
founding of the AAUP. It was very likely, then, that many presidents
regarded them as different facets of the same insurgency and responded
to both with the same alarm.

But even administrators who were cognizant of the difference
between a bid for executive and legislative control and a bid for judicial participation might not have considered the latter a natural or
innocuous progression from the current way. To presidents opposed to
predismissal hearings of any sort, predismissal hearings by the faculty
were not a small step but two giant steps in the wrong direction. Moreover, many must surely have perceived that a faculty trial would not
be just another bureaucratic bridging mechanism but the staging of a
drama that would require a reversal of statuses and roles. A president
who became a charge maker rather than a discharge maker would put
himself on a level with the person he accuses; a president who must
plead as a humble adversary for the favorable judgment of the staff in
robes would suffer yet more severe displacements. A great deal was
being asked of the executive ego: it was being asked to concede that
high should be low, unequals equal, precisely at the most perilous
junction—at the point where superior and subordinate have a falling-
out. And this was being asked at a time when the executive ego was
notably not of the shrinking sort.

Without fresh provocations, it was quite possible that professors
would not have forced the issue. Standing in isolation, the Ross case
might well have lost its flavor as a controversy and never gained its
power as a paradigm. Indeed, between 1901 and 1913, as a lull
seemed to settle on the academic freedom front, interest in judicial tenure seemed as well to flag. But then, quite suddenly, a new rash of
dismissals broke out across the country, and the fight for judiciality

gained a new lease on life. The incident that was probably most re-
animating was not at all a replay of the Ross affair: it occurred at a
relatively minor institution, it raised a rather archaic academic freedom
issue, it was not caused by the intrusion of a rich trustee. But therein
lay its potency: it showed that faculty hearings might have utility even
in situations that did not attain the appalling stature of the Ross dismissal and that did not reflect, with anything like the clarity of that
archetype, the conflict between scholarship and purse.

In January 1913, Willard C. Fisher, professor of economics at
Wesleyan University, resigned his post at the peremptory demand of
the president. The reason for that demand was a speech he had delivered in another city in which he had urged less rigid observance of
the Sabbath and the subordination of church-going to good works.
President William A. Shanklin, after reading a newspaper account of
the speech, had written Fisher that his opinions were "so far out of
harmony with the spirit of the college which, though in no wise sectarian, is, and always has been, profoundly in sympathy with the
Christian churches" that his continuance in his position was "undesirable." In reply, Fisher had conceded that "a college with the history
and constituency and support of Wesleyan is not exactly the place for
a man who holds such views as mine and who cannot suppress them";
he had assured the president that he would sever his sixteen-year connection with the institution "without a trace of ill-will toward any-
body."[83] The concession waived the academic freedom principle; the
grace note promised no publicity; and here the matter might have
ended, a footnote to the saga of avoided battles, had the constituency
of the college been as uniform or its history as insulating and one-sided
as Fisher had assumed. But Wesleyan was one of a large number of
denominational institutions that faced in two directions—toward a
partially outgrown parochialism (it had broken its formal church connection but still relied on Methodist support) and a not yet fully realized secularity (it hankered for the prestige of research scholars,
though it still regarded the president's office as a curacy and still
labored for the redemption of student souls). As head of an institution
that had felt the gusts of change without gaining the surety of a trans-

<hr>

[83] W. A. Shanklin to W. C. Fisher, January 27, 1913; Fisher to Shanklin,
Janaury 27, 1913. In *American Economic Review*, March 1913, *3*, 258.

formation, the president shuttlecocked between the values of diverse publics: he enforced a canon of conformity to win sectarian approval, yet when he was challenged by a distinguished scholar and alumnus, the Princeton economist E. W. Kemmerer, he denied that Fisher had been punished for his unorthodoxy and vaguely blamed his character defects. Fisher, to preserve his status as a heretic, sent the original correspondence to the journals *Science* and *American Economic Review*, and the case, initially headed for obscurity, came into public view. Some militant professors took advantage of the opportunity to indict a president from his own inculpating text.[84] Others, however, held back, unwilling to act as partisans in what appeared to be a clouded case. Professor J. E. Creighton could not induce his Cornell colleagues to sign a strong pro-Fisher statement because of their contention, "repeated more than once, that we did not know all the facts."[85] Kemmerer encountered much the same resistance when he tried to rally the economists he knew. He wanted to go beyond remonstrances: while he did not believe that Fisher's allies should "go about the country . . . advising people not to accept the position," he did propose that the leading figures of the discipline should refuse to recommend a substitute until such time as the university made restitution or removed liable personnel. Assisted by the chairman of his department, Frank A. Fetter, one of those who had resigned from Stanford for the sake of conscience, Kemmerer did succeed in obtaining some pledges of support for his passive boycott.[86] But he could not draw an effective cordon around the institution. Henry C. Emery, returning to his professorship at Yale after serving on the United States Tariff Commission, stopped off at Middletown to fill Fisher's shoes for a semester; in the fall, Charles A. Tuttle, a Heidelberg Ph.D. from Wabash College, accepted an invitation to become Fisher's permanent replacement. Emery's was the key defection because it not only spared the institution a hiatus but gave it a qualitative gain. The Wesleyan president had assured him, Emery explained to his nettled colleagues, that academic freedom had not been violated; without authoritative findings

[84] Creighton to E. W. Kemmerer, March 16, 1913. In Kemmerer Papers, Princeton University.

[85] Creighton, "Academic Freedom," *Science*, March 21, 1913, *37*, 450.

[86] Kemmerer to Walter F. Willcox, March 6, 1913. In Kemmerer Papers.

to the contrary, he saw no reason not to trust this *ipse dixit*.[87] Authoritative findings, as it happened, never did emerge. The organized economists again set an inquiry into motion, an inquiry headed by Columbia's E. R. A. Seligman, the chief investigator and reporter in the Stanford case. But it yielded no publicized result, mainly because the chairman became convinced that Fisher had not been faultless in conduct and because he wished to reserve full reportage for the worthy pure. The stymying of this investigation had a lot to do with rallying the economists around the idea of an ecumenical organization that would render assistance even to less-than-saintly victims. And the reappearance of an unresolved freedom riddle, wrapped in a motive mystery, caused that organization from the start to demand faculty involvement in dismissal trials.

To what precise institutional innovations did the AAUP commit itself? When one reviews the decretals of the association, one finds that it did not hold consistently to one position but adopted as many as four, more or less sequentially, as it gathered experience from its investigations, rode the tide of such events as depression and war, negotiated agreements with administrators, and changed the character of its leadership ('lost some philosophers and gained more lawyers). Giving each of these positions a rough descriptive tag and placing them in chronological order, one might say that the 1915 General Report on Academic Freedom and Academic Tenure '(the philosophical birth cry of the Association)' adopted the model of the guild; that the 1925 Conference Statement '(the first joint effort of the AAUP and the Association of American Colleges, an administrative organization)' adopted the model of the expert counsel; that the 1940 and 1958 Statements '(also interorganizational agreements)' adopted the model of the Civil Service and the model of the criminal court. The last two schemes have taken over and now dominate academic thinking on this subject, but it may be useful nonetheless to glance at the conceptual alternatives that have fallen along the way.

When Lovejoy and company set down rules for "fair procedures" in dismissal cases (this was the phrase they used and not "due process,"

---

[87] Emery to J. McKeen Cattell, n.d. In "Wesleyan College Case File," AAUP Papers, Washington, D.C.

which was the coinage of model four), they sought to accomplish two objectives. First, they tried to establish, as firmly as they dared, the right of the faculty as a body to judge the fitness of a current member when it was brought into dispute: "Every university or college teacher should be entitled, before dismissal or demotion, to have the charges against him stated in writing in specific terms and to have a fair trial on those charges before a special or permanent committee chosen by the faculty senate or council, or by the faculty at large.[88] It should be noted that they envisioned a faculty tribunal separate from the administration, a court of immediate jurisdiction, in which the professional spirit could have full and unembarrassed play. And then? The first AAUPers did not dispute the legal power of the board to review the findings of this lower court. Neither did they refuse to concede to lay authority an independent competence to determine whether a scholar was guilty of misconduct in a case that bore no other tinge. But they held that those not "trained for a scholar's duties" could not intervene in cases involving ideas or the expression of ideas "without destroying, to the extent of their intervention, the essential nature of the university." They thought it "inadmissible that the power of determining when departures from the requirements of the scientific spirit and method have occurred should be vested in bodies not composed of members of the academic profession. . . . Such bodies necessarily lack full competency to judge of these requirements; their intervention can never be exempt from the suspicion that it is dictated by other motives than zeal for the integrity of science; and it is, in any case, unsuitable to the dignity of a great profession that the initial responsibility for the maintenance of its professional standards should not be in the hands of its own members."[89]

Here, in the throat of the professional could be heard the still audible voice of the master. In the area of academic freedom, the first leaders of the AAUP sought the closest approximation to guild autonomy they could possibly lay claim to and still accept the legal impregnability of the charters and the political inevitability of lay control. Later, however, this claim would be weakly staked; in academic free-

[88] "General Report of the Committee on Academic Freedom and Academic Tenure," presented at the annual meeting of the association, December 31, 1915, AAUP *Bulletin*, 1915, *1*, 41–42.
[89] "General Report . . . ," pp. 38–39.

dom matters, the AAUP would ask not as much for faculty control as for greater trustee courtesy; conflicts on this score would arise, but would never be joined by the association with this natal clarity.

Up to this point, the articles spoke only to judicial method. The second object of this early statement was to forge a link between tenure and judiciality. In a footnote, the authors informed the reader that a refusal of reappointment would not be regarded as a dismissal and would not be covered by judicial rules. While they enjoined the administration to seek "the advice and consent" of some faculty body before refusing to resume a term appointment, they made it clear that the judicial entitlements of tenure would not go to everyone on the faculty but only to those who had earned them, either by promotion to the two highest ranks or by service as assistant professor for a period of ten years or more. The logic of this dichotomy, which was not spelled out in the document, could be read between the lines. The dismissal procedure here envisioned (all placating argument to the contrary notwithstanding) was intended to make academic discharges much more difficult than they usually had been. The interposition of a faculty body between the administration and the board (a faculty trial *before* dismissal) was designed to break the auricular communication that had contributed in the past to unjust dismissals; the required method of initiation (specific *charges* put in *writing*) was designed to make the administrative accuser bear the full burden of proof; the indicated handling of this business (a *separate* faculty trial, a *fair* hearing on *all* the charges) assured a full ventilation of grievances and a lengthy litigatory plot. As the founders saw it, it would have been unwise to have universalized these procedures—unwise as a matter of politics, for they had to concede something to managerial reluctances in order to overcome them; but especially unwise as a matter of principle. In their view, to grant the academic teacher judicial privileges that would entrench him before he proved his worth would be to diminish the power of the institution to correct initial errors, to perpetuate serious misalliances between academic persons and positions, to turn a calling meant to reward the highest talents into a sinecure for the green and so-so man. But these concerns for quality and merit, while they did credit to the conscience of the profession, left unanswered one tantalizing question—how may the rights of the unentitled, including the right of academic freedom, be protected under a two-class system such as this? The quest for answers to that question would test the ingenuity of every professional generation from the first day it was posited to now.

In tone and substance, the 1925 Conference Statement marked a significant retreat by the association from its primal hopes and demands. To be sure, it was the first code of judicial tenure to be subscribed to by a body of college presidents; consequently, it reflected a mellowing of potentate opinion when it declared that predismissal hearings by the faculty were "desirable," that charges based on extramural utterances should be "submitted" to a faculty committee, and that decisions not to renew appointments should be taken in conference with the department involved. In certain respects, indeed, it added strengthening touches to the procedure: thus, it provided (as the 1915 Statement did not)` that the "accused teacher should always have an opportunity to face his accusers." But in this statement, a faculty trial was merely deemed desirable, not required; in academic freedom matters (here limited to extramural utterances)`, the faculty, though necessarily involved, would not necessarily render conclusive judgments; in the termination of limited appointments, the faculty was to be consulted but was not empowered to veto actions simply by withholding its consent. Nor was it mandated that the charges be specific and put into writing: despite certain safety catches, the crucial triggering device could be worked with greater ease. These changes were indicative of a shift of rationale: here, the aim of a faculty hearing was not so much to block or expose intolerance as to inform the distant and unknowing board. The difference between models one and two, between an argument for faculty prerogative and an argument for faculty counsel, is pointed up by the permission granted in the 1925 document for summary dismissals by the board in cases of "gross immorality or treason, when the facts are admitted." When, in short, there was no apparent need for faculty advice, there was no need for a faculty (or any)` trial.[90] It was in this document, too, that terminations because of financial exigency were first recognized as legitimate, provided they were undertaken as a last resort.

On the question of who qualified for these attenuated judicial rights, all that the 1925 Statement held was that persons on perma-

---

[90] Reproduced in AAUP *Bulletin,* Spring 1959, *45,* 110–111.

nent or long-term appointments did and that persons on temporary or short-term appointments did not, but it did not say when or at what rank such appointments and their corresponding privileges would necessarily ensue. It thus not only accepted a two-track system of tenure, but invited institutions of higher learning to keep their faculty members, of whatever title or seniority, permanently on the lesser track. The 1915 Statement had created a normative distinction between tenure and nontenure which resolved into a class distinction between judicial haves and have nots. The 1925 Statement retained the class distinction, but removed its normative basis by letting seasoned members as well as tyros remain in an indigent state.

We may glean the reasons for this fallback from 1915 from the records of the negotiations and from the temper of the times. The records show that it was the representatives of the AAC who insisted on unlimited probationary periods, the financial exigency exemption, and the inclusion of that world war relic, "treason," among the grounds that would justify removal. But the representatives of the AAUP were not tough bargainers on these or other questions. Their mood of conservatism and conciliation reflected the changes that had occurred within a decade: the decline of progressive fervor, the extinction of syndicalist ideas, the fatigue that often follows a rousing organizational birth. Whatever else may have been the cause, it is clear that the effect of the 1925 agreement was to give the profession rather limp defenses against the economic havoc that would soon descend.

In 1940, the two associations, after several years of negotiation, agreed to a new Statement of Principles, one that was destined to become the most widely endorsed and most influential of all such formularies. This statement embodied two important rationales, neither of which had heretofore been prominent. One of these absorbed the emphasis on the routinization of job security that might have been picked up from Civil Service situations. For example, this statement was the first to use the term *probationary* to describe the pretenure stint, thus making it clear that it *was* a pretenure stint and not a collection point for a supply of cheap, submissive, and unhopeful labor. This statement was the first to dissociate tenure from rank and tie it exclusively to years of service; moreover, so that all need not start afresh in each new employment, it was the first to include in the reckoning all the years spent in the profession (though by written agreement only a three-year portion of outside service might be allowed to count). As a result, it became possible for the first time to advance the notion of *de facto* tenure—tenure that would accrue to the faculty member not by institutional say-so but by many turns of the working clock. Also featured in the 1940 Statement were several efforts to plug the holes left in the dikes of tenure by the 1925 agreement. Except in the case of financial exigency, all dismissals were to be for cause and all were to be judicially determined. Except for the statement that faculty hearings were to be provided if possible (the qualification was inserted to cover the very small institution, where colleagues might be too close to colleagues to wish to serve), everything in this document suggested that the faculty had to judge to make the action truly judicial. And—without ceremony—the frightful and frightening word *treason* was dropped.[91]

Not everything in the 1940 Statement went to shoring up security. Considerable attention was paid to competing values—institutional flexibility, quality control. Thus, it reaffirmed the proposition that tenure alone conferred judicial citizenship and that probationers could be let go at the expiration of a term appointment, provided due notice had been sent. It dropped all reference to faculty review of such nonrenewals; it did not revive the notion of determinative faculty verdicts when issues of freedom were involved. It set the maximum period of probation at seven years, which was shorter than the AAUP founders had suggested but longer than the fledgling unions then proposed. Moreover, by setting up a purely temporal yardstick, it made the institution reach the in or out question without delay or equivoca-

---

[91] Aside from an oblique reference to moral turpitude and a suggestion as to how incompetence should be judged, this statement did not define adequate cause for dismissal. Neither had the 1915 Statement, though it thought that a substantive definition should be high on subsequent agendas; nor have later documents in any systematic way. This failure to set forth a penal code should not be attributed to laziness or inadvertence. Though silence by the organized professions leaves each institution to its own devices, it is probably more protective of freedom and tenure than a listing of capital offenses. Such an enumeration might contain provisions that would outlive the occasion that gave them pertinence, might be applied with so much literalness that no room would be left for judging motives or considering the defendant's record as a whole, might invite the addition of new prescriptions whenever contemporary excitements led to misconducts not itemized on the list.

tion, after the requisite interval had elapsed. Even so, this statement was of all the most security minded. It went further than any other in broadening tenure coverage, making it accessible to the still-youthful mass where once it had been reserved for the titled few. And it made tenure not just codable, but enforceable.

In the previous statements, very little had been said about how predismissal hearings should be conducted. As far as faculty hearings were concerned, this omission may have reflected self-romanticization: the AAUP founders in particular seemed to believe that academics were equipped by career-long training to deal with knotty human questions, that all that was needed to deliver justice was to ensure that they would have the right to judge. To some extent, too, this omission may have reflected the lack of legal talent at the drafting table, a lack that Ralph Himstead, the first lawyer to serve as general secretary of the association, would repair in the later round. In any event, the 1940 Statement was the first to make a serious effort to approximate what may be called the trial hearing, in contradistinction to the looser, less regulated, and more extemporaneous scholarly research type. It reverted to the demand for written charges; it added the right of the accused to an adviser who might act as counsel; it provided for a full and accessible stenographic record of the proceedings. Its sequel, the 1958 Statement on Procedural Standards in Faculty Dismissal Hearings, went much further in this direction, providing for preliminary hearings, prespecification of procedural standards, limited cross-examination, explicit findings on every charge, and a method of articulating the faculty's proximate judgment with the trustees' review and final vote.[92] These efforts to judicialize the dismissal process by adding to it the techniques worked out in the courts may be said to have had rather mixed effects. Insofar as they have served to remind the faculty and the governing boards that they trade in reputations and must carefully test their wares, these efforts may have been on the whole quite salutary. But insofar as they suggest that academic trials and criminal trials are more than cousins and might be twins, insofar as they threaten to increase the due process pollution of the environment, they have the

[92] AAUP, *Policy Documents and Reports* (Washington, D.C., 1969): "1940 Statement of Principles" and "1958 Statement on Procedural Standards in Faculty Dismissal Proceedings." See also, "1968 Recomended Institutional Regulations on Academic Freedom and Tenure."

capacity to be pernicious. There is much to praise in a lawyerly approach, but there is much to deplore in the signs of creeping legalism. The story of judicial tenure after 1940 is the story of an idea that gains in favor, even in regions that were once inhospitable to it. With variations, the basic protocol came to be enacted in all but two categories of institution—those that were so dominated by administrations that faculty initiatives of any kind were objectionable and those that were so protected by genteel custom that faculty dismissals by any ceremony were unthinkable. To account for the success of this idea, one might cite a number of promoting agencies. Among the important abetting factors was the work of the AAUP—its case reports and public censures that named and shamed transgressors into correction; its control of the 1940 Statement, which it could apply with scriptural fidelity or interpret with Talmudic ingenuity. Another factor was the overthrow of the Holmesian doctrine that public employment was a privilege that could be conditioned or retracted without infringing on rights protected by the Fourteenth Amendment. Having done this, the courts gave public academic teachers leave to claim that while they may not have a constitutional right to be seen, they do have a constitutional right to be heard by the state in its role as employer and before a dismissal takes effect. Still another facilitating factor was the elaboration of procedural safeguards in many different kinds of employment: academic due process did not seem strange when school teachers got the right to predismissal hearings under state tenure laws and when workers covered by union contracts were accorded an elaborate right to grieve.

But one cannot fully explain why judicial tenure gained ascendancy in this period—and even less why it is now thought by some to have passed its apogee—unless one also takes into account an unwitting factor—the swings of the academic economy. The depression of the 1930s caused a contraction of academic employment and academic services; the war and postwar inflation that followed served to ravage real academic incomes; by the mid-fifties, after these successive setbacks, the academic system was not meeting the demands of a growing population, and the talented people of this society were refusing to follow the scent of such poor rewards. At this point, the nation embarked upon a crash program of expansion and enrichment, and a new economic cycle was begun. Helped by enormous largesse from the states, steep rises in federal support, the seed millions of the Ford Foundation, the success of innumerable alumni fund drives, and public willingness to pay the tuition and other college attendance costs, the academic system more than doubled its capacity within a decade, and the academic work force, much expanded, more than recouped its earlier income loss. No matter that these new moneys sometimes financed mediocrity or that the giving was sometimes more inspired by the specter of Soviet accomplishment than the sight of professorial impoverishment. The fact remains that in this period (which is sure to glow in memory the more it recedes in time), there arose two unprecedented phenomena: American colleges and universities faced with plenty, and an American professoriate almost able to afford the middle-class style to which it had so long aspired. Inevitably, the fortunes of judicial tenure rode high upon this arc. The instant creation of new universities increased the number of parvenu institutions that would offer tenure along with other perquisites just to prove to the world that they had arrived. The shortage of top-flight applicants in relation to top-flight jobs changed the buyer-seller balance all down the line and made the promise of firm if not easy tenure an essential part of the bargains that were struck. Wealthier institutions were able to consider the positive sides of tenure and not dwell on its alleged inefficiencies and money costs; professors in those institutions could take their tenure rights for granted and forget that all institutions keep their work force only as long as they can pay their bills. But most of all, prosperity and expansion relieved the tensions generated by the probation system: they permitted enough mobility in the system to reduce the penalizing effects of failure; they provided a sufficiency of jobs and prizes to tempt the young into the waiting game.

Alas, the flourishing academic life, as soon as it became remarkable, began to disappear: the salvaging of this profession, which began as a Herculean effort, wound up as the Perils of Pauline. Starting in 1966, and growing worse each year thereafter, a new recession has taken hold—the third in the space of the last forty years. In some ways, it embodies the worst features of the other two. It severely reduces the number of academic openings: in this respect, it resembles the depression of the thirties. And, like the world war and Korean war recessions, it is accompanied by a ravenous inflation, which eats away faculty compensation, measured by what the dollar buys. To be sure, by starting at a higher plateau, this recession recapitulates the others with somewhat less intensity. A profession of half a million can generate a larger absolute number of openings than can a profession of seventy thousand, which was the number of academic practitioners in 1930. And the previous and continuing rise in nominal incomes makes the cheapening of the dollar somewhat less hard to take. But this is only to say that misfortune is experienced at a different threshold, not that it is exaggerated or unreal. If there are more open jobs today than in 1930, there are also many more candidates competing for them since the graduate schools also expanded. And if inflation attacks a larger paycheck, it might do so with a crueller impact because it supervenes upon an affluence—or at least an expectation of affluence—that faculties do not dare abandon and deeply dread to lose.

Predictably, as the economy continues to hurtle down, the voices of opposition to tenure rise. Some of these voices have been heard before: to those who never wished this system well, either because it seeemed to give professors undue privileges or because it placed administrators under undue constraints, the recession simply provides an opportunity to inveigh against it—this time on the ground of costs. But by no means are all complainers opportunists. One can hear, in this rising chorus, the authentic moans of those who are being hurt. With chances for reemployment much cut down, with institutions freezing tenure lines in order to stabilize their own living costs, with the graduate schools still turning out an oversupply of postulants for the increasingly rare awards of ordination, there must needs be conflict on class lines. In many faculties a new antipathy between seniors and juniors has developed, an antipathy that is generational and ideological in rhetoric, but largely economic at its base. Rather than be cast out into an unwelcoming world, some academic journeymen, with encouragement from unions and to some extent from the courts, are demanding judicial rights that would make them the equals of their tenured work fellows. Others, rather than concede to rival colleagues a life-and-death control over their careers, appear willing to take their chances on limited appointments for everyone—and let the best or the cagiest survive. Still others, with some administrative and veteran support, are urging periodic evaluations of the tenured faculty, say at five- or ten-year intervals (but if an institution can afford the man hours that would have to be invested in such search-and-possibly-de-

stroy operations, it has either an extraordinarily productive faculty or
a grossly underused one!). The calls for no tenure, instant tenure,
tenure for the nonce but not forever merge illogically into one loud
utterance—a vote of no confidence in the system it has taken sixty—or
perhaps six hundred years—to build.

In the opinion of this writer, it is essential to separate the problems raised by a pinched economy from the problems raised by the
tenure system. Each presents its own analytic difficulties, each calls for
its own responsive strategies. For the first, one would have to debate
the goods and bads of growth and then decide whether the proper
answer lies in adjusting the labor supply to a circumscribed demand
or in laying hold of fresh resources that would permit us to escape the
harsh predicaments of zero-sum. For the second, one would have to
calculate the benefits we get (still essentially libertarian)' against the
costs (still centered on efficiency)'. The costs of judicial tenure have
not always been well assessed by either its proponents or its detractors.
Some who defend the system have said that it does not in the least
impede the dismissal of professors for incompetence, that it can be as
easily used to throw the inadequate scholar out as to keep the heretical
scholar in. But general observation does not support this argument.
Operationally if not formally, the faculty hearing does act as a brake
on administrative venturesomeness as well as on administrative arbitrariness. In fact if not always by rule, it is the display of evil character,
not the display of weak ability, that calls the mechanism into play. To
use the terminology of this chapter, judicial tenure has raised the level
of assurance from presumptive competence to presumptive permanence.
On the other side, some would have us believe that judicial tenure is
a major reason why professors grow ignorant and slack. This view has
been encapsulated in a metaphor: the university, it is said and said
again, contains and (under the tenure rules) cannot divest itself of
dead wood. It cannot be denied that faculty members may grow
moribund. But whether they do so because of tenure is another point.
If they did, one would find that the most lifeless faculties in the nation
are in institutions where tenure is most secure—namely in the major
universities. It would also follow that the American professoriate of
1900, which was not supplied with this protection, made a more significant contribution to scholarship and rated higher on the world
exchange than does the American professoriate today. Since both con-

clusions are extremely dubious, one has cause to doubt the complaining premise. May there not be a close association between the use of positive incentives and the rise in scholarly ambitions, an association closer than that between the use of negative sanctions and a faculty on its toes? The trouble with the warehouse metaphor, which conceives of the university as a lumber yard, collecting and sorting finished products, is that it ignores the ways the university functions as a society that shapes the very materials it holds. Take University X, which goads its faculty into animation with a mixture of diverse rewards and tacit but merciful expectations. Compare it with University Y, which offers no broader vista after tenure than payments scaled to longevity and no better models than a faculty that does the least it can. Neither is saved or destroyed by its tenure system. The warehouse metaphor is thus in double error. It understates the extent to which men rise or sink to the level of their circumstances. And it wrongly assumes, against all the facts of work psychology, that one stick—expulsion—and no carrot is the governor of what we aim for and achieve.

IV

Legal Dimensions
of Tenure

Victor G. Rosenblum

In their 1959 study of tenure in American higher education Byse and Joughin stressed as the "essential characteristic of tenure," not any concrete legal norm, but, rather, "continuity of service." They saw continuity, in turn, as a product of the relinquishment, through legal obligation or moral commitment, of the freedom or power the educational institution otherwise would possess to terminate the teacher's services.[1] A more recent comprehensive

[1] C. Byse and L. Joughin, *Tenure in American Higher Education* (Ithaca: Cornell University Press, 1959), p. 71.

survey of developments in the law of academic freedom contains a similar paucity of definitive legal content regarding tenure and is forced to substitute admonition for settled doctrine: "Once a professor has tenure, his rights *should* be well protected."[2] At best, it would be a serious mistake to think of the legal dimensions of tenure as a series of specific codified rules or principles subject uniformly to enforcement in the courts. On the contrary, reluctance, amorphousness, a substantial degree of diversity, and even a modicum of whimsy have marked judicial conceptions and appraisals of tenure over the years.

In discussing these legal dimensions, we must first of all distinguish between judicial approaches to tenure in public and in private institutions. A tenure plan promulgated by a governing board of a public institution is generally considered a form of sublegislation having the force of law. A finding that a discharge was contrary to the tenure plan of a public institution can generally be followed by an order to reinstate the teacher, since the discharge was, in effect, beyond the board's authority and contrary to state law. In a private institution, any right to tenure is contractual rather than statutory. The principle that courts will not decree specific performance of personal service contracts is likely to prevail even when money damages do not provide an adequate remedy. Hence, a specific order of reinstatement will not ordinarily follow a conclusion that a contract has been breached through failure to observe its tenure provisions. The wide range and public-private dichotomies of court approaches to tenure led Byse and Joughin to observe that "continuity of employment extended by an institution with a long and honorable tradition of academic freedom and tenure often will be much more meaningful than an express legal obligation grudgingly assumed by a lesser institution."[3]

To the extent that regularities have emerged in legal construction of rights of faculty members, the following general observations and propositions would apply: (1) Questions of tenure as such have played comparatively minor roles in judicial development of applicable norms and doctrines. (2) Courts have been less interested in allocating rights on a stratified basis between tenured and nontenured

[2] "Developments in the Law—Academic Freedom," 81 *Harvard Law Review* 1045 at 1102 (1968).
[3] Byse and Joughin, p. 75.

faculty than in examining basic due-process and First Amendment questions that can affect the whole academic community, at least in the public sector. (3) The courts have stressed procedure in public institutions, entitling faculty there to adequate notice, hearing, and opportunity for representation before they can be dismissed. (4) Judicial recognition has been accorded the principle that public employees should not lose their jobs because of their exercise of substantive constitutional rights such as free speech. (5) Dismissal or firing is not equated legally with nonrenewal of a teaching appointment. (6) Constitutional procedural protection is assured tenured faculty in public institutions, but nontenured faculty can be certain of constitutional protection only against dismissal in the course of an employment contract. (7) Constitutional procedural protection is available to a nontenured faculty member contesting nonrenewal of a contract if he can show initially that nonrenewal was due to his exercise of a constitutional right. (8) These developments with regard to public institutions do not have automatic counterparts in private institutions in the absence of contractual provisions or demonstrable customs embodying them. (9) Thus courts can offer little certainty of protection to the aggrieved professor in the private sector who feels that his tenure rights have been invaded; for the distinctive quality of the typical private institution's tenure system is "what is in substance private grievance machinery operating under privately developed standards."[4]

---

[4] "Developments in the Law—Academic Freedom," 81 *Harvard Law Review* 1045 at 1102. Other valuable compilations and analyses of judicial approaches to tenure are found in Harry Pettigrew, " 'Constitutional Tenure': Toward a Realization of Academic Freedom," 22 *Case Western Reserve Law Review* 475 (1971); William Van Alstyne, "The Constitutional Rights of Teachers and Professors," *Duke Law Journal* 841 (1970); the chapter on "Law and the Faculty" in K. Alexander and E. Solomon, *College and University Law* (1972), pp. 342–409; the chapter on "Faculty Academic Freedom, Procedural Due Process, The First Amendment and Tenure" in C. Byse and S. Nahmod, *Cases and Materials on the Role of Law on the Campus* (mimeo, 1971); the chapter on "Faculty" in J. S. Brubacher, *The Courts and Higher Education* (San Francisco: Jossey-Bass, 1971), pp. 46–75; the section on teacher tenure in N. Edwards, *The Courts and the Public Schools*, 3rd ed. (1971), pp. 467–473; the section on tenure in *The Teacher's Day in Court*, published annually by the research division of the National Education Association; and the *Notes* and *Journal* of the National Organization on Legal Problems of Education.

Roth and Sindermann Decisions

The most recent examination by the U.S. Supreme Court of the rights of faculty members took place in a pair of cases (decided in June 1972) in which nontenured teachers in public colleges sought to contest the nonrenewal of their appointments. Although the court's decisions in the Roth[5] and Sindermann[6] cases do not provide clear and explicit norms of tenure, the reasoning, nuances and implications of the decisions are important because they appear to establish an authoritative context within which judicial review of questions of tenure will operate in the future.

In five-to-three decisions, Justice Powell not participating, the court decided that allegation of First Amendment or due-process issues does not preempt or control basic norms of property and contract governing relationships between faculty and administrations. The majority reached comprehensive, though not necessarily irrevocable, conclusions about the criteria for determining whether and when faculty members in public institutions have a right to a statement of reasons and an opportunity for a hearing in cases of nonreappointment.

Essentially, the contract between the faculty member and the school and the customary practices of the school in administering it were held to determine the extent of the property interest of the faculty member in reappointment. In the absence of charges against the teacher by the administration, or the imposition of a stigma or other disability foreclosing the faculty member's freedom to take advantage of other employment opportunities, a state school owes a nontenured faculty member no hearing or statement of reasons for nonreappointment. The net effect of the decisions in *Roth* and *Sindermann* was thus to stress that basic responsibility for allocating teachers' rights belongs to academic institutions themselves. The courts will not ordinarily substitute their notions of equity for the by-laws, rules, and contracts of the schools. At the same time, the justices reminded state college and university officials that the meaning of an institution's by-

---

[5] Board of Regents of State Colleges *v.* David F. Roth, 405 U.S.—, 92 S.Ct. 2694, 40 *Law Week* 5079 (1972).

[6] Charles R. Perry *v.* Robert P. Sindermann, 405 U.S.—, 92 S.Ct. 2694, 40 *Law Week* 5087 (1972).

laws, rules, and contracts must be measured by realities rather than formal façades in administration-faculty relationships and practices.

In the course of the decisions, Justice Stewart, who wrote the majority opinion in both cases, ended prior constitutional distinctions between rights and privileges in public employment and created opportunities for social scientists to undertake empirical research that might modify the court's present interpretations at some later date. He was careful to avoid sweeping doctrinal generalizations, emphasizing instead the importance of the particular facts of each case to what he regarded as the applicable legal rules.

Since the facts were central to the outcomes, they are worth detailing. David Roth was hired in 1968 for his first teaching job as an assistant professor of political science at Wisconsin State University at Oshkosh. He had no formal contract of employment beyond his official notice of appointment, which the court construed as the equivalent of an employment contract. Roth's notice of appointment stated that he was hired for a fixed term of one academic year. The notice of appointment also informed Roth that "regulations governing tenure are in accordance with Chapter 37.31, Wisconsin statutes. The employment of any staff member for an academic year shall not be for a term beyond June 30 of the fiscal year in which the appointment is made." Chapter 37.31, to which the notice of appointment referred, states that "all teachers in any state university shall initially be employed on probation. The employment shall be permanent, during efficiency and good behavior, after four years of continuous service in the state university system as a teacher." Rules promulgated by the board of regents provide that a nontenured teacher must be informed by February 1 of retention or nonretention for the ensuing year. The regents' rules add: "During the time a faculty member is on probation, no reason for nonretention need be given. No review or appeal is provided in such case." The president of Wisconsin State University at Oshkosh informed Roth before February 1, 1969, that he would not be rehired for the 1969–70 academic year. He gave Roth no reason for the decision and no opportunity to challenge it.

Professor Roth, claiming that his First and Fourteenth Amendment rights were infringed by the decision not to rehire him, brought suit in a federal district court. He alleged that the true reason for nonreappointment was to punish him for statements criticizing university officials. He also alleged that the university's failure to notify him of any reason for nonretention or to allow him a hearing violated his right to procedural due process.

The district court agreed with Professor Roth that procedural due-process guarantees should apply in his case and ordered university officials to provide him with reasons and a hearing. It did not reach the merits of the claim that the professor was being punished for his criticism of university officials. The basis for the district court's ruling was essentially that a balancing of the weights of the respective interests involved warranted the conclusion that the professor's interest in reemployment outweighed the university's interest in summarily denying him reemployment.[7]

With one judge dissenting, the court of appeals affirmed the district court's order requiring that reasons and a hearing be given Professor Roth.[8] The court of appeals accepted the district court's assumption that nonretention by one university or college creates concrete difficulties for a professor in his subsequent academic career. The stigma of nonretention was believed sufficiently to limit future employment opportunities as to warrant invocation of procedural due-process guarantees. In any event, opportunity for a hearing and a statement of reasons were required here "as a prophylactic against nonretention decisions improperly motivated by exercise of protected rights."[9]

Professor Sindermann had a much longer employment record with his institution than Professor Roth. In 1965, after teaching for two years at the University of Texas and for four years at San Antonio Junior College, he became a professor of government and social science at Odessa Junior College in Texas. He was employed at Odessa for four successive years under a series of one-year contracts, including service for a time as cochairman of the department. During the 1968–69 academic year, Sindermann, in his capacity as president of the Texas Junior College Teachers Association, publicly disagreed with policies of the board of regents. His 1968–69 employment contract terminated in May 1969, and the board of regents, having voted not to offer him a new contract for the next academic year, issued a press

[7] Roth v. Board of Regents, 310 F.Supp. 972 (1970).
[8] Board of Regents v. Roth, 446 F.2d 806 (1971).
[9] Regents v. Roth, 809–810.

release alleging that Sindermann had defied his superiors by attending legislative committee meetings when college officials had explicitly refused to permit him to leave his classes for that purpose.

Odessa Junior College has no formal tenure program; but, according to its *Faculty Guide: "Teacher Tenure:* Odessa College has no tenure system. The administration of the college wishes the faculty member to feel that he has permanent tenure as long as his teaching services are satisfactory and as long as he displays a cooperative attitude toward his coworkers and his superiors, and as long as he is happy in his work." This provision, in Professor Sindermann's view, is tantamount to a de facto tenure program; and he alleged that he had tenure pursuant to it. Moreover, he claimed legitimate reliance on Guidelines of the Coordinating Board of the Texas College and University System, which provides that a teacher like himself has some form of job tenure after employment in the state college and university system for seven years or more. Included in the Guidelines of the Coordinating Board is this provision:

Beginning with appointment to the rank of full-time instructor or a higher rank, the probationary period for a faculty member shall not exceed seven years, including within this period appropriate full-time service in all institutions of higher education. This is subject to the provision that when, after a term of probationary service of more than three years in one or more institutions, a faculty member is employed by another institution, it may be agreed in writing that his new appointment is for a probationary period of not more than four years (even though thereby the person's total probationary period in the academic profession is extended beyond the normal maximum of seven years).

In a claim similar to Professor Roth's, Professor Sindermann filed suit in a federal district court. He alleged that the regents' decision not to rehire him infringed his right to freedom of speech and that their failure to accord him an opportunity for a hearing violated the Fourteenth Amendment's guarantee of procedural due process. The district court ruled that Sindermann had "no cause of action . . . since his contract adopted the tenure system." Summary judgment was rendered for the regents. The court of appeals reversed the judgment of the district court, ruling that nonrenewal of Sindermann's contract would violate the Fourteenth Amendment if it was, in fact, due to his exercise of free speech. The actual reason for the regents' decision having been found "in total dispute," the court of appeals remanded the case to the district court for a full hearing on the contested issue of fact. The court of appeals also held that, despite Sindermann's lack of tenure, the failure to allow him a hearing would violate procedural due process if Sindermann could show that he had an "expectancy" of reemployment. The issue of expectancy was thus to be aired on remand along with the issue of whether Sindermann's nonreappointment was due to his exercise of free speech.[10]

The majority of the Supreme Court reversed the appellate tribunal's decision in the Roth case and affirmed, while indicating disagreement with some of the cited reasons, in the Sindermann case. The tones of the two opinions varied even though written by the same Justice. It was not simply that Roth lost and Sindermann won in the Supreme Court. Rather, it was that Stewart's opinion in the Sindermann case focused on the factors that can include nontenured teachers within the boundaries of constitutional protection; in the Roth opinion, in contrast, he stressed the points that led to exclusion of the professor's case from constitutional protection.

A substantial section of Justice Stewart's opinion in the Roth case was devoted to analysis of the boundaries of the words *liberty* and *property* in the due-process clause of the Fourteenth Amendment. Describing them as "broad and majestic terms," Stewart proceeded to invoke the late Justice Frankfurter's statement that liberty and property are among the great constitutional concepts "purposely left to gather meaning from experience."[11] But, in Justice Stewart's opinion, neither experience nor precedent warranted application of the district court's balancing test in determining whether protected interests of liberty or property were present. To determine whether due-process requirements apply in the first place, said Stewart, "We must look not to the 'weight' but to the *nature* of the interest at stake." As an indicator of the court's recognition that concepts do gain meaning from experience, Stewart declined to sustain the argument that procedural due-process guaran-

---

[10] Sindermann v. Perry, 430 F.2d 939 (1970).

[11] Justice Frankfurter dissenting in National Insurance v. Tidewater, 337 U.S. 582 at 646.

tees are inapplicable to public employees because public employment is a "privilege" rather than a "right." Instead, he took the occasion to declare that "the court has fully and finally rejected the wooden distinction between 'rights' and 'privileges' that once seemed to govern the applicability of procedural due-process rights."[12]

Stewart recognized also that property interests protected by procedural due process "extend well beyond actual ownership of real estate, chattels, or money" and that, by the same token, liberty means more than freedom from bodily restraint.[13] The right of individuals to contract, to engage in the common occupations, to acquire useful knowledge, to marry and bring up children, and to worship God according to the dictates of conscience are among liberty's denotations. Stewart added: "In a constitution for a free people, there can be no doubt that the meaning of 'liberty' must be broad indeed." He postulated, however, that "certain boundaries" to the scope of procedural due process must be observed. Although he acknowledged that a state's refusal to renew employment might occur "under such circumstances that interests in liberty would be implicated," he held that Roth's was not such a case.

In examining why Roth did not qualify for due-process protection, Stewart contended that the state did not make any charges against him that might jeopardize his standing and associations in his community. Had Roth been charged with something like dishonesty or immorality, "this would be a different case." Nor did the state invoke any regulations to bar Roth from all other public employment in state universities or to foreclose his freedom to take advantage of other employment opportunities. On the record before the Supreme Court, "all that clearly appears is that the respondent was not rehired for one

---

[12] See, for example, Bailey *v.* Richardson, 182 F.2d 46 (1950), affirmed by an equally divided Supreme Court, 341 U.S. 918 (1951). Justice Holmes's unfortunate dictum as a member of the Supreme Judicial Court of Massachusetts, in a case involving employment rights of a policeman, helped to reinforce the right-privilege dichotomy in constitutional law for many years. "The petitioner may have a constitutional right to talk politics," said Holmes, "but he has no constitutional right to be a policeman" McAuliffe *v.* City of New Bedford, 155 Mass. 216 (1891).

[13] Board of Regents *v.* Roth, 92 S.Ct. 2701 at 2706.

year at the university." "It stretches the concept too far," Stewart concluded, "to suggest that a person is deprived of 'liberty' when he simply is not rehired in one job but remains as free as before to seek another."[14]

Having disposed of the "liberty" argument, Stewart went on
to demolish the contention that Roth was entitled to due-process protection to safeguard his property interest in reemployment. A property
interest in a benefit requires "a legitimate claim of entitlement to it"
rather than merely "an abstract need or desire for it" or "a unilateral
expectation of it." Although property interests may take many forms,
the Fourteenth Amendment's procedural protection of property em-
braces the security of interests "already acquired" by a person in specific benefits. Welfare benefits, for example, cannot be summarily re-
voked, since the recipient who has once met eligibility standards has
already acquired an interest in continued receipt of those benefits.[15]
Similarly, in the realm of public employment, a tenured professor has
already acquired an interest in continued employment, which is safeguarded by due process.[16] Nontenured college professors and staff members dismissed before the expiration of their periods of employment are
equally protected against summary action that fails to provide a hearing.[17] According to Stewart, Roth had acquired no property interest
beyond his one-year appointment. Property interests are "not created
by the constitution" but rather are created and defined in their dimensions by "existing rules or understandings that stem from an independent source such as state law." The terms of Roth's appointment created and defined his property interest in employment at Wisconsin
State University at Oshkosh. "Those terms secured his interest in employment up to June 30, 1969." They specifically provided that his
employment was to terminate on June 30, and "they made no provision for renewal whatsoever."[18] Thus, neither the terms of Roth's appointment nor the contents of any state statute or university rule or

[14] Regents v. Roth, 2708.
[15] Goldberg v. Kelly, 397 U.S. 254 (1970).
[16] Slochower v. Board of Education, 350 U.S. 551 (1956).
[17] Wieman v. Updegraff, 344 U.S. 183 (1952); Connell v. Higgen-
botham, 403 U.S. 207 (1971).
[18] Board of Regents v. Roth, 2709.

policy secured his interest in reemployment or created any legitimate claim to it. In such circumstances, Roth "surely had an abstract concern in being rehired," but an abstract concern could not constitute "a property interest sufficient to require the university authorities to give him a hearing when they declined to renew his contract of employment."[19]

The argument that Roth was denied First Amendment rights of free speech was disposed of in a footnote, which also slapped down the court of appeal's position that a hearing should be required as a prophylactic against improperly motivated nonretention decisions. Since the courts had not found that Roth's nonretention was based on his exercise of the right of free speech, there could be no analogy drawn to cases requiring notice and hearing before an injunction is issued against the holding of rallies or public meetings or before a state makes a large-scale seizure of a person's allegedly obscene books or magazines. "Whatever may be a teacher's rights of free speech, the interest in holding a teaching job at a state university, *simpliciter,* is not itself a free speech interest."[20] The judgment of the court of appeals was reversed, and the case was remanded "for further proceedings consistent with this opinion."

Justices Douglas, Marshall, and Brennan dissented, the first two writing separate opinions and Brennan recording his dissent. Douglas rejected the majority's distinction between nonrenewal and dismissal cases. He insisted that when violation of First Amendment rights is alleged, "the reasons for dismissal or for nonrenewal of an employment contract must be examined to see if the reasons given are only a cloak for activity or attitudes protected by the constitution." Nonrenewal of a teacher's contract is tantamount to dismissal, he continued, comparing nonrenewal to "a blemish that turns into a permanent scar" and effectively limits any chance the teacher has of being rehired.[21] He favored initial hearings before school-constituted review bodies, with the district court making the final determination whether nonrenewal of the teacher's contract was in retaliation for his exercise of First Amendment rights.

[19] Regents *v.* Roth, 2710.
[20] Regents *v.* Roth, Court's footnote 14, 2708.
[21] Regents *v.* Roth, 2713.

Justice Marshall, disagreeing with the majority over their definitions of liberty and property, maintained that federal and state governments are restrained by the constitution from acting arbitrarily with respect to any and all employment opportunities they offer or control. "In my view, every citizen who applies for a government job is entitled to it unless the government can establish some reason for denying the employment." This is the essence of the "property" right protected by the Fourteenth Amendment, as well as of the "liberty" to work that manifests the personal freedom and opportunity secured by the Fourteenth Amendment. Since employment is one of the greatest benefits that governments offer in modern-day life, "the government may not reward some citizens and not others without demonstrating that its actions are fair and equitable." If the demand for reasons were to become exceptionally great, summary procedures could be devised that would provide adequate information to all persons. In any event, "as long as the government has a good reason for its actions, it need not fear disclosure."[22]

The function of Justice Stewart's opinion for the majority in *Roth* was to cut off constitutional support for positions such as Marshall's and Douglas's in dissent. Stewart, in effect, was setting constitutional boundary lines around the territory covered by procedural due process. In doing so, he made it clear that Douglas's joinder of nonrenewal cases with dismissal cases where free speech issues are alleged, Marshall's assumptions about the citizen's entitlement to government employment, the district court's utilization of a balancing test to determine the applicability of due-process rights, and the court of appeals' "prophylactic" argument for requiring hearings when nonretention may have been occasioned by improper motives were all beyond the boundaries of "liberty" and "property" interests subject to protection by procedural due process under the Fourteenth Amendment.

If the Roth decision concentrated on fixing constitutional boundaries in implementation of the view that "the range of interests protected by procedural due process is not infinite," the Sindermann case focused on mapping the terrain within those boundaries—a terrain that remains extensive, albeit rocky in parts.

[22] Regents *v.* Roth, 2716.

At the outset of his Sindermann opinion, Justice Stewart rejected the position of the board of regents that the professor's lack of a contractual or tenure right to reemployment must defeat his claim that the nonrenewal of his contract violated the First and Fourteenth Amendments. Here Stewart drew analogies to cases of improper denials of tax exemptions, unemployment benefits, welfare payments, and other public employment;[23] and he expressly reaffirmed previous Supreme Court holdings that forbade predicating nonrenewal of a nontenured public school teacher's one-year contract on his exercise of First and Fourteenth Amendment rights.[24] Stewart concluded, therefore, that the government "may not deny a benefit to a person on a basis that infringes his constitutionally protected interests" even though the person may have no "right" to that benefit and even though the government could deny him the benefit for other reasons. If a benefit could be denied because of constitutionally protected speech or association, a person's "exercise of those freedoms would in effect be penalized and inhibited. This would allow the government to produce a result which it could not command directly. Such interference with constitutional rights is impermissible."[25]

Since there was a genuine dispute as to whether the regents had refused to renew Sindermann's contract as a reprisal for his exercise of free speech, it was improper for the district court, by summary judgment, to foreclose the teacher's opportunity to make this showing. Sindermann's allegations that his nonretention was due to his testimony before legislative committees and his other public statements critical of the regents' policies presented "a bona fide constitutional claim" entitled to full exploration in the district court.

With regard to Sindermann's procedural due-process claim, Stewart examined in detail the conditions under which the general rule "that the constitution does not require opportunity for a hearing before the nonrenewal of a nontenured teacher's contract" may be modified. The conditions for modification were a showing by the

---

[23] Perry v. Sindermann, 92 S.Ct. 2694 at 2697.

[24] Shelton v. Tucker, 364 U.S. 479 (1960); Keyishian v. Board of Regents, 385 U.S. 589 (1967).

[25] Perry v. Sindermann, 92 S.Ct. 2694 at 2697.

teacher "that the decision not to rehire him somehow deprived him of an interest in 'liberty' or that he had a 'property' interest in continued employment despite the lack of tenure or a formal contract."[26]

Although the mere proof that he was not rehired in one particular job could not by itself amount to a loss of liberty, and although the court of appeals was wrong in suggesting that the teacher's allegations of First Amendment infractions gave him a due-process right to some kind of hearing, the appellate tribunal was right in remanding the case to the district court for determination of Sindermann's assertion that the college had a de facto tenure program by virtue of rules and understandings promulgated and fostered by the school officials and that he had tenure under that program. Sindermann's possible property interest in continued employment could not be based on any subjective "expectancy," as the court of appeals had held; nonetheless, Sindermann must be given an opportunity to prove the legitimacy of his claim of entitlement to continued employment in light of the actual policies and practices of the institution.

Institutional policies and practices can, of course, be evidenced by written contracts; "yet absence of such an explicit contractual provision may not always foreclose the possibility that a teacher has a property interest in reemployment."[27] Agreements may be implied even though not formalized in writing. At this juncture, Stewart cited the sections of Corbin's *Treatise on Contracts* pointing out that explicit contractual provisions may be supplemented by other agreements implied from the promisor's words and conduct in light of the surrounding circumstances and that the meaning of the promisor's words and acts is found "by relating them to the usage of the past."[28] A teacher like Sindermann, who has been employed for a number of years by the same institution, might be able to show from the circumstances of his service and from other relevant facts that there is an "unwritten 'common law' " in his university that certain employees shall have the equivalent of tenure. In addition to Corbin, Stewart cited the section of Byse and Joughin's *Tenure in American Higher Education* dealing

[26] Perry v. Sindermann, 2698.
[27] Perry v. Sindermann, 2699–2700.
[28] Perry v. Sindermann, citing 3 *Corbin on Contracts,* sections 561–562.

with tenure granted in practice but without official commitment.[29] In short, the court ruled that Sindermann should have the opportunity to prove that, in light of surrounding circumstances, the words, conduct, customs, and usage of state school officials gave him a legitimate entitlement to tenure.

In a separate concurring opinion, Chief Justice Burger summed up the majority's conclusion: "A state-employed teacher who has a right to reemployment under state law, arising from either an express or implied contract, has, in turn, a right guaranteed by the Fourteenth Amendment to some form of prior administrative or academic hearing on the cause for nonrenewal of his contract."[30] The relationship between a state institution and one of its teachers, Burger emphasized, is essentially a matter of state concerns and state law; federal courts, therefore, should abstain from deciding whether a teacher is constitutionally entitled to a prior hearing if relevant state contract law is unclear.

Brennan, Douglas, and Marshall dissented in part, stating that they would favor directing the district court to enter summary judgment for Sindermann, entitling him, without further proceedings there, to a statement of reasons why his contract was not renewed and to a hearing on the disputed issues of fact.[31]

The Roth and Sindermann rulings are obviously complementary and should be construed as a unit. *Roth* held explicitly that allegations by a nontenured teacher that nonrenewal of his contract by a public institution was based on his exercise of First and Fourteenth Amendment rights do not warrant judicial orders that reasons and a hearing be given the teacher by school officials. At the same time, *Sindermann* held explicitly that such allegations by a teacher are entitled to full exploration in the district court in order to determine whether the college refused to renew the teaching contract on an impermissible basis. With regard to "property," *Roth* held that the Fourteenth Amendment's procedural protections cannot be invoked unless the facts show that the teacher has already acquired interests in specific benefits. *Sindermann* added that the acquisition of interests sub-

[29] Byse and Joughin, pp. 17–28.
[30] Perry *v.* Sindermann, 2717.
[31] Perry *v.* Sindermann, 2700, 2717–2718.

ject to protection can be shown not only by formal rules or contracts but by agreements implied from words and conduct in light of the surrounding circumstances. These statements of the applicable law are clear. Two other aspects of the Roth and Sindermann rulings are not explicit but may be at least as significant. One concerns burden of proof; the other concerns the receptivity of the judiciary to relevant empirical research.

Burden of Proof

The issue of burden of proof arises at two stages in the proceedings and may determine whether a teacher's interest in continued employment can really be protected by due process or whether protection is largely illusory. The first stage is at the trial court level; at this level, according to the Roth and Sindermann rulings, the teacher having a genuine dispute with the school administration over whether nonrenewal occurred as a reprisal for his exercise of constitutionally protected rights must be given an opportunity to prove the legitimacy of his claim. A key point to bear in mind is that such proof by the teacher would not entitle him to reinstatement at that stage. In the absence of such proof, the teacher has no right whatever to reasons and a hearing before school officials on his nonrenewal. With such proof by the teacher, the school officials then become obligated to grant him a hearing at his request. Thus, in order to be entitled to a hearing on the grounds of nonretention, the nontenured teacher must prove that he has a constitutionally protected interest in reemployment or that the school officials refused to renew his contract on an impermissible basis.

Justice Stewart indicated that the burden of proof remains on the teacher's shoulders once a hearing is required, for he described such an administrative hearing for the teacher as one "where he could be informed of the grounds for his nonretention and challenge their sufficiency."

It could be argued that even the district court judge and the dissenting Supreme Court justices in *Roth* accepted the proposition that the burden of proof is on the teacher. In requiring that the university give Roth a statement of reasons for nonretention as well as a hearing on those reasons, the district court judge had made clear that "the burden of going forward and the burden of proof rests with the professor. Only if he makes a reasonable showing that the stated reasons are wholly inappropriate as a basis for decision or that they are wholly without basis in fact would the university administration become obliged to show that the stated reasons are not inappropriate or that they have a basis in fact."[32] Justice Douglas stressed the importance of providing the teacher with reasons for his nonretention and with "an opportunity to rebut those reasons," suggesting his acceptance of the view that the teacher bears the burden of proof.

The district court judge and the dissenters, however, were speaking of burden of proof in a single stage. In their view, the teacher alleging that nonretention was based on constitutionally impermissible reasons is entitled, without further proof, to a statement of reasons and a hearing. At that hearing, the teacher would have to show that the reasons were inappropriate or inaccurate. The burden of proof would then shift to the school officials to show that the reasons were factual or appropriate. The teacher would thus bear the burden of proof at one stage only. Justice Stewart's formulation of the sequence of events appears to place the burden twice upon the teacher. The double burden on the employee seems unwarranted and out of step with the Supreme Court's decision on the same day in another academic institution case involving burden of proof.

In Healy v. James,[33] a unanimous court invalidated a state school's refusal to authorize the establishment of a local chapter of Students for a Democratic Society. In the court's opinion, the procedures followed by school officials had improperly shifted the burden of proof over compliance with valid school regulations from the school administration to the organizers of the proposed SDS chapter.

Writing for eight members of the court (Rehnquist concurred in the result but did not join in Powell's opinion), Justice Powell prefaced his analysis of the applicable law with this observation: "As the case involves delicate issues concerning the academic community, we approach our task with special caution, recognizing the mutual interest of students, faculty members, and administrators in an environment free from disruptive interference with the educational process. We are also mindful of the equally significant interest in the widest latitude for free expression and debate consonant with the maintenance of or-

[32] 310 F.Supp. 972 at 979–980.
[33] 405 U.S.—, 92 S.Ct. 2338, 40 *Law Week* 4887 (1972).

der. Where those interests appear to compete, the First Amendment, made binding on the states by the Fourteenth Amendment, strikes the required balance."[34] After a review of First Amendment precedents, Powell noted that they leave the court no room for the view that First Amendment protections should apply with less force on campuses than in the community at large. Quite to the contrary, "the college classroom with its surrounding environs is peculiarly the 'marketplace of ideas,' and we break no new constitutional ground in reaffirming this nation's dedication to safeguarding academic freedom."[35] Denial of official recognition to college organizations, without justification, would abridge the First Amendment right of association, even though an SDS chapter might survive through informal meetings of individuals on campus and through distribution of materials off campus.

Having delineated the applicable contours of the First Amendment, Powell proceeded to the issue of burden of proof. Both the district court and the court of appeals had assumed that the supporters of the proposed SDS chapter had the burden of showing entitlement to recognition by the college. While the organizers of the chapter were obliged to file an application for recognition in conformity with the rules of the college, final rejection of their application could not rest on their failure to prove their propriety to the administration. Powell concluded: "Once petitioners had filed an application in conformity with the requirements, the burden was upon the college administration to justify its decision of rejection."[36]

It is difficult to see why the burden of proof similarly should not be on school officials to justify a decision of nonrenewal of a faculty member's appointment once the teacher has shown that he has a constitutionally protected interest in reemployment or that the school officials refused renewal on an impermissible basis. The proper standard for dismissal of a tenured faculty member has traditionally been that "the administrative official should have the burden of proving the charges by a preponderance of the evidence."[37] No cogent reasons appear for subjecting the nontenured faculty member to a two-stage

[34] Healy v. James, 2341.
[35] Healy v. James, 2346.
[36] Healy v. James, 2347.
[37] Byse and Joughin, p. 149.

burden of proof that may deal a crushing blow to vindication of his rights.

Since burden of proof was not formally an issue in the Roth case, Stewart's remarks could be classified as gratuitous conjecture or dictum. Nonetheless, it would be appropriate, before Stewart's views take root through oversight, to initiate legal tests that could lead to substitution of Powell's observations on burden of proof in *Healy* for Stewart's in *Roth*. The adoption of Powell's standard would go a long way toward heightening the conviction in academic circles that constitutional juices still flow in the oft-quoted judicial remark that "vigilant protection of constitutional freedoms is nowhere more vital than in the community of American schools."[38]

Empirical Research

Stewart's opinion in *Roth* seemed to leave the door open to enlarging the applicability of "liberty" and "property" protections of procedural due process through research findings. Two observations in footnotes about the record in the district court warrant the conjecture, at least, that empirical findings (1) on the actual consequences for teachers of nonrenewal of contracts and (2) on the actual contract-renewal practices of school officials in the case of year-to-year employees could affect the court's conclusions about the right to reasons and a hearing. After commenting, in his text in *Roth,* that no state statute or university rule or policy secures the teacher's interest in reemployment or creates any legitimate claim to it, Stewart added in footnote 16: "To be sure, the respondent does suggest that most teachers hired on a year to year basis by the Wisconsin State University [at] Oshkosh are, in fact, rehired. But the district court has not found that there is anything approaching a 'common law' of reemployment."[39] If valid research produced the finding that year-to-year employees customarily were rehired, a district court presumably would be justified in concluding that there is "a common law of reemployment" and in ordering school officials, consequently, to provide reasons and a hearing for the nonrenewal teacher, pursuant to Stewart's reasoning.

[38] Shelton *v.* Tucker, 364 U.S. 479 at 487.
[39] Court's footnote 16 in Board of Regents *v.* Roth, 92 S.Ct. 2701 at 2710.

The court's footnote 13 in *Roth,* without explicitly committing the majority to changing their stance in light of any empirical findings, nonetheless went to great pains to make it clear that the court could not accept "assumptions" about the consequences of nonrenewal. Both the district court and the court of appeals had accepted the premise of a "substantial adverse effect" of nonretention on the career of the teacher. Stewart's response was that "even assuming *arguenda* that such a 'substantial adverse effect' under these circumstances would constitute a state-imposed restriction on liberty, the record contains no support for these assumptions. There is no suggestion of how nonretention might affect the respondent's future employment prospects."[40]

The court did not draw a visible line between proof of "substantial adverse effect" on a teacher's career interests, which could presumably invoke due-process protection, and "mere proof . . . that his record of nonretention in one job, taken alone, might make him somewhat less attractive to some other employers," which would not qualify for constitutional protection. The line of demarcation here between the protected and the nonprotected interest might be found in the record of effort in seeking other employment as a teacher. The narrower the teacher's quest for professional employment elsewhere, the more vulnerable his case would be to evaluation as not constitutionally protected. The more extensive his unsuccessful quest, the greater the likelihood of a finding of "substantial adverse effect," entitling the teacher to due-process protection.

The practical problem, of course, for the teacher whose contract is not renewed is that, by the time he could show substantial adverse effect, the pressures on him to find means of economic survival might well outweigh his interest in due-process vindication or, at least, his ability to finance a suit. Professional studies of the consequences of nonrenewal of contracts could remove a potent barrier from the path of the typical nonreemployed teacher seeking redress and could provide, at the same time, relevant data for judicial decision making about the due-process rights of teachers. The sooner the realities of practices in the academic marketplace can be documented through empirical research, the sooner judicial assumptions, misperceptions, or whimsies will fade in applying constitutional norms to college and university

[40] Regents *v.* Roth, footnote 13, 2707.

communities. If "friends of the court" would spend more time gathering and reporting on empirical data relevant to the judiciary's decision-making roles rather than on sheer doctrinal advocacy, the *amicus curiae* function, as well as the clarity and quality of the court's ensuing opinions, could be materially enhanced.

Private School Faculty

The Roth, Sindermann, and Healy cases all concerned state colleges or universities. Since the First and Fourteenth Amendments do not restrict purely private action, an obvious question arises as to what redress, if any, the plaintiffs in these cases would have had if private institutions had been involved. A majority of the present Supreme Court probably would not have found sufficient state control over the programs or policies of private institutions to justify invocation of the First and Fourteenth Amendments.

In the first place, even Justice Douglas, in his dissent in *Roth*, acknowledged that "there may not be a constitutional right to continued employment if private schools and colleges are involved."[41] The First Amendment is clearly violated, in his view, when public school authorities discharge a teacher because of his or her philosophical, political, or ideological beliefs. "The same may well be true of private schools also, if through the device of financing or other umbilical cords they become instrumentalities of the state." Proof that the nominally private college or university has become an "instrumentality" of the state would thus be a prerequisite to garnering the vote even of one of the court's most avid proponents of expanding constitutional protection. The majority of the Burger court—less prone than Douglas, Brennan, and Marshall to expand the jurisdiction of the Fourteenth Amendment—might well require an umbilical cord made of piano wire before concluding that relationships between the state and any private institution were so extensive or pervasive as to make the institution's actions tantamount to those of the state.

Two recent lower federal court cases dealing with private academic institutions and a Supreme Court decision in 1972 in a related area reinforce the view that application of the state-action concept to the private university is far from imminent, despite the argument of

[41] Regents *v.* Roth, 2711.

scholars such as Professor Robert O'Neill that "public and private components have been so intermingled in private colleges and universities that they are no longer realistically separable" and that "the function of private higher education is so essentially public that a governmental standard should judge its performance."[42]

In Grossner v. Trustees of Columbia University[43] a group comprised of students, a part-time faculty member, and nonstudents using Columbia's facilities alleged that policies of Columbia's president and administration in dealing with campus sit-ins were offensive to principles of due process and were designed to deter plaintiffs from exercising their First Amendment rights on the campus. Judge Frankel of the federal district court had no difficulty finding that plaintiffs failed the threshold test of showing that there was sufficient evidence of state action to warrant jurisdiction in the court. He was unimpressed by evidence of federal and state financial assistance to Columbia, observing that receipt of money from the state is not, without a good deal more, enough to make the recipient a state agency or instrumentality. There was no significant state participation or involvement in the direction or control of any of Columbia's activities. Hence, the university did not meet the Supreme Court's criterion in Burton v. Wilmington Parking Authority,[44] holding that state action exists whenever a state has so insinuated itself into a position of interdependence with a nominally private enterprise that it must be recognized as a joint participant in the challenged activity. Finally, Judge Frankel responded to the argument that Columbia was performing a "public function," which may be likened to the activities of a company town subject to the Fourteenth Amendment, by stressing that "nothing supports the thesis that university (or private elementary) education as such is state action."

The U.S. Court of Appeals for the Second Circuit dealt with a more complex version of the issue in Powe v. Miles.[45] The case involved students at Alfred University, a private institution which, in

---

[42] "Private Universities and Public Law," 19 Buffalo Law Review 155 (1970). See also R. Schubert, "State Action and the Private University," 24 Rutgers Law Review 323 (1970).

[43] 287 F.Supp. 535 (1968).

[44] 365 U.S. 715 (1961).

[45] 407 F.2d 73 (1968).

addition to its privately financed divisions, operated the New York
State College of Ceramics on contract with the state. Some of the students were enrolled in Alfred's other schools and some in the New York
State College of Ceramics. The state of New York paid all the direct
expenses of the ceramics school as well as a stipulated sum per credit
hour for courses taken in the "private sector" by the ceramics students.
The "private sector," in turn, paid for instruction its students received
in the ceramics school. New York also paid Alfred a pro rata share of
the entire administrative expense of the university, including salaries
of the president and other administrative officials. At the time the case
arose, the state was paying 20.75 percent of the total Alfred University
budget. As in the Columbia case, it was alleged that Alfred's student
disciplinary procedures and actions constituted state action depriving
students of their rights to free speech.

  Judge Friendly ruled that state action was present in the operations affecting the ceramics college but not in Alfred's other schools.
"The seemingly simple but entirely sufficient reason that the state has
willed it that way" accounted primarily for the finding as regards students of the ceramics college. "The very name of the college identifies
it as a state institution." Furthermore, New York's statutes make it an
integral part of the state university; they even designate Alfred University officials who administer discipline to the ceramics college students "the representatives of the state university trustees."[46] With regard to the Alfred students from the "private sector," however, there
was no state action, because the state was in no way involved in the
activity that caused the alleged injury. Outside of direct payments for
the ceramics college, accounting for about 3 percent of the budget of
almost $7,000,000 for the "private section" schools and the adminis-
tration, the state's aid to Alfred was held "a long way from being so
dominant as to afford basis for a contention that the state is merely
utilizing private trustees to administer a state activity."[47]

  [46] Powe v. Miles, 82–83. On the merits, Judge Friendly ruled that the
petitioning students from the college of ceramics were not denied any rights,
privileges, or immunities secured by the constitution, as the result of actions by
the Alfred administration establishing guidelines for demonstrations and procedures for the enforcement of the guidelines.
  [47] Powe v. Miles, 81.

In 1972, in Lloyd Corporation *v.* Tanner,[48] the Supreme Court examined the boundaries between state action subject to Fourteenth Amendment controls and private action immune from such controls. In this case, the owners of a fifty-acre shopping center (containing department stores and other commercial and professional stores and offices and accommodating more than one hundred vehicles in its parking areas) held that the private status of the center entitled them to bar the distribution of handbills on the property. Tanner had successfully sought an injunction in a district court against the owners' ban on handbill distribution, the district court having emphasized that the center is "open to the general public" and is "the functional equivalent of a public business district." The operational equivalence of the center's actions to state action made the handbill prohibition a violation of Tanner's First Amendment rights.[49]

The court of appeals agreed with the district court, but the Supreme Court reversed the ruling in a five-to-four vote, with Marshall, Douglas, Brennan, and Stewart dissenting. Justice Powell, writing for the majority, ruled that the distribution of handbills inviting the public to a meeting to protest the draft and the Vietnam War is not constitutionally protected. The shopping center does not lose its private character merely because the public is generally invited to use it for designated purposes. "In addressing this issue," Powell emphasized, "it must be remembered that the First and Fourteenth Amendments safeguard the rights of free speech and assembly by limitations on *state* action, not on action by the owners of private property used nondiscriminatorily for private purposes only."[50] The majority explicitly rejected the argument that all members of the public have the same right of free speech in the shopping center's facilities as they would have in similar public facilities in the streets of a city or town.

In his dissenting opinion, Justice Marshall pointed out that Lloyd Center allows organizations to parade on Veterans Day and to have speeches on the meaning of the holiday and the valor of our soldiers; that the American Legion is given permission annually to sell

---

[48] 405 U.S.—, 92 S.Ct. 2219 (1972).
[49] Tanner *v.* Lloyd Corporation, 308 F.Supp. 128 (1970).
[50] Lloyd Corporation *v.* Tanner, 92 S.Ct. 2219 at 2228.

poppies; and that Presidential candidates are permitted to speak without restriction on any issue of the day, "which presumably includes war and peace." In light of these facts, he perceived no basis for depriving Tanner and his associates of "the opportunity to distribute leaflets inviting patrons of the center to attend a meeting in which different points of view would be expressed than those held by the organizations and persons privileged to use Lloyd Center as a forum for parading their ideas and symbols." In striking a balance between the freedom to speak and the freedom of a private property owner to control his property when the competing interests are fairly weighted, "the balance can only be struck in favor of speech."[51]

A shopping center, of course, is not a university campus; and the difference between a commercially oriented private institution and an educationally oriented one could be significant in a subsequent test of the applicability of the First and Fourteenth Amendments to private colleges and universities. In the Lloyd case, Justice Powell placed some emphasis on the fact that the handbill had no relation to any purpose for which the shopping center was built and being used. It could certainly be maintained that the exercise of free speech on campuses, public or private, is related directly to the objectives and purposes of education. No doubt the First and Fourteenth Amendments could be construed to reach the private campus without doing violence to the reasoning in *Lloyd*. Nonetheless, the probability of extending the umbrella of the amendments to private campus life is reduced materially by the Supreme Court's rejection in *Lloyd* of the interpretations of state action by the district court and the court of appeals. It would require the special insights and imperviousness to adverse information of a Pangloss to find in the present thrust of the Supreme Court or in recent school cases like *Grossner* and *Powe* support for extension of constitutional protection to tenure practices on the private campus.

Judicial Intervention in Campus Affairs

Many academicians would maintain, of course, that there is nothing remotely Panglossian about their enthusiasm for the maintenance of a low judicial profile vis à vis the campus. The role of legal norms in regulating campus life is obviously a matter of controversy

---

[51] Lloyd, 2234.

and sensitivity. For example, several years ago James Perkins, then president of Cornell, cautioned the educational community about the dangers it would confront if resort to legal action became a campus routine. Among other horrors, academic careers and institutions could be ground to a standstill while months or years of court delay froze the status quo. The cost of legal procedures would be a nightmare for both the individual and the institution. Institutional autonomy, "the surest guardian of academic freedom," could be destroyed. If the educational establishment is viewed as cautious, conservative, and bureaucratic now, "they haven't seen anything compared to what it could be if every move and every conversation were liable to replay in the courtroom." In short, judicial review of campus affairs could prevent academic institutions from making individual qualitative decisions, and institutional autonomy could be so damaged as to threaten the survival of academic freedom. Perkins urged the academic community "as an educated and presumably civilized body of men and women . . . to work out a modus vivendi that will free them from the fear of daily encounter with the summons server."[52]

Certainly Dr. Perkins was correct in insisting that qualitative decisions—the "sorting out" of human talent by a "continuous matching of institution and program on the one hand with individual aspiration and capability on the other"—are essences of academic life. He was equally correct in emphasizing that "not all the courts in the country, working full time on academic problems, could ever construct the peculiar environment in which a well-balanced learning community can either function or flourish." He may even have overlooked other major drawbacks to pervasive imposition of judicial review. As Clark Byse has noted, expanding judicial review could deter academic decision makers from exercising their independent judgment and, by shifting the focus of inquiry from what is desirable or wise to what is constitutional or legal, lead them to abandon the primacy of educational objectives.[53] Nonetheless, an appraisal of judicial review of campus life

[52] J. A. Perkins, *The University and Due Process* (American Council of Education, 1967). Reprinted in C. Byse and S. Nahmod, *Cases and Materials on the Role of Law on the Campus* (1971), pp. 54–67.
[53] "The University and Due Process: A Somewhat Different View," *AAUP Bulletin,* Summer 1968, pp. 143–148.

cannot appropriately be confined to its dangers. Of equal importance
is the question whether judicial review must inevitably take on the dimensions of a pandora's box for the academic community or whether
it can nourish rudimentary standards of fairness in academic decision
making while recognizing the necessity for diversity and even idiosyn-
crasy as components of educational creativity and achievement.

Just as litigious faculty can rush to court prematurely in efforts
to enjoin or confound administrators with whom they are feuding, so,
too, school officials in some communities may still seek to equate a
faculty member's exercise of free speech with insubordination or incompetence. Experience, unfortunately, shows that archaic regulations
and authoritarian administrative styles are not biodegradable. The
facts of cases like Epperson v. Arkansas (involving statutory prohibition of the teaching of evolution) and Pickering v. Board of Education
(involving the dismissal of a teacher for writing a scathing letter to the
local newspaper about the utilization of funds by school officials)[54]
might seem to be products of nineteenth-century conceptions of educational roles rather than illustrations of modern practices that could
have been perpetuated but for decisions of the Supreme Court.

Marvin Pickering, a teacher at Township High School in Will
County, Illinois, wrote a letter to his local paper after a tax increase
for educational use was defeated for the second time. In his letter,
Pickering attacked the school board's allocation of financial resources,
following voter approval several years earlier of a $5,500,000 bond
issue, for unduly favoring athletics to the detriment of the educational
programs. He also charged the superintendent of schools with attempting to prevent teachers in the district from criticizing or opposing the
board's policies. The board dismissed Pickering for writing and publishing the letter. At a subsequent hearing, required by Illinois law,
the board found that false statements in the letter unjustifiably im-
pugned the motives, honesty, integrity, responsibility, and competence
of the board and school administrators so as to make Pickering's retention detrimental to the best interests of the school.

The teacher's claim that his letter was protected by the First
Amendment was rejected by the Illinois court on the ground that his

[54] Epperson v. Arkansas, 393 U.S. 97 (1968); Pickering v. Board of
Education, 391 U.S. 563 (1968).

acceptance of the job as teacher in the public schools obliged him to refrain from statements about the school, "which in the absence of such position he would have an undoubted right to engage in."[55] The Supreme Court chided the Illinois court and reversed its ruling. Justice Marshall declared: "To the extent that the Illinois Supreme Court opinion may be read to suggest that teachers may constitutionally be compelled to relinquish the First Amendments rights they would otherwise enjoy as citizens to comment on matters of public interest in connection with the operation of the public schools in which they worked, it proceeds on a premise that has been unequivocally rejected."[56] Applying the standard developed in New York Times v. Sullivan[57] in 1964, when major aspects of libel law were brought under the First Amendment, the court held that Pickering's erroneous allegations—in the absence of proof that they had been knowingly or recklessly made—could not serve as the basis for his dismissal any more than they could serve as a basis for tort recovery against him for defamation.

In the Epperson case (decided in 1968, soon after the Pickering case), the Supreme Court reversed an Arkansas statute substantially similar to the Tennessee statute that had produced the Scopes trial four decades earlier. Forbidding both the teaching that mankind ascended or descended from a lower order of animals and the use in the public schools of any textbook teaching such a theory, the statute was defended by Arkansas officials with the blatant claim that the Fourteenth Amendment does not restrict the state in its relations with its own employee-teachers. In response, Justice Fortas commented simply, "It is much too late to argue that the state may impose on the teachers in its schools any conditions that it chooses, however restrictive they may be of constitutional guarantees."[58] The court struck down the statute, however, not as an invasion of the rights of the teacher but as a law respecting an establishment of religion. The overriding fact, said Fortas, "is that Arkansas law selects from the body of knowledge a particular segment which it proscribes for the sole reason

[55] Pickering v. Board of Education, 36 Ill.2d 568, 225 N.E.2d 1 (1967).
[56] 391 U.S., 568.
[57] 376 U.S. 254 (1964).
[58] Epperson v. Arkansas, 393 U.S. 97 at 106.

that it is deemed to conflict with a particular religious doctrine, that is, with a particular interpretation of the Book of Genesis by a particular religious group."[59]

The most obvious point illustrated by the Pickering and Epperson cases is that basic constitutional rights of faculty, otherwise in jeopardy, can be protected through judicial review. A second point, important both to the faculty member seeking redress and to the administrator wary of the incursions of the judiciary into academic traditions, is that the courts offered neither party a *deus ex machina* capable of extricating him painlessly or with certainty from an otherwise untenable position. The state supreme courts in both cases had upheld the school officials against the teachers. Vindication of the teachers' rights had high prices attached—costs for legal services and material and emotional investments of time and effort. If in clear-cut invasions of the First Amendment the judicial path to vindication is lined with obstacles, what can be expected when issues raised with the judiciary are more amorphous, esoteric, or indigenous to academia, such as interpretation of principles of tenure?

Courts have generally been reluctant to interpose their authority to develop a special subfield of substantive law for academic tenure. If the overt hostility to principles of tenure of the South Dakota Supreme Court in Worzella *v.* Board of Regents[60] was something of an aberration, the Illinois Supreme Court's ready acceptance of termination, pursuant to state tenure rules, and the U.S. Supreme Court's subsequent denial of certiorari in Koch *v.* Board of Trustees[61] may present more of a prototype of present-day judicial response to pleas for substantive protection.

Dr. Worzella, a professor of agronomy at South Dakota State College since 1943, was discharged by the board of regents in 1958. According to the board, Dr. Worzella was guilty of insubordination and of involvement in serious personal disputes and activities that

[59] Epperson *v.* Arkansas, 103.

[60] 77 S.D. 447, 93 N.W.2d 411 (1958). See C. Byse, "Academic Freedom, Tenure and the Law: A Comment on Worzella *v.* Board of Regents" 73 *Harvard Law Review* 304 (1959).

[61] 34 Ill. App.2d 51, 187 N.E.2d 340 (1962), Cert. denied 375 U.S. 989 (1964).

made him a "controversial character" whose retention would not be in the best interest of South Dakota State College.

To Dr. Worzella's contention that he had permanent tenure under a tenure policy approved by the board of regents, the South Dakota Supreme Court answered that the tenure policy, which prevented the board from removing a faculty member without prior approval of the president of the college and the faculty tenure committee, was an unlawful delegation of power by the board of regents. Worzella was not entitled to have a writ of mandamus compelling the board to reinstate him because, said the unanimous court, "such delegation of authority to subordinates is an unlawful encroachment upon the board of regents' constitutional and statutory power of control over such college."[62] In the course of his opinion, Judge Hanson added that "the exact meaning and intent of this so-called tenure policy eludes us. Its vaporous objectives, purposes, and procedures are lost in a fog of nebulous verbiage."

Dr. Koch, a biology professor at the University of Illinois, did not have to endure an exercise in tortured constitutional or statutory construction or in gratuitous critiques of academic policy as did Dr. Worzella. By the time the Illinois trustees and the Illinois courts had effectuated his separation from the university, however, he must surely have wondered what is distinctive about the protection accorded by tenure rules. Koch was not, in fact, a tenured faculty member. In March 1960, in his fifth year of teaching at the university (under a contract that would have terminated in September 1961), he wrote a letter to the school paper asserting that premarital sexual intercourse among college students is not, in and of itself, improper. The proceedings that followed were the same as those required for terminating tenured faculty, pursuant to the dismissal provisions of Section 38 of the University of Illinois statutes.

The president of the university charged him with "conduct seriously prejudicial to the university through deliberate infraction of commonly accepted standards of morality," one of the explicit criteria of the university statutes for termination of tenure "for cause." Dr. Koch was served with a written statement of the charges and was granted

[62] Worzella v. Board of Regents, 93 N.W.2d 411 at 414.

a hearing before the university senate's committee on academic freedom prior to proceedings before the board of trustees. The senate committee, whose powers are advisory only, recommended unanimously that Dr. Koch be reprimanded but not discharged. The trustees declined to follow the recommendation of the top-ranking academic and administrative personnel who comprised the senate committee; after conducting a hearing at which Dr. Koch was represented by counsel, they ordered that he be discharged as of August 31, 1960, a year before the expiration of his contract.

In his appeal to the courts, the professor alleged that First Amendment rights to free speech were at issue, since the sole accusation against him was that his views, as expressed in the *Daily Illini,* were repugnant to commonly accepted standards of morality and could be interpreted as an encouragement of immoral behavior. The Illinois courts rejected his constitutional argument and proceeded to rule that there was no violation of his contractual rights, since he had been granted detailed procedural protection, including formal hearings and representation by counsel.[63] Certiorari was denied by the Supreme Court.

Cases like *Worzella* and *Koch* contrast sharply with the widespread view that tenure rules anoint or weld faculty members in their positions. If there is any truth to the conception of tenure as unbreakable, it is because of institutional practices rather than because of precise protective doctrines developed by the courts. Nothing in the rationales, norms, or rules of tenure legally shields any faculty member from accountability for performance as teacher, scholar, and colleague. In general, tenure rules enhance procedural rights, and the burden of proof over retention shifts in most institutions when tenure is achieved. The probationary faculty member must convince his colleagues and administration by his performance and continued promise that he merits tenure; any doubts must usually be resolved against him. With tenure, the presumption customarily is that he is performing at least competently unless and until proof to the contrary is introduced. If conspiracies of silence protect the once-distinguished faculty member who has become professionally incompetent because of alcoholism,

---

[63] 187 N.E.2d 340 at 343.

family problems, encroaching senility, or sheer indifference, that poses a problem for the integrity of internal governance of the institution rather than for the validity of the conception of tenure.

The approaches to law regulating tenure that we have examined are hardly likely to impress academics as cheaper or more effective in the protection of basic rights than private persuasion, bargaining, and organizational rule making. There has, of course, been some progress in judicial delineation of the First Amendment rights of teachers. As Van Alstyne has noted,

> *The drive of the judicial process has . . . severely restricted the use of political litmus tests for teaching eligibility and checked the tendency of school boards and legislators to police the extramural political utterances and private lives of teachers through threats of their jobs. Specifically, political disclaimer oaths, bans on membership in feared or hated political organizations or unions, discharge for extramural criticism, and dismissal or revocation of teaching certificates for private behavior not specifically shown to affect the teacher's professional competency, his intramural working relationships, or his classroom integrity gradually have all been rolled back by judicial decree.*[64]

The Roth and Sindermann cases—along with *Koch, Worzella,* and others—affirm, however, that vindicating First and Fourteenth Amendment rights through the judicial process remains costly, complex, and uncertain.

For the tenured faculty member in a public institution, it is fair to say, the law requires—as a matter of constitutional right—pretermination notice, hearing, and orderly inquiry into continued fitness to teach. The nontenured faculty member in a public school has the same protection with regard to dismissal before the end of a contract term but not with regard to nonrenewal. The Supreme Court's present view of the state-action concept offers no basis for assuming that constitutional due-process or First Amendment guarantees will be extended to faculty in private universities. Negotiation, contract, and

[64] W. Van Alstyne, "The Constitutional Rights of Teachers and Professors," 1970 *Duke Law Journal* 841 at 846–847.

custom, rather than constitution, must be relied on as avenues of redress for faculty in the private sector.

On the whole, courts may be more effective as a looming presence to prevent cases from arising than as an avenger to redress particular inequities. The fact that a teacher has rights potentially subject to enforcement "may strengthen the hand of the conscientious administrator or trustee when public pressure unjustifiably seeks discharge of the teacher."[65] The reality of substantive judicial protection is subject to evaporation, however, when the methodology of discharge accords, in public institutions, with procedural due process and, in private institutions, with whatever procedures are specified in by-laws and contracts governing employment.

An Unresolved Question and Task for the Academic Community

The courts have not even begun to determine, as Nathan Glazer has put it, "what a university requires and may properly demand of a faculty, quite independent of any constitutional standard."[66] Glazer's construction of tenure distinguishes sharply "between a man's role as a citizen and his role as a member of an institution with some autonomy." Like Perkins, he is fearful of putting the university at the mercy of lawyers and judges, who may, in the course of developing their legal positions, "come to views of the limits of free speech and the proper tests that may determine these limits that are in one way or another contradictory to the essential purposes of a university." Although the constitution fully protects a professor's speech in his role as citizen, Glazer argues that it should not protect him fully in his academic role. Tenure cannot allow professors to urge a university's physical destruction, for example, regardless of whether such speech breaches constitutional standards.

In a similar vein, Lewis Mayhew has maintained that the university—as an institution formed to induct young people into adult society and to search for truth—has to protect itself "when the resources to serve those purposes or when [the] achievement [of those purposes] is threatened by the action of individuals."[67]

---

[65] Byse and Joughin, p. 75.
[66] "Why a Faculty Cannot Afford a Franklin," *Change,* June 1972, p. 41.
[67] "Dissent: A Campus View," *Change,* June 1972, pp. 45–47.

If the notion of a university's inherent right to self-preservation includes its yielding to demands for the sacrifice of faculty whose words or actions threaten the continuity of financial support for the institution, we reach a crucial point in delineation of tenure principles—a point where courts are totally inadequate. Tenure standards that cave in before the onslaught of donors would be at least as unconscionable as standards that pander to the whims of student or faculty revolutionaries. Especially as the era of homogeneity of campus values fades, colleges and universities must be prepared to formulate and implement specific standards governing the multiple facets of tenure. The academic community has more to gain by explicitly asserting the principles, processes, and values its members deem essential to intellectual integrity and a climate of creativity than by encouraging—or allowing by default—a judicial *in loco parentis* to take control. If we academics find the task too onerous or distasteful, there will be no feasible alternative to judicialization.

꧁꧂ **V** ꧁꧂

Faculty Unionism and Tenure

William F. McHugh

꧁꧂꧁꧂꧁꧂꧁꧂꧁꧂꧁꧂꧁꧂꧁꧂

As everyone with the capacity to face reality now recognizes, faculty unionism has arrived at a number of academic institutions and is likely to spread to others. The impact of faculty unionism on tenure can best be considered in the light of following questions: What are the causes of faculty unionism?[1] What constitutes a tenure system and what are the relevant problems it cre-

---

[1] For a discussion of the causes of faculty unionism, see W. F. McHugh, "Faculty Unionism," in B. L. Smith and Associates, *The Tenure Debate* (San Francisco: Jossey-Bass, 1972).

ates? What are the general elements of the collective bargaining process? Is tenure negotiable?

Major Features of Tenure

There is by no means a uniform tenure system in higher education. Some institutions have no system of tenure at all, and the faculty serves at the pleasure of the institution. Others have de facto tenure policies, developed through practice and custom but never written down. Some institutions have highly detailed policies with elaborate notice requirements; others have simply endorsed and imported the AAUP tenure policies or guidelines.[2] In some public institutions, typically state teacher colleges, tenure is detailed by the state legislature in statutory law; in others, college governing boards have promulgated detailed tenure systems. In spite of this diversity, most tenure systems may be described along the following lines.

There are three coordinate elements in a tenure system. First of all, tenure is part and parcel of academic freedom, since it frees a faculty member from restraints and pressures that otherwise would inhibit independent thought and action. The modern idea of academic freedom, as Hofstadter and Metzger[3] have noted, was developed by men who absorbed analogous ideas from the larger life of society: from modern science, the notion of the empirical search for truth, verified by objective processes; from commerce, the notion of free competition of ideas; from politics, the idea of free speech and free press as essential to perspectives in a pluralistic society; from religious liberalism, the spirit of tolerance. Second, tenure represents a kind of communal acceptance into the professorial guild, acceptance by one's peers. Rooted in the medieval guild, it entails a vow akin to the ministry or priesthood; hence, the very term "professor." This aspect of tenure presently seems in eclipse at many institutions. Third, tenure is a means for providing job security to promote institutional stability and loyalty and to reward individual service and accomplishment.

In addition to these common features, there are usually two

---

[2] C. Byse and L. Joughin, *Tenure in American Higher Education* (Ithaca, N.Y.: Cornell University Press, 1959), p. 9.

[3] R. Hofstadter and W. Metzger, *Academic Freedom in the United States* (New York: Columbia University Press, 1955), pp. 61–62.

basic types of academic appointments relating to tenure: *term appointments,* which confer security against dismissal for a fixed term; and *continuing appointments,* which confer such status for as long as the professor remains in good standing at the institution. Both are subject, of course, to formal dismissal proceedings for cause.

Although the de facto decision of appointment, reappointment, or tenure is as a practical matter a faculty decision, nonetheless, in the American university the de jure authority to grant appointment and tenure is almost always vested in the trustees by statue, charter, or by-laws, depending upon whether the institution is public or private. Tenure provisions are typically spelled out in written trustee policies or faculty handbooks adopted by the college trustees. Usually, the institution is required to make tenure decisions within a prescribed period of time—for example, after a faculty member has completed no more than seven years of service. Usually also, the institution is required to give notice of nonrenewal within a specified time; the longer the service, the longer the notice requirement—perhaps six months' notice for two-year appointments and a year's notice for three-year appointments. In addition, written trustee policies sometimes establish broad criteria (teaching, scholarly research, mastery of subject matter, university service) for promotion.[4] These criteria are then applied to the particular tenure-review case.

The tenure-appointment-review process characteristically entails a pyramid of reviewing committees; the process originates in the academic department and culminates with a recommendation from a campus-wide committee (usually including deans or academic vice-presidents). The president then presents the recommendation to the governing board for approval. These review procedures—frequently developed by departments, faculties, and schools and usually not passed upon by the governing board—are a combination of written policy and de facto practice and tailored to the special needs of the faculty or departments involved. Sometimes, however, trustee policies or by-laws will expressly delegate an advisory or consultative role to the faculty in the appointment and promotion process; or the by-laws might

---

[4] See *State University of New York Trustee Policies 1971,* Article XII, Title B, Sec. 2, p. 19.

even give faculty authority to establish and apply the criteria upon which tenure is awarded.

In addition to regulating appointments and promotion, trustee policies frequently make provision for dismissal of faculty. A dismissal proceeding is different from a tenure-review process. Specifically, in a dismissal proceeding, the institution brings charges against a faculty member (charges such as inadequate performance of duties, incompetence, or misconduct) with the clear design of ridding itself of an undesirable employee. Such a proceeding may be brought during the term appointment of term appointees or against a tenured faculty member. It typically requires notice and a formal adjudicatory hearing, usually with right to counsel. The hearing frequently takes place before a faculty committee, which makes findings of fact and recommendations to the president or board. It is likely to be an adversary proceeding, concerned only with the issues raised by the charges. A tenure review, in contrast, is concerned with whether or not to grant tenure in light of the departmental or academic program needs, prevailing economic and budget considerations, the qualities of the particular candidate, and the existing job market. Tenure review obviously never applies to a person who already has tenure, whereas a dismissal proceeding could. Theoretically, separation from an institution because tenure was not granted carries no professional stigma; dismissal for cause clearly does. One of the purposes behind a dismissal procedure ensuring due process is to protect the academic freedom of tenured faculty members and those on term appointments. The tenure-review process has different objectives. Frequently, where there is a confusing factual situation, administration and faculty fail to keep this distinction in mind.

Possibly some of the confusion between these two processes results from two opposing views of the term appointment. One view characterizes a term appointment as fundamentally a contractual obligation on the part of the institution for the term period in return for services rendered by the faculty member. Admittedly, an individual may be considered for a continuing appointment at some future point; but this view holds that the term-appointment relationship carries no implied expectancy of continuing employment. According to this view, the individual is fully protected when there are notice requirements and when a tenure decision is required after a prescribed period of service. When an individual receives notice that his appointment will not be renewed upon expiration, it does not necessarily follow that he is inferior or inadequate or that he has done something wrong. In short, since the institution is not obligated to renew appointments, it is not obligated to give written reasons or a hearing to an individual whose term appointment has been nonrenewed.

The term appointment, according to this traditional view, facilitates the pursuit of institutional excellence by ensuring institutional flexibility to react to economic realities, desirable market conditions, access to higher-quality faculty, shifting emphasis in academic programs. From the faculty point of view, it provides job security for a fixed term, opportunity for self-development by leaving open the opportunity for promotion to a continuing appointment (tenure), and security against arbitrary or unlawful dismissal during the term of the appointment.

This view of the term appointment has been attacked by many faculty and faculty organizations as subjective, elitist, and institutionally oriented. Most important, it makes no provision for challenging nonrenewals founded on unlawful, capricious, subjective, or punitive reasons. They ask at the bargaining table: Why not tell a man why you are not renewing his appointment; why not give him an opportunity to improve? Why after seven years—and perhaps a pattern of promotion and a series of salary increases—is he suddenly undesirable? Have you no obligation to him after years of service to your institution; are you just going to turn him and his family out into the streets? Shouldn't there be at least some due-process procedure to ascertain whether the reasons for his nonrenewal are capricious, unconstitutional, or irrational? The view underlying this argument emphasizes the probationary aspect of the term appointment, the job-security aspect. According to this view, the individual on term appointment is— from the moment of his appointment—on a tenure track that leads to a continuing appointment at the institution. That is, where the university has policies relating to notice requirements and requires a tenure decision after a prescribed period of service, it follows that an initial term appointment may create an institutional obligation to grant tenure if certain conditions are met. There is, then, an implied obligation on the part of the institution to grant tenure, provided the individual measures up to expressly articulated institutional standards and does not do something wrong. It is further argued that in cases where nonrenewal amounts to denial of tenure, the burden should logically shift to the institution to show the reasons for nonrenewal or to show where the faculty member has failed to measure up to expressed institutional criteria and therefore is denied a continuing appointment otherwise available.

Some consider that failure to give reasons for nonrenewals is equivalent to a dismissal for cause except that the nonrenewed individual is deprived of the due process normally provided in a dismissal proceeding. This argument is often made in cases where an institution or faculty appears to be ridding itself of a "troublemaker" by merely waiting out the expiration of his term appointment, or where the particular candidate is controversial, or where circumstances suggest an arbitrary or capricious decision. Accordingly, many faculty members have been urging institutions to establish policies requiring written reasons for nonrenewal of a term contract or for denial of tenure, and providing a forum for challenging tenure decisions. Thus, a candidate who feels wronged can trigger a review of the tenure decision before an impartial committee, which will presumably limit its scope of review to the question of whether appropriate evaluation procedures were followed.[5]

Because of the growing lack of confidence in the tenure evaluative process—which has, in turn, opened it up to greater faculty criticism —the AAUP has been trying to develop a procedure that will afford maximum evaluative flexibility with broad exercise of peer-group discretion to preserve high academic standards, while at the same time harnessing that discretion to prevent capricious or unlawful abuse of the evaluative process in cases of nonrenewal of term contracts. There has also been a rash of court cases[6] concerned with the problem—most notably, two recent decisions of the U.S. Supreme Court in the Roth and Sindermann cases (see Chapter Four).

---

[5] See the elaborate review procedure endorsed by the AAUP in its "Statement on Procedural Standards in the Renewal or Nonrenewal of Faculty Appointments," *AAUP Bulletin,* 1971, 57, 206–210.

[6] Lucas *v.* Chapman, 430 F.2d 945 (5th Cir. 1970); Greene *v.* Howard University, 412 F.2d 1128 (U.S. App. D.C. 1969); but see Jones *v.* Hopper, 412 F.2d 1323 (10th Cir. 1969); Bolmar *v.* Keyes, 162 F.2d 136 (2nd Cir. 1947).

Characteristics of Bargaining Process

For our purposes here, four general characteristics of the bargaining process should be kept in mind. First, it clearly contemplates
an *adversary relationship* and assumes a divergence of faculty and institutional interests, raising the possibility of a power struggle. In private institutions, which are covered by the National Labor Relations
Act (NLRA), and in public institutions in states where there is par-
tial authorization for strike (Pennsylvania and Hawaii), the ultimate
weapons are the threat of strike on the one hand and employer willingness to take a strike on the other. In most public institutions where
the strike is not authorized by state law, the ultimate weapon usually
is the threat of public fact-finding report, which may gain the political
support of the public. The adversary relationship assumes a well-de-
fined dichotomy between the faculty and those who manage the institution. That is, management sets and pursues institutional objectives;
faculty interests may conflict with these goals and priorities, or (in
public institutions) with those established by external governmental
agencies. The bargaining agent's objective, whether rationalized on
the basis of what is best for the institution or not, is to further the collective interest of the faculty it represents and to circumscribe managerial auhority to that extent.

Second, implicit in the adversary relationship is the assumption
of a *bilateral relationship*. The NLRA and most state collective bargaining laws increase the faculty's legal status by requiring the university to recognize the exclusive representative status of a duly elected
faculty bargaining agent and to bargain with it in good faith, whether
or not agreement is reached. Implicit in bilateralism is the assumption
of a two-party contractual relationship between the faculty and the
university. Therefore, at a unionized campus the general framework
and many incidents of the faculty-university relationship are established in a negotiated contract and during contract implementation.
By comparison, at nonunionized campuses board policies governing
faculty-university relationships are, legally speaking, unilaterally established; that is, the faculty has no legal right to bargain about them.
Of course, many faculties have in fact, "collegially negotiated" through
traditional channels the board policies governing faculty-university relations.

Third, the collective bargaining process is premised upon a *collective relationship;* that is, organizations of employees sharing a community of interest are represented *exclusively* by an elected representative. Competing organizations may thus be excluded from negotiating with the institution and are relegated to a back-seat status on major institutional issues. It is a democratic process in the sense that everyone in the bargaining unit (including nontenured faculty) has an equal opportunity to vote whether there will be bargaining and, if so, on who the bargaining agent will be. The agent is dependent upon, and must be responsive to, the majority of those it represents. It has no legal obligation to make distinctions within its own organization (distinctions based, for example, upon such things as academic rank or senior faculty status—a critical matter when the majority of faculty in the bargaining do not have tenure)'.

This collective relationship stresses the dynamics of politics and organizational behavior, which become major factors in faculty-university relations and which may reach beyond the campus, especially when an elected bargaining agent is affiliated with national or state organizations which have legal, financial, and other staff organized and financed to confront institutional action or directives and policies in the courts, legislative halls, or elsewhere. The character of faculty leadership is likely to change as a result of this collectivism. It requires considerable investment of time, with increasing emphasis upon an institutional perspective of faculty, school, or discipline. It requires individuals able to lead in a political context and attuned to the majority of the constituency.

Fourth, the bargaining process depends upon *third-party neutrals* when efforts at mutual accord break down. It relies upon mediation, fact finding, and arbitration to resolve impasses during contract negotiations or grievance impasses arising from the administration and application of the contract. A third-party mediator tries to persuade the parties to resolve their differences. An arbitrator, in a more formal adjudicatory proceeding, determines the merits of the impasse issues and presents his findings in a written decision, which may serve as a precedent for comparable future issues. Arbitration decisions in other labor disputes (for instance, in cases involving teachers in public schools)' may serve as precedents in analogous faculty-university disputes and thus influence an arbitrator's decision in, say, a community college faculty dispute. Binding arbitration, as contrasted with advisory arbitration, means that the parties will be bound by the arbitrator's decision. Binding arbitration is relatively common as the terminal step in a grievance system (grievance arbitration) but less commonly used to resolve impasses that arise during the negotiations themselves (interest arbitration), especially when there is the right to strike. Parties are frequently reluctant to be bound by an arbitrator's decision on a negotiation-impasse issue where the strike leverage is available.

Fact finding—virtually the same as advisory arbitration—is often utilized in negotiation impasses where the strike is not authorized (as in New York, New Jersey, and Michigan). The theory behind fact finding is that publication of the fact finder's report clarifies the issues and informs the public and the legislative decision makers. It gives the parties an opportunity to assess public reaction to their respective positions. Thus, the fact finder's report, although not binding, places public pressure on the parties to settle their differences or upon the legislative body to accept the fact finder's report.

Third-party neutrals are usually selected by the parties themselves or appointed by a public-employment-relations board, or some conciliation service, from panels of experienced mediators, fact finders, and arbitrators. Private institutions are likely to resort to the Federal Mediation Service or the American Arbitration Association, while public institutions are likely to deal with state-board-controlled conciliation services.

Tenure Negotiability

For a number of reasons tenure is likely to be a major negotiable issue when faculty unionism arrives on campus. Many of the conditions conducive to unionism are the same as those that encourage tenure negotiation. The Roth and Sindermann decisions will likely increase pressure by faculty to negotiate contractual rights to written reasons for nonrenewal of term contracts and review procedures patterned after recent AAUP policy. At institutions with a high concentration of nontenured faculty, and certainly at institutions with no tenure system at all, the bargaining agent will be under considerable political pressure to deliver on job security, especially where economic conditions threaten job mobility.

Two major problems arise, however, when the bargaining process is applied to academic institutions. One is the difficulty of establishing a clearcut adversary relationship, of separating the management-rights function from the professional responsibility of the faculty. The other, related, problem is the predisposition of faculty to seize upon unionism as a kind of governance system. There is a widely held view by faculty today that they should have wide discretion in the conduct of their professional activities and some form of "shared authority" in the governance or formulation of institutional policies. This notion—stemming from medieval times but gaining momentum over the past twenty years during a time of unusual faculty autonomy—is part and parcel of academic freedom and institutional autonomy. When aggressively pursued, the commitment to shared authority projects into the bargaining relationship a much wider spectrum of matters than are customarily associated with collective bargaining in private industry or in the public sector. Forced to draw lines between management and faculty rights, the collegial tradition paradoxically tends to draw a broad range of issues, many noneconomic, into the bargaining process.[7] According to a study by the American Association for Higher Education, "economic factors per se have [not] been an important consideration underlying recent expressions of faculty unrest. . . . A meaningful application of the concept of 'shared authority' should involve a wide variety of issues. The issues include educational and administrative policies; personnel administration; economic matters ranging from the total resources available to the compensation for

[7] CUNY Contracts, articles. I, V, VII. In the State University of New York representation proceeding before PERB, Kugler, President, New York State AFT College and University Council, testified that the following subjects would be the subject of negotiation: merit increases, number of students, promotions, compensation for extracurricular activity, TV and radio tape residuals, research staff, office space, secretarial services, travel funds, academic calendar, evening and extension assignments, sabbatic leave, leaves of absence, maternity and sick leave, tenure policies, grievance procedures, general regulations pertaining to campus affairs, consultation on educational matters, curriculum, admissions, student activities, choice of administrators (including deans, chairmen, presidents), pensions, health benefits, life and disability insurance, salary policy, moving expenses, tuition waiver for dependents, central faculty authority, master plan formulation, educational policy governing entire university, establishment of new campuses, intercollege agreements, and selection of the chancellor and other central administrators.

particular individuals; public questions that affect the role and functions of the institutions; and procedures for faculty representation in
campus governance."[8]

The American Association of University Professors, in its October 1969 policy statement, also has recognized the "significant role
that collective bargaining may play in bringing agreement between
faculty and administration on economic and academic issues." Negotiation of a collective agreement, then, may "provide for the eventual
establishment of necessary instruments of shared authority."

Accordingly, the three national faculty organizations (the AFT,
the AAUP, and the NEA) reflect in their campaign literature and
bargaining agreements a concept of negotiable issues covering a range
of matters: admissions, class size, workload, calendar, procedures for
budget formulation, participation in institutional planning and allocation of resources, procedures for the selection of certain administrators
and department chairman, traditional economic items, and tenure
matters.

The legal environment offers no major obstacles to negotiating
aspects of tenure. The NLRA and most state public-employment-relations acts typically permit negotiations with respect to salaries, wages,
hours, and other terms and conditions of employment. But what constitutes "terms and conditions of employment" with respect to faculty
in a college or university? In other words, what is the scope of negotiation? None of the reported decisions have squarely faced the issue
of whether or to what extent a tenure system might be negotiated. It
is fair to generalize, however, that matters relating to job security have
traditionally been considered within the definition of "terms and conditions of employment" under most collective bargaining laws.[9] Generally speaking, scope of negotiations has been liberally construed to
include in the bargaining process a variety of matters of logical concern to affected employees. However, the mere fact that a tenure matter may be negotiable under a given labor statute does not mean that
it must be negotiated or that, if it is negotiated, agreement has to be

---

[8] American Association for Higher Education, *Faculty Participation in Academic Governance,* (Washington, D.C., 1967), p. 1.

[9] See, for instance, *In the Matter of State of New York* (State University of New York), 2 PERB 4183, p. 4 (August 12, 1969).

reached. All that is required is that the parties negotiate the issue
in good faith. It is left for the parties to work it out between themselves.

Accordingly, scope of negotiations is determined also by actual
practice and experience between the parties as to what classes of issues
have been in fact negotiated, agreed upon, and provided for in the
contract. While written negotiated agreements do not necessarily coin-
cide in scope with the potential field of negotiation, they do represent
accessible documentation on current practice. Negotiated agreements
at community colleges, four-year institutions, and universities indicate
that faculty are negotiating a tenure system with contract provisions
covering the following matters: prescribed notice requirements; specification of evaluation criteria; promotion committees and their composition; access to and content of personnel files upon which promotion
and tenure decisions are based; the requirement of written reasons in
nonrenewal cases; academic-rank ratios; a procedure for appealing
tenure decisions; a dismissal-for-cause procedure; and an institutional
commitment to principles of academic freedom usually contained in
general contract provisions.[10] Academic freedom, frequently couched
in general terms, is alluded to in numerous contracts:

> All parties to this agreement recognize the importance of aca-
> demic freedom to the fulfillment of the college's educational pur-
> poses and therefore endorse the 1940 Statement of the Ameri-
> can Association of University Professors on Academic Freedom
> [Dutchess Community College, N.Y.].

> It is the policy of the college to maintain and encourage full free-
> dom, within the law, of inquiry, teaching, and research. This
> freedom shall include the right to belong to any legal organiza-
> tions and to promote such organization, and to hold and make
> public any view or opinion involving, but not limited to, social,
> economic, political, and educational issues [Fulton-Montgomery
> Community College, N.Y.].

> The parties incorporate herein by reference the 1940 Statement
> of Principles on Academic Freedom and Tenure of the Ameri-

[10] Moskow, M., "The Scope of Collective Bargaining in Higher Education," *Wisconsin Law Review*, 1971, *1971*(1).

*can Association of University Professors in accordance with the
endorsement of the board of trustees of the university on January 15, 1968 [St. John's University].*

*During the life of this agreement the university-wide policies on
the following matters shall be changed only after special conference: (1) Academic Freedom, (2) Academic Tenure . . .
[Central Michigan]*

With respect to community colleges the foregoing conclusions
are supported by a January 1971 survey of twenty-two New York
community college contracts and a 1969–1970 survey of twenty-four
Michigan community college contracts as well as the Chicago community college system agreement. Since there is nothing to suggest
otherwise, it seems fair to conclude that the trend to negotiate tenure
in unionized community colleges will continue—especially where there
are authoritarian administrative styles, no tenure system, or tenure
largely dependent upon informal practice.

Experience in the four-year colleges and universities is somewhat less extensive, but developments so far show little difference from
the community college agreements in regard to negotiation of tenure
provisions. In some respects, however, these agreements cover a wider
range of related tenure matters than do the community college contracts.

Given negotiability of tenure, such matters as student or faculty
senate interests in evaluation and promotion committees, personnel
file guidelines, the validity of departmental guidelines on promotion
and tenure, study committees on faculty personnel matters will all
somehow have to be related to the bargaining relationship on unionized campuses. The faculty bargaining agent will no doubt play a
prominent part in such matters. All of this is, of course, somewhat
speculative at this point because there are no available studies concerning the impact of contract administration upon tenure.

Implications of Tenure Negotiability

Policies of Governing Boards. Faculty members at schools
like St. John's, SUNY, and Boston State are negotiating into their
contracts the status of existing written tenure policies of their governing boards. Accordingly, the collective bargaining agreement can, in

practical effect, bake into a contract portions of board policies relating to tenure (St. John's contract) or can require reopened negotiations on board tenure policies when such policies are intended to be changed by the trustees (SUNY contract) or can actually incorporate such tenure-related policies as academic-freedom provisions (Rutgers). Thus, unionized faculties have been seeking, by expressed provisions in the contract, to preserve favorable existing institutional policies concerning tenure or to negotiate desired changes in them. Open-ended provisions allow considerable latitude to faculty in this regard; such a provision is illustrated by the language of the St. John's University contract: "The parties agree to continue all practices of the administration currently adhered to by it. 'Practices' refers to those practices of the office of president, offices of the vice-presidents, offices of the deans, based upon written policies of the board of trustees and the university senate. . . . All of the provisions of the statutes presently in effect relating to tenure and promotion remain in full force and effect with the following modifications . . ."

Changed Legal Relationship. Where tenure matters are negotiated, the result will change the fundamental legal relationship between faculty and the institution. In the past, many institutions made favorable changes in tenure policies because the faculty pressured for improvement or because the institution hoped thereby to enhance its recruitment efforts. Such policies were developed during a time when political and financial constraints upon the institution were not significant. Many of the tenure provisions were predicated upon AAUP policy.

In *public* institutions, tenure rules or policies promulgated by action of the governing board of the institution have the force and effect of administrative regulations and are not usually contractual rights as such. They may be changed or eliminated by similar action of the board. Collectively speaking, the faculty has no legally vested right to prevent a change in the policies. But where an authorized bilateral agreement is collectively negotiated between the faculty and the public institution, the legal relationship is one of contract; it may not be unilaterally changed by the governing board during the contract term. In *private* institutions, legal relationships with respect to tenure matters have always been contractual—derived from the letter or form of appointment and read in the light of existing institutional policies. However, in both public and private institutions, unionism probably will result in establishing tenure relationships through the collective agreement rather than through an individually negotiated agreement. To some extent, a collective agreement disenfranchises the individual faculty member from negotiating his own comprehensive contract. On the other hand, such comprehensive contracts—particularly concerning tenure matters—are not commonly negotiated on an individual basis. Most agreements or letters of appointment characteristically recite the salary, rank, and length of appointment with specific reference to institutional policies regarding tenure in the faculty handbook or trustee policies. In private institutions so-called individual contracts in the majority of cases are contracts of adhesion and are tied to already established institutional policies. The individual has no negotiating leverage over these. Depending on the policies and form of appointment, the institution may well have the right unilaterally to change its tenure policies without causing a breach of individual contract.

Most of the collective bargaining agreements so far prohibit individual faculty contracts from being inconsistent with the collective agreement. Although this prohibition does not necessarily preclude an individually negotiated salary arrangement, such an arrangement seems unlikely. Collective bargaining in both public and private institutions, then, probably will diminish if not eliminate the individual contract concept and shift tenure matters from the board policies to the collective contract itself. This will reduce the flexibility of the board to unilaterally change such policies during the term of the collective bargaining contract.

Increased Bilateralism. If collective bargaining trends so far suggest a businesslike and detailed litany of tenure rights spelled out in the collective bargaining contracts instead of in policies, handbooks, written interpretations, or everyday practice, it is reasonable to assume that there will be a tendency to homogenize practices relating to tenure and reduce discrepancies in practice between departments, schools, and faculties. Unilateral flexibility by the institution and its subdivisions to change signals with respect to appointment and tenure because of economic or other considerations will be reduced in both public and private institutions where existing policies and the status quo become baked into collective bargaining agreements. For example, at institutions where the majority of faculty are nontenured, institutional attempts to limit all new term appointments to one year with a practice of one-year rollovers may well be resisted at the bargaining table. Likewise, a series of nonrenewals to take advantage of favorable market conditions may result in efforts to establish rank ratios, rigorous review procedures on nonrenewals, and a policy of "promotion from within." Retrenchment of "fat programs" will result in pressure for contract retrenchment criteria with, perhaps, built-in seniority concepts tied to tenure status.

This is not to say that collective bargaining will necessarily mean institutional ineritia. Quite the contrary: the bilateralism implicit in the bargaining process, if knowledgeably handled, can work as a constructive force. The process lends itself to mutual problem solving and can result in a more disciplined presentation of detailed personnel data necessary to informed institutional tenure policies, and may help produce an institutional perspective on the problem of tenure.

In the absence of bilateral checks, fiscal crises can result in haphazard and ad hoc personnel decisions and cause a breakdown in faculty trust. Confronted with this bilateralism, institutions will have to be better prepared to rationalize and justify decisions and policies relating to tenure—especially with respect to retrenchment and in the faculty evaluation process.

Managerial Attitudes.   The rule that every action has an equal and opposite reaction may well apply at some unionized institutions. Bilateralism is a two-way street, and the scope of negotiations raises basic questions about management's rights and prerogatives. Reduced to simplest terms, management rights with respect to tenure are those matters which management has not negotiated away.

Management-rights provisions in existing contracts typically take this line:

> *The legislature and the trustees, separately and collectively, hereby reserve unto themselves all powers, authority, duties, and responsibilities and the adoption of such rules, regulations, and policies as they deem necessary in the management, direction, and administration of all operations and activities of the college . . . limited only by the specific and express terms of this agreement [Genesee Community College, New York].*

*Except as expressly limited by other provisions of this statement,
all of the authority, rights, and responsibilities possessed by the
state are retained by it [State University of New York].*

*Oakland has the legal responsibility and, subject to the terms of
this agreement, the right to manage its operations, including but
not limited to the right to (a) hire, assign, promote, schedule, discipline, and discharge faculty members; (b) determine and schedule the academic year; (c) locate or relocate its present facilities
and equipment; (d) control all of its property [Oakland Uni-
versity].*

How managements-rights provisions could or would encroach
upon additional faculty practice in regard to tenure is pure specula-
tion at this point. Contract administration experience is not extensive
enough or adequately documented to permit reliable conclusions. Assertion of management rights is likely to surface during contract administration in the event of a program cut where the contract makes
no provision for faculty retrenchment or where management policy
declares a moratorium on new positions in combination with a high
attrition rate and increased workload.

It is also too early to tell whether aggressive unionism will induce a polarized response from boards of trustees and state governments toward a "management's rights" psychology.[11] Sustained and militant pursuit of unionism by faculty, however, probably will induce a
more aggressive management attitude on the part of university officials.
For, in practical effect, faculty unionism circumscribes—by means of
a legally enforceable contract—the legal authority of the board of
trustees and the executive responsibility wherever it might lie. Faculty
unionism is a frontal attack upon the legal control and ultimate institutional responsibility vested in the lay board of trustees or the executive authority of governmental officials. Thus, at some institutions,
existing governance schemes, collegial attitudes, and prebargaining faculty prerogatives, as we have known them, simply will not survive the
advent of militant unionism. This raises the chicken and egg argument: if there had been "collegiality" and faculty participation in the
first place, there would not have been militant faculty unionism; the

[11] Lieberman, M., "Professors, Unite!" *Harper's*, October 1971, p. 61.

heavy exercise of managerial authority, especially by officials in large public institutions, has been a primary cause of faculty unionism. Nevertheless, confronted by self-conscious faculty unions seeking to secure "rights" signed, sealed, and delivered in a written contract, some institutions may respond with an escalated "management" reaction and a major redefinition of institutional authority vis-à-vis faculty.

Managerial authority could be asserted in contract checks on faculty appointment, promotion, and rank ratios negotiated to protect ultimate board authority. Hardened managerial attitudes in negotiations could force faculty to trade off prebargaining rights by conceding them as management rights in exchange for salaries and job security. It could be manifest in institutional counterproposals for experimentation in types of academic appointments such as five-year term appointments, or committees to review the merits of tenure in the context of the particular institution. It may increase pressure for greater institutional scrutiny and justification in the initial academic appointment process. There may be institutional efforts to place centralized control over personnel funds, which departments would otherwise control, or new types of pay incentives based on productivity concepts to induce larger-scale experimentation in teaching methodology. It could well resurrect the merit concept, with more centralized control over merit funds. Management initiatives might encourage sporadic employment relationship by greater use of part-time faculty. Forces, of course, are already building in this direction; but unionism could accelerate the trend.

It is simply too early to tell whether positions will harden and polarize. The importance of skill and sophistication in the art of compromise and uses of the bargaining process must not be underestimated. For undue contentiousness and ill will arise more often from the actions of those on both sides who are ill equipped to function responsibly in the a collective bargaining context. Much depends upon the faculty tradition and the prebargaining relationships at a particular institution. In many cases, faculty representatives and institutional officials will be reluctant—because of strong institutional traditions, if not their trained incapacities to do otherwise—to shrug off collegial relationships characteristic of yesterday for the confrontation styles of unionism seen in some schoolteacher experiences.

Grievance. There is a difference between the traditional academic grievance system and the grievance procedure typically contained in negotiated academic contracts. Academic grievance systems usually entail review by joint faculty-administrative committees, which make recommendation to the dean, president, or trustees, whose decision is final. The procedure is informal and based upon behind-the-scenes consensus. The purpose is to adjust individual problems and not collective or institutional matters and rarely involves the use of outside third parties. Collective bargaining grievance is quite different. Its purpose is to provide a method for challenging institutional actions on matters that the parties have defined in the collective bargaining agreement as "grievable." It is typically designed in three or four stages, becoming progressively more formal and adversarial at the latter stages and culminating in a final administrative decision which is often subject to review and binding arbitration by an outside third-party arbitrator. It involves not only individual grievances but also institutional or collective grievances. Thus, the challenged interpretation placed upon a grievable contract provision relating to tenure can affect basic faculty-institutional relationships and entail substantial costs.

If grievance is limited only to contract provisions, there will probably be less scope for challenge than if grievance is defined to include policies of the governing board or other written administrative policies in addition to the contract. By the same token, the scope of grievance is less critical where there is no binding arbitration and where final decision is reserved to the governing board. There is a definite trend toward binding arbitration of grievances. There is, however, also a consistent effort to keep the academic merits of a tenure decision out of the grievance machinery.

One approach provides for review of procedural violations in evaluation but keeps the review before an in-house committee with no provision for arbitration (Central Michigan). The New Jersey State College contract—although it contains detailed tenure promotion procedures, personnel file procedures, and promotional criteria—expressly excludes from the grievance procedure "decisions involving the nonreappointment of probationary or nontenure personnel."

Another approach often used where the contract has binding grievance arbitration is to limit the arbitrator's scope of review in tenure grievances. That is, the arbitrator decides only whether procedural violations occurred in the evaluative process; he does not evaluate the academic merits of the decision itself. CUNY, SUNY, and St. Johns are examples of this approach.

Resistance to hashing out the academic merits of a tenure decision through the adversary grievance machinery by limiting the arbitrator's scope of review may prove impractical. Tenure matters, such as evaluative criteria and procedures, can become so detailed and cumbersome that implementation may almost guarantee their violation, especially where evaluative authority is highly diffused to departments and schools within the institution. The problem is inflamed by the practical difficulty in distinguishing between procedural violation and academic merits. The difficulty in hewing the line between a review of evaluative procedures and the academic merits is compounded in cases where the arbitrator must decide whether "errors of fact, gross prejudice, capricious action, or factors violative of academic freedom influenced the [tenure] decision" [Central Michigan], or whether there was "an arbitrary or discriminatory application of or a failure to act pursuant to [contract or board provisions]" [St. John's].

Because of the bird-dogging instincts of a new union trying to establish itself, the availability of contract grievance machinery, and access to union attorneys and staff, the volume on campus of challenges to nonrenewals and promotional decisions probably will initially increase. Recourse to a grievance system will be more attractive than court action where it offers greater procedural safeguards than those required by the Roth and Sindermann decisions. Initially, an inordinate amount of time and energy probably will be spent on grievances over tenure matters. In some instances, the procedures may be downright intimidating, with a tendency to discourage nonrenewals of term contracts in borderline cases because of the potential hassle involved.

On the other hand, grievance machinery offers the potential over the long pull to resolve abuses in the faculty evaluative process. Once academics become familiar with the grievance machinery, many disagreements will be settled at the informal stages. Properly administered, grievance procedures will highlight weaknesses that can be corrected in the evaluative process and will encourage thorough justification of appointment and evaluation decisions. All of this may be an improvement over traditional academic grievance systems, which have been characterized by long delays, imprecise definition of grievance, inexperienced and untrained hearing bodies. Some institutions simply have no grievance procedure at all.

Collective bargaining grievance is usually designed to encompass the following features: a precisely defined procedure, objectivity in selection of hearing bodies, credibility (because bilaterally negotiated), timely disposition of cases, professionally skilled persons to administer it, and continuity in interpretation of policies.

In sum, it is clear that matters pertaining to tenure and promotion will become increasingly subjected to contract grievance machinery. It will encourage, initially, challenges to nonrenewal and promotional matters. These challenges will entail formal hearings, written decisions, interpretations of promotional criteria, and precedent-setting interpretations of key contract or board policy provisions relating to tenure. It has, however, the long-term potential of reducing disputes and promoting stability.

Academic Tenure and Contract Systems

♪❈♫❈♪❈♫❈♪❈♫❈♪❈♫❈♪❈♫❈♪❈♫❈♪❈♫❈♪

In April 1972 the Commission on Academic Tenure requested the Higher Education Panel of the American Council on Education to conduct a brief descriptive survey of tenure policies and practices in American higher education. An instrument of ten questions was developed, in which each respondent was asked to indicate whether a tenure or term appointment system existed at his institution. The questionnaire (Figure 1) and resulting data are included in this chapter.

The questionnaire was mailed to 511 institutions of the Higher Education Panel, a sample of 20 percent of the total population of 2543 institutions. This population of institutions was the base of the American Council on Education's 1971 survey of entering freshmen. Excepted from this base are those institutions requiring undergraduate credits for admission to their first class. Responses were received from 413 institutions, for a response rate of 81 percent.

215

FIGURE 1.   ACADEMIC TENURE QUESTIONNAIRE

In many of the questions below, the phrase "full-time faculty" is used. It refers to current full-time faculty members and other full-time staff members who hold faculty appointments (e.g., administrators). Specifically excluded from this definition are graduate students who act as teaching assistants or teaching fellows.

1. A full-time faculty member may be granted tenure at this institution: Yes............
    [If "no," skip to question 7]   No ....
2. This institution has a probationary period for tenure: Yes............
    [If "no," skip to question 3]   No ....
    a. Maximum length of probationary period: ....years
    b. Maximum years of prior service accepted as part of the proba-
       tionary period: ....years   [No prior service accepted...........]
    c. Typical length of contracts awarded a faculty member during the
       probationary period: First contract ....years   Succeeding
       contracts ....years
    d. What percent of those faculty members considered for tenure in
       the spring of 1971 actually receive tenure?   ....percent
3. In what ranks may tenure be held? [Check as many as apply]
    Professor........... Associate........... Assistant........... Instructor........... Other...........
    [Specify   ....]
    If your faculty is unranked, check here...........
4. Percent of current full-time faculty with tenure: ....percent
5. Does your institution limit the percent of tenured faculty?   Yes...........
                                                                  No ....
6. Is the tenure system currently under review for change on your
    campus?   Yes........... No...........
7. FOR THOSE INSTITUTIONS WITH *ONLY* TERM
    APPOINTMENT (CONTRACT) SYSTEMS
    [Other institutions skip to question 8]:
    a. What has been the typical length of contracts:
                                          First contract...........years
                                          Succeeding contracts...........years
    b. What percentage of those faculty whose contracts expired in 1971
       were renewed? ....percent
    c. Is your institution planning to establish a tenure system?   Yes...........
                                                                     No ....
    [Continue to 8]
8. Does your institution give formal written reasons to the faculty

member concerned for nonrenewal of contracts (probationary or recurring term apointments) or for denial of tenure? Always........... Sometimes.......... Never...........

9. Does your institution have procedures under which a faculty member whose contract was not renewed or who was denied tenure may appeal? Yes.......... No..........

   a. If yes, how often have any of these procedures been used since September 1969?   ....times

10. Is there a recognized faculty bargaining agent on your campus?
                                                    Yes.......... No..........

Weights for the sample institutions were established in accordance with ACE weighting procedures used in earlier surveys. The reporting unit for this survey is the institution. The total population has been stratified into thirty-six cells, each defined by a combination of institutional size, type of control, and selectivity based on achievement-test scores of entering freshmen. Cell weights were established as a ratio of the number of institutions in the sample to the number of institutions in the appropriate cell. Response frequencies from each institution were then weighted by the appropriate cell weight. Differential weighting for subgroups of institutions with tenure systems, contract systems, collective bargaining contracts, and the like, was impossible because the distribution was unknown. Indeed, one of the purposes of this survey was to establish those patterns of distribution. A more detailed explanation of the sampling and weighting procedures can be found in the pamphlet *Faculty Tenure and Contract Systems— Current Practice,* by W. Todd Furniss (ACE Special Report, 27 July 1972).

For convenience, the sample and population breakdown is provided in Table 2. The weighted estimates of percentage distributions of the responses to the survey are presented in three tables. Table 3 shows percentage distributions of responses to those questions applicable to all institutions (questions 1, 8, 9, and 10 on the questionnaire). Table 4 shows percentage distributions of responses to those questions applicable only to institutions with tenure practices (question 2, 3, 4, 5, and 6). Table 5 shows the percentage distributions of responses to the question applicable only to institutions with term appointment or contract systems (question 7). The first part of question 7 is not included in Table 5, since all institutions with contract systems reported

Table 2. Survey on Tenure—Population Distribution

| | Universities | | Four-Year Colleges | | Two-Year Colleges | | All Institutions | | |
	Public	Private	Public	Private	Public	Private	Public	Private	Total
Number of institutions in sample responding	28	31	49	224	49	32	126	287	415
Total population of institutions	119	67	360	963	796	238	1275	1268	2543
Number of faculty as percent of all faculty in 1969[a]	37.3	13.6	17.3	18.5	10.3	2.9	65.0	35.0	100.0

[a] Data on faculty members for 1972 are not available. However, the Office of Education, HEW, estimates that the total size of the faculty increased by 7.5 percent during the period 1969–1972. It is unlikely that this increase will be evenly distributed across the various types of institutions. The percentage of faculty in two-year colleges will probably exhibit the greatest increase.

Table 3. CHARACTERISTICS OF ALL INSTITUTIONS (Percentage Distributions)

	Universities		Four-Year Colleges		Two-Year Colleges		All Institutions		
	Public	Private	Public	Private	Public	Private	Public	Private	Total
Institutions with tenure practices	100.0	100.0	100.0	94.1	68.3	68.2	80.3	89.5	84.9
"Does your institution give formal written reasons to the faculty member concerned for nonrenewal of contracts (probationary or recurring term appointments) or for denial of tenure?"									
All Institutions:									
Never	13.3	19.4	26.9	14.5	14.0	.0	17.5	12.0	14.7
Sometimes	50.8	61.3	34.9	46.9	18.0	58.8	26.0	50.0	38.0
Always	35.9	19.4	38.2	38.5	68.1	41.2	56.6	38.1	47.3
Institutions with tenure practices:									
Never	13.3	19.4	26.9	14.9	17.5	.0	20.3	13.0	16.4
Sometimes	50.8	61.3	34.9	49.9	19.5	53.3	28.7	51.0	40.5
Always	35.9	19.4	38.2	35.2	63.0	46.7	51.0	36.0	43.1
Institutions without tenure practices:									
Never	NA[a]	NA	NA	8.5	6.3	.0	6.3	3.6	5.4

Table 3. Characteristics of All Institutions (Percentage Distributions) (cont.)

	Universities		Four-Year Colleges		Two-Year Colleges		All Institutions		
	Public	Private	Public	Private	Public	Private	Public	Private	Total
Sometimes	NA	NA	NA	.0	14.6	70.5	14.6	40.1	23.5
Always	NA	NA	NA	91.5	79.1	29.5	79.1	56.2	71.1
"Does your institution have procedures under which a faculty member whose contract was not renewed or who was denied tenure may appeal?" (Percent who said "Yes")									
All institutions	86.7	83.9	91.4	81.1	93.1	77.6	92.0	80.6	86.3
Institutions with tenure practices	86.7	83.9	91.4	80.7	93.2	95.2	91.8	83.0	87.1
Institutions without tenure practices	NA[a]	NA	NA	13.6	7.1	60.3	7.1	59.8	18.7
"How many times have the appeals procedures at your institution been used since September 1969?"									
All institutions:									
None	26.1	23.1	33.3	52.8	63.5	82.1	51.0	56.7	53.7
One	18.0	23.1	20.0	24.6	10.5	6.3	14.0	21.2	17.5
Two and three	26.1	19.2	20.3	17.4	19.1	4.2	20.1	15.1	17.7

Four to six	14.4	11.5	7.9	3.7	7.0	7.4	7.5	4.9	6.3
Seven or more	12.6	19.1	18.4	1.3	.0	.0	7.2	3.0	4.7
Did not answer	2.7	3.8	.0	.0	.0	.0	.3	.2	.2
Institutions with tenure practices:									
None	26.1	23.1	33.3	52.7	56.4	81.1	44.9	55.8	50.4
One	18.0	23.1	20.0	23.1	6.8	5.0	12.7	20.1	16.4
Two to three	26.1	19.2	20.3	18.5	25.3	5.0	23.6	16.4	19.9
Four to six	14.4	11.5	7.9	4.2	9.4	8.8	9.5	5.4	7.4
7 or more	12.6	19.1	18.4	1.5	2.2	.0	9.1	2.1	5.5
Did not answer	2.7	3.8	.0	.0	.0	.0	.5	.2	.3
Institutions without tenure practices:									
None	NA[a]	NA	NA	52.9	78.8	87.1	78.8	65.9	75.5
One	NA	NA	NA	47.1	15.7	12.9	15.7	34.1	20.4
2 or more	NA	NA	NA	.0	5.5	.0	5.5	.0	4.1
"Is there a recognized faculty bargaining agent on your campus?"[b]									
All institutions	2.3	.0	11.9	.2	8.7	.0	9.0	.2	4.6
Institutions with tenure practices	2.3	.0	11.9	.2	12.8	.0	11.2	.2	5.3
Institutions without tenure practices	.0	.0	.0	.0	.0	.0	.0	.0	.0

[a] Not applicable, since all universities and public four-year colleges reported that they operated under a tenure system.

[b] Since it was determined that many respondents misinterpreted this question, these data are unreliable. However, they are included here merely to show the responses received. Similar studies have revealed that collective bargaining is in use in about 10 per cent of all instu-tions; cf. *Chronicle of Higher Education*, 1972, *6* (32), 2.

Table 4. CHARACTERISTICS OF INSTITUTIONS WITH TENURE PRACTICES (Percentage Distributions)

	Universities		Four-Year Colleges		Two-Year Colleges		All Institutions		
	Public	Private	Public	Private	Public	Private	Public	Private	Total
Maximum length of probationary period:									
Three years or less	7.8	6.5	5.9	7.2	47.8	22.2	28.7	9.3	18.2
Four years	7.8	.0	12.1	4.5	17.5	10.8	14.4	5.1	9.5
Five years	28.9	9.7	24.4	18.1	15.1	20.4	20.0	18.0	19.0
Six years	11.7	16.1	28.7	20.7	.0	14.4	11.3	19.5	15.7
Seven years or more	43.7	67.7	28.9	49.4	19.5	32.3	25.8	48.0	37.6
Maximum years of prior service accepted as part of probationary period:									
None	32.8	37.9	69.4	40.8	69.7	73.7	65.1	45.4	54.7
One to two	5.6	.0	10.7	6.8	8.8	2.4	9.0	5.7	7.3
Three	40.8	48.3	9.8	35.5	17.2	10.8	17.5	32.5	25.5
Four or more	20.8	13.7	10.0	16.9	4.4	13.2	8.4	16.2	12.5
Typical length of contracts awarded a faculty member during probationary period:									
First contract:									
One year	66.4	64.5	93.5	90.5	98.0	100.0	92.5	90.5	91.5
Two years	18.0	3.2	5.1	6.2	.0	.0	4.0	5.1	4.6
3 years or more	15.6	32.3	1.4	3.3	2.0	.0	3.5	4.4	3.8

Succeeding contracts:									
One year	64.0	61.3	94.9	84.0	96.0	91.6	91.7	83.9	87.5
Two years	18.0	3.2	.0	9.2	2.0	.0	3.3	7.5	5.5
Three years or more	18.0	35.5	5.1	6.9	2.0	8.4	5.0	8.6	6.9
Faculty members considered for tenure in spring 1971 who actually received tenure (percentage):									
None	.0	.0	9.3	12.5	2.4	16.8	4.5	12.4	8.7
One to forty	4.6	12.9	5.7	6.6	.0	5.4	2.6	6.8	4.8
Forty-one to seventy	11.0	9.7	11.7	16.9	6.8	2.4	9.0	14.6	11.9
Seventy-one to eighty	10.2	19.4	9.8	10.6	13.5	10.8	11.8	11.1	11.4
Eighty-one to ninety	11.7	16.1	18.5	4.1	4.0	2.4	10.0	4.3	7.0
Ninety-one to ninety-nine	18.0	9.7	7.3	.9	14.8	.0	12.6	1.2	6.5
One-hundred	14.8	9.7	32.3	41.0	54.2	62.3	41.8	42.4	42.1
Did not answer	29.7	22.6	5.3	7.5	4.4	.0	7.8	7.2	7.5
Faculty ranking									
Ranked	100.0	100.0	100.0	95.4	47.8	50.9	72.4	89.3	81.4
Unranked	.0	.0	.0	4.6	52.2	49.1	27.6	10.7	18.6
"If your faculty is ranked, in what ranks may tenure be held?":									
Professor	100.0	100.0	100.0	100.0	100.0	100.0	100.0	100.0	100.0
Associate professor	100.0	100.0	100.0	100.0	100.0	100.0	100.0	100.0	100.0
Assistant professor	69.5	58.1	89.8	83.7	100.0	78.8	89.9	81.8	85.2
Instructor	43.0	19.4	41.8	22.7	50.0	52.9	44.9	25.0	33.3
Other	7.8	.0	12.2	1.0	22.5	.0	15.0	.9	6.8

Table 4. Characteristics of Institutions with Tenure Practices (Percentage Distributions) (cont.)

	Universities		Four-Year Colleges		Two-Year Colleges		All Institutions		
	Public	Private	Public	Private	Public	Private	Public	Private	Total
Percentage of current full-time faculty with tenure:									
Thirty or less	7.0	3.2	16.6	17.3	35.0	30.6	25.3	18.5	21.6
Thirty-one to forty	13.3	.0	17.2	14.6	6.8	29.9	11.2	16.0	13.7
Forty-one to fifty	28.9	32.3	23.0	28.1	2.0	13.8	12.6	26.3	19.9
Fifty-one to sixty	25.0	38.7	16.1	17.2	21.5	7.8	20.1	17.0	18.4
Sixty-one to seventy	15.6	19.4	23.3	12.6	6.4	2.4	13.4	11.5	12.4
Seventy-one or more	5.5	3.2	3.8	7.3	28.2	15.6	17.0	8.2	12.3
Did not answer	4.7	3.2	.0	3.0	.0	.0	.6	2.6	1.6
"Does your institution limit the percent of tenured faculty?":									
Yes	5.5	6.5	7.5	9.5	.0	2.4	3.3	8.3	5.9
No	94.5	93.5	92.5	90.5	100.0	97.6	96.7	91.7	94.1
"Is the tenure system currently under review for change on your campus?":									
Yes	48.4	41.9	36.6	54.1	28.6	40.1	33.8	51.5	43.2
No	51.6	58.1	63.4	45.9	71.4	59.9	66.2	48.5	56.8

Table 5. CHARACTERISTICS OF INSTITUTIONS WITH TERM-APPOINTMENT (CONTRACT) SYSTEMS (Percentage Distribution)

	Four-Year Colleges	Two-Year Colleges		All Institutions		
	Private	Public	Private	Public	Private	Total
"What percentage of those faculty whose contracts expired in 1971 were renewed?":						
Forty or less	.0	.0	5.1	.0	2.9	1.0
Forty-one to eighty	.0	.0	17.9	.0	10.2	3.6
Eighty-one to ninety	8.5	9.4	6.4	9.4	7.3	8.7
Ninety-one to ninety-nine	25.4	83.5	34.6	83.5	30.7	65.0
One hundred	66.1	7.1	35.9	7.1	48.9	21.7
"Is your institution planning to establish a tenure system?":						
Yes	28.8	14.6	.0	14.6	12.4	13.8
No	71.2	85.4	100.0	85.4	87.6	86.2

Note: All universities and public four-year colleges reported that they operate under a tenure system.

that the typical length of the initial contract was for one year, while succeeding contracts were for one year in all two-year colleges and in 71 percent of all four-year colleges. Finally, all nonrespondents are listed as "Did Not Answer" in the appropriate table.

VII

Faculty Attitudes and Tenure

In 1969, the Carnegie Commission on Higher Education, in conjunction with the American Council on Education and the Survey Research Center at the University of California, Berkeley, initiated a broad series of surveys of students, faculty, and administrators in institutions of higher learning in order to provide normative data for research purposes. In one of these surveys, a twelve-page questionnaire was mailed to a national sample of regular faculty at 303 colleges and universities in the United States. Usable returns were received from more than sixty thousand faculty members, and weights were developed so that the resulting data could be generalized to the total population.[1]

[1] A complete description of weighting procedures and sampling design can be found in A. E. Bayer, *College and University Faculty: A Statistical Description,* (Washington, D.C.: American Council on Education, 1970), pp. 3–6. Prepared by the staff of the Commission on Academic Tenure.

227

In December 1971, the Commission on Academic Tenure developed a set of hypotheses concerning faculty attitudes and characteristics which theoretically could be tested on the basis of the data from this faculty survey. Accordingly, the commission requested the assistance of the Office of Research of the American Council on Education to develop cross-tabulations of the data. First, a series of questions dealing with tenure, institutional governance, and faculty goals and interests were selected from the original questionnaire as the basis for the study. Since the purpose of the study was to describe differences among faculty members with regard to the selected questions, the weighted responses were distributed into various categories. The first category represents the broad range of institutional types: universities, four-year colleges, and two-year colleges. These institutions were then defined by their type of control—public or private. Then, because it was desirable to differentiate further among universities and four-year colleges, these institutions were delimited by their degree of selectivity based on the achievement-test scores of their entering freshmen; those institutions with entering freshmen averaging higher than 500 on achievement-test scores were placed in the high selective category, while those with entering freshmen averaging below 500 were placed in the low selective category. Next, the weighted responses were distributed among relative age brackets according to the respondent's age: 35 and under, 36 to 50, and 51 and over. Finally, the responses were distributed according to whether or not the respondent held tenure.

Weighted estimates of percentage distributions of college and university faculty on the selected items are shown in Tables 6, 7, and 8. Table 6 portrays the weighted percentage distributions of faculty members by type of institution and according to tenure status, age, and rank. Thus, this table defines the population and serves to qualify the responses in succeeding data. Table 7 and 8 show the weighted percentage distributions of faculty by institutional type, control, and selectivity, and by faculty age and tenure status on the items selected from the questionnaire. In Table 7, the items shown are reprinted verbatim from the questionnaire. Each respondent was given four possible choices for answering: strongly agree, agree with reservations, disagree with reservations, and strongly disagree. For convenience, these answers were collapsed into two possibilities, agree or disagree; and the percentage distributions of faculty who agree are shown. In Table 8, the items are again verbatim. However, each respondent was asked to rate personal and institutional goals on the basis of first, second, and third choices. For the sake of brevity, only the percentage distributions of the first choice are shown.

On each item, a small number of respondents either skipped the question or gave an unreadable response. These unusable responses have been omitted, and the computations of percentage distributions is based only on readable responses. Finally, the tenure status of faculty members in two-year colleges should be qualified. Since some two-year colleges (approximately 30 percent) do not have tenure systems at all, the item related to tenure status is irrelevant in these institutions. Thus, some faculty in these institutions may have responded to this item as nontenured when, in fact, the item is not applicable.

In their attitudes toward themselves, their colleagues, their institutions, and their profession, tenured and nontenured faculty display significant differences; but study of the tables suggests that differences apparently associated with age or type of institution are often as important as those associated with tenure.

In general, the tenured faculty member, regardless of age, is more likely than the nontenured to think that the undergraduate curriculum has suffered from faculty specialization, that the administration in his institution has taken a clear stand in support of academic freedom, that respect for the academic profession has declined over the past twenty years, and that departmental decisions on other than personnel questions are normally made by vote of the entire department, including junior members.

On the other hand, the nontenured faculty member is more likely to think that he has no opportunity to influence the politics of his department or of the institution, that the administration of his department is very or somewhat autocratic, that junior faculty members have too little say in the running of departments (although most faculty, including nontenured, agree that departmental decisions on other than personnel matters are normally taken by vote of all members, including the junior members), and that a small group of senior professors has disproportionate power in departmental decision making.

On a number of topics of crucial importance in the operation of tenure policies and in any plan for their improvement, the tenured and nontenured faculty members are in substantial agreement:

1. In response to the statement "Teaching effectiveness, not publications, should be the primary criterion for promotion of faculty,"

nearly 80 percent of all faculty agree strongly or agreed with reservations. The proportion is highest, as might be expected, in the two-year colleges, where it approaches 100 percent for both tenured and nontenured faculty of all ages. It is lowest, also as one would expect, in the most selective universities, public and private. But it is significant that in these schools it is the younger tenured faculty who agree least often; the senior tenured faculty are far more likely to rate teaching effectiveness over publications.

2. With the statement "Faculty promotion should be based in part on formal student evaluations of their teachers," a clear majority of all faculty—58.5 percent—also agree. Here there is very little difference in attitude among faculty in different types of institutions, but the younger faculty are generally more receptive to student evaluation as a formal part of the promotion process than are their older colleagues, and the nontenured are substantially more favorable to student evaluation of teaching than the tenured faculty, in institutions of all types.

3. Most of those who believe that promotion should be based in part on student evaluation of teaching evidently envisage an arrangement under which those evaluations would be considered by faculty promotion committees rather than an arrangement in which students would be formally included in the promotion process. When asked what role undergraduate students should play in faculty appointments and promotion, .3 percent favor control by students, 5.7 percent favor giving them voting power, 15 percent advocate formal consultation, 25 percent favor informal consultation, and more than half—54 percent—think that students should have little or no role. Faculty members show somewhat greater willingness to give graduate students voting power (10 percent) or to consult them informally (20.5 percent) or formally (26 percent), but 43 percent thought they too should have little or no role. In general, the 21 percent who favor control, voting power, or formal consultation with students in the appointment and promotion process are more likely to be the younger nontenured faculty.

4. If such a large majority of faculty members believe that publication should take second place to teaching effectiveness in promotion decisions, how do they view the criteria actually being used? Faculty were asked to react to the statement that "In my department

it is very difficult for a man to achieve tenure if he does not publish."
In view of the widespread belief that "publish or perish" is the rule in
American higher education, it is perhaps surprising that less than half
of all faculty members agree, either strongly or with reservations; 56
percent disagree. Even in universities, whose commitment to scholarship and research has traditionally seemed to necessitate publication as
a condition of tenure status, 36 percent of the faculty do not believe
that publication is necessary for tenure in their departments. But the
nontenured university faculty, and especially the younger ones, are on
the whole more likely than those who have already achieved tenure
to believe that publication is crucial to promotion. In four-year public
colleges only a third of the faculty members believe that publication is
essential for tenure; in private colleges, only 28 percent. Here too, those
who are younger and who do not have tenure are most likely to agree.
In two-year colleges less than 10 percent believe that publication is a
prerequisite to tenure. "Publish or perish," then, is apparently as much
myth as reality, in the judgment of faculty members themselves. Nonetheless, it is striking that 78 percent of faculty members believe that
teaching effectiveness and not publication should be the primary
criterion for promotion, while 44 percent say that tenure is in fact
very difficult to achieve for the person who does not publish. Clearly,
the tenure system is not now operating to reflect in personnel decisions
the priorities generally espoused by the faculty. This identifies one
major objective of any reform of the tenure system.

The prospects for such reform are enhanced by the fact that
faculties themselves are aware of the discrepancy between what they
believe should be done and what is done. Since faculties usually make
the essential determinations about promotion, they can, if they will,
bring their own practices into conformity with their declared priorities.
And there is further encouragement in the fact that among those with
tenure it is the senior members, whose influence is often of greatest
weight in personnel decisions, who believe most strongly that teaching
effectiveness should be the primary criterion for promotion.

The following tables, then, provide a background for the
discussion in the text. A complete copy of the questionnaire is appended
to *College and University Faculty: A Statistical Description,* cited
earlier.

Table 6. CHARACTERISTICS OF FACULTY MEMBERS BY SELECTIVITY,

	Universities				Four-Year Colleges
	Public		Private		Public
	High (Selectivity)	Low (Selectivity)	High (Selectivity)	Low (Selectivity)	High (Selectivity)
Proportionate distribution of faculty members (total across = 100.0)	20.5	16.8	12.6	1.0	11.0
Tenure Status:					
Tenure	53.3	52.6	48.7	35.2	49.9
Nontenure	46.7	47.4	51.3	64.8	50.1
Total	100.0	100.0	100.0	100.0	100.0
Age of Faculty:					
Thirty-five and under	31.7	33.8	28.5	37.1	35.2
Thirty-six to fifty	45.6	43.3	46.0	35.7	45.3
Fifty-one and over	22.7	22.9	25.5	27.2	19.5
Total	100.0	100.0	100.0	100.0	100.0
Age and Tenure Status:					
Thirty-five and under					
Tenure	5.0	6.4	3.0	4.5	5.7
Nontenure	26.7	27.4	25.5	32.6	29.5
Thirty-six to fifty					
Tenure	28.6	26.9	25.3	13.7	27.8
Nontenure	17.0	16.4	20.7	22.0	17.5
Fifty-one and over					
Tenure	19.6	19.3	20.3	17.1	16.4
Nontenure	3.1	3.6	5.2	10.1	3.1
Total	100.0	100.0	100.0	100.0	100.0

CONTROL, AND TYPE OF INSTITUTION (Percentage Distributions)

Four-Year Colleges			Two-Year Colleges		All Institutions	
Public	Private		Public	Private		
Low (Selectivity)	High (Selectivity)	Low (Selectivity)			High (Selectivity)	Low (Selectivity)
6.3	11.9	6.6	10.3	2.9	56.1	43.9
43.8	43.9	43.2	50.9	32.5	49.7	48.9
56.2	56.1	56.8	49.1	67.5	50.3	51.1
100.0	100.0	100.0	100.0	100.0	100.0	100.0
35.4	31.6	33.5	36.0	32.6	31.6	34.5
37.6	43.0	39.2	44.2	34.4	45.1	41.3
27.0	25.4	27.3	19.8	33.0	23.3	24.2
100.0	100.0	100.0	100.0	100.0	100.0	100.0
4.7	3.6	5.8	9.6	5.6	4.4	6.7
30.7	28.0	27.7	26.4	27.0	27.2	27.8
17.3	21.6	18.4	26.9	14.2	26.3	23.2
20.3	21.4	20.8	17.3	20.2	18.8	18.1
21.8	18.7	19.0	14.4	12.7	19.0	18.0
5.2	6.7	8.3	5.4	20.3	4.3	6.2
100.0	100.0	100.0	100.0	100.0	100.0	100.0

Table 6. CHARACTERISTICS OF FACULTY MEMBERS BY SELECTIVITY,

	Universities				Four-Year Colleges
	Public		Private		Public
	High (Selectivity)	Low (Selectivity)	High (Selectivity)	Low (Selectivity)	High (Selectivity)
Rank of Faculty:					
Professor	28.0	24.7	29.1	18.7	20.5
Associate professor	23.0	22.1	22.4	20.1	24.6
Assistant professor	30.9	30.1	26.7	23.2	33.5
Instructor	12.4	19.3	13.8	25.8	13.4
Lecturer	2.7	2.0	4.5	11.2	6.3
No ranks designated	.4	.2	.4	.0	.2
Other	2.6	1.6	3.1	1.0	1.5
Total	100.0	100.0	100.0	100.0	100.0
Rank and Tenure Status:					
Professor					
Tenure	26.6	22.8	27.1	14.7	18.9
Nontenure	1.4	1.9	2.0	4.0	1.6
Associate Professor					
Tenure	18.7	17.2	15.4	14.2	18.9
Nontenure	4.3	4.9	7.0	5.9	5.7
Assistant Professor					
Tenure	4.7	8.5	3.0	2.5	8.0
Nontenure	26.2	21.6	23.7	20.7	25.5
Instructor					
Tenure	1.2	2.6	1.0	3.1	1.6
Nontenure	11.2	16.7	12.8	22.7	11.8
Lecturer, No Ranks, Other					
Tenure	1.2	.8	.8	.0	1.1
Nontenure	4.5	3.0	7.2	12.2	6.9
Total	100.0	100.0	100.0	100.0	100.0

Four-Year Colleges			Two-Year Colleges		All Institutions	
Public	Private		Public	Private		
Low (Selectivity)	High (Selectivity)	Low (Selectivity)			High (Selectivity)	Low (Selectivity)
15.9	21.1	19.2	5.5	8.8	25.3	16.9
18.7	22.4	19.6	10.9	10.9	23.0	17.8
27.2	32.5	29.0	16.5	12.7	30.8	25.0
25.0	17.9	23.4	40.0	42.2	14.1	27.3
10.6	2.9	2.8	.3	3.1	3.9	3.2
.8	1.3	4.5	22.7	14.4	.5	7.1
1.8	1.9	1.5	4.1	7.9	2.4	2.7
100.0	100.0	100.0	100.0	100.0	100.0	100.0
13.5	18.6	15.0	4.8	4.6	23.5	14.7
2.4	2.5	4.2	.7	4.2	1.8	2.2
12.6	14.8	12.4	7.8	6.2	17.1	12.9
6.1	7.6	7.2	3.1	4.7	5.9	4.9
11.9	14.3	8.4	5.7	6.2	5.4	8.2
15.3	18.2	20.6	10.8	6.5	25.4	16.8
4.1	2.9	3.2	15.3	7.7	1.2	6.3
20.9	15.0	20.2	24.7	34.5	12.9	21.0
.9	1.5	4.0	17.0	7.2	1.2	5.1
12.3	4.6	4.8	10.1	18.2	5.6	7.9
100.0	100.0	100.0	100.0	100.0	100.0	100.0

Table 7. FACULTY ATTITUDES BY AGE AND TENURE; AND SELECTIVITY,

	UNIVERSITIES											
	PUBLIC											
	High (Selectivity)						Total	Low (Selectivity)				
	Tenure			Nontenure				Tenure			Nontenure		
	—35	36–50	51+	—35	36–50	51+		—35	36–50	51+	—35	36–50	51+
PER CENT OF FACULTY WHO AGREE STRONGLY OR WITH RESERVATIONS WITH THE FOLLOWING STATEMENTS:													
I have no opportunity to influence the politics of my department.	4.8	4.3	5.7	11.5	10.0	12.3	8.5	7.9	5.6	6.3	13.5	11.4	18.0
I have no opportunity to influence the politics of this institution.	37.7	26.3	27.4	55.1	45.6	50.8	40.1	50.5	36.5	29.5	61.3	50.5	49.5
I am in frequent communication with people in my own academic specialty in other institutions.	72.0	76.5	72.2	56.9	61.2	54.9	66.4	63.4	70.6	70.2	52.4	55.6	43.2
The undergraduate curriculum has suffered from faculty specialization.	49.3	53.9	61.0	47.3	55.2	57.2	53.6	49.0	53.9	58.0	47.7	53.6	67.4
The administration of my department is very or somewhat autocratic.	29.5	29.5	26.2	40.5	37.1	30.8	33.3	36.9	36.7	29.8	45.7	38.9	32.5
Junior faculty members have too little say in the running of my department.	30.9	25.0	22.4	44.9	39.8	34.6	33.7	35.1	27.1	23.2	46.6	40.9	35.2
A small group of senior professors has disproportionate power in decision making in this institution.	48.1	37.7	33.5	56.6	51.0	48.6	45.4	39.8	34.7	27.8	56.4	47.1	39.8
The administration here has taken a clear stand in support of academic freedom.	78.8	84.1	89.2	68.9	77.9	79.1	79.2	56.9	61.1	74.7	45.6	57.5	75.2
Respect for the academic profession has declined over the past 20 years.	50.5	58.0	66.6	52.9	60.1	65.9	58.5	59.3	59.5	64.8	53.5	59.8	73.2
My field is too research oriented.	22.0	20.8	25.0	27.6	24.2	23.6	24.2	24.9	23.4	22.1	28.4	22.2	30.2
Many of the highest paid university professors get where they are by being "operators" rather than by their scholarly or scientific contributions.	49.0	46.8	46.1	54.4	49.3	44.4	49.3	51.2	52.0	44.4	54.3	46.4	48.9
Teaching effectiveness, not publications, should be the primary criterion for promotion of faculty.	50.0	55.3	70.1	64.6	72.6	86.2	64.5	61.0	67.4	76.9	73.6	79.4	93.6
Faculty promotions should be based in part on formal student evaluation of their teachers.	60.1	57.0	53.0	64.3	60.5	57.5	59.2	52.7	55.2	51.2	61.6	58.7	51.7
In my department it is very difficult for a man to achieve tenure if he does not publish.	68.7	68.8	66.5	71.6	68.2	65.6	69.2	46.5	47.8	43.9	60.5	50.5	48.2
Decisions in my department other than personnel matters are normally made by the vote of the whole department including junior members.	66.4	66.9	70.2	58.6	57.6	58.0	63.0	62.8	59.7	65.8	51.1	53.3	53.3

CONTROL, AND TYPE OF INSTITUTION (Percentage Distribution)

		UNIVERSITIES															Total
Total					PRIVATE											Total	
Total		High (Selectivity)						Total	Low (Selectivity)						Total		
		Tenure			Nontenure				Tenure			Nontenure					
		—35	36–50	51+	—35	36–50	51+		—35	36–50	51+	—35	36–50	51+			
10.2	9.3	4.6	5.3	6.1	13.2	14.7	13.0	10.8	33.3	9.6	6.1	17.6	14.0	2.9	14.1	11.1	9.7
46.7	43.1	33.4	26.3	22.9	54.0	51.0	50.2	40.8	85.4	54.1	30.1	72.0	65.3	36.2	59.5	42.1	42.8
61.2	64.1	76.1	76.8	73.2	56.2	59.8	62.7	65.9	72.7	76.0	86.0	47.4	55.5	55.9	60.6	65.6	64.5
53.3	53.5	43.2	47.3	57.6	48.8	55.8	58.0	52.0	40.9	54.2	42.0	54.5	48.4	49.5	51.0	51.9	53.1
37.9	35.3	33.5	31.7	25.8	44.3	45.3	33.5	36.9	56.3	44.8	35.6	60.7	39.0	19.1	44.4	37.4	35.9
35.1	34.3	37.7	32.4	26.8	49.7	47.2	43.1	40.0	77.1	42.5	24.9	68.0	54.8	51.5	52.2	40.9	36.1
42.0	43.9	45.5	41.1	35.6	59.0	56.3	49.0	48.4	79.2	66.4	58.6	81.1	72.5	59.8	70.4	49.9	45.5
58.8	70.0	87.8	88.3	92.7	78.6	80.7	85.1	84.7	47.9	52.4	82.9	32.8	45.7	75.2	53.3	82.5	73.3
59.4	58.9	41.7	52.0	63.1	48.7	58.8	69.9	56.0	85.4	81.5	80.8	66.4	72.2	68.0	73.5	57.2	58.5
24.7	21.1	18.8	18.0	21.5	24.2	19.7	18.3	21.0	17.8	22.8	12.4	22.2	33.3	19.4	22.8	24.4	23.6
50.4	49.8	47.7	43.9	41.5	52.2	49.3	44.3	46.8	83.3	58.9	36.0	69.4	52.3	48.0	57.7	47.5	49.2
73.9	68.7	44.2	48.1	63.6	63.4	73.5	86.0	62.9	77.1	79.5	81.9	82.2	87.4	90.5	84.9	64.5	67.6
56.5	58.0	56.5	49.8	42.1	64.5	60.1	55.7	55.0	45.8	54.1	55.9	75.8	62.3	75.5	64.2	55.7	57.4
51.4	61.2	67.9	70.9	68.3	77.8	73.8	61.3	72.3	82.5	63.7	71.1	75.6	63.3	73.3	66.8	71.9	64.0
57.3	60.5	60.9	58.6	62.7	50.5	42.0	46.8	52.6	52.1	63.6	74.1	70.8	65.7	70.5	68.3	53.8	58.7

Table 7 (cont'd). FACULTY ATTITUDES BY AGE AND TENURE; AND

FOUR-YEAR COLLEGES

PUBLIC												
High (Selectivity)						Total	Low (Selectivity)					
Tenure			Nontenure				Tenure			Nontenure		
—35	36–50	51+	—35	36–50	51+		—35	36–50	51+	—35	36–50	51+

PER CENT OF FACULTY WHO AGREE STRONGLY OR WITH RESERVATIONS WITH THE FOLLOWING STATEMENTS:

Statement	—35	36–50	51+	—35	36–50	51+	Total	—35	36–50	51+	—35	36–50	51+
I have no opportunity to influence the politics of my department.	5.8	4.0	5.2	9.9	10.2	6.8	8.2	8.2	5.6	5.1	9.7	13.4	14.5
I have no opportunity to influence the politics of this institution.	37.6	19.5	24.7	48.1	40.8	42.6	35.8	33.3	28.0	22.9	53.2	46.8	45.7
I am in frequent communication with people in my own academic specialty in other institutions.	53.5	58.1	56.7	46.0	51.9	56.8	52.3	54.4	61.8	65.0	44.7	56.1	46.2
The undergraduate curriculum has suffered from faculty specialization.	40.8	48.7	56.6	44.7	46.6	49.8	47.9	36.5	50.9	49.6	44.3	60.5	50.5
The administration of my department is very or somewhat autocratic.	34.9	25.4	24.5	38.5	36.3	20.3	31.2	33.9	23.1	20.9	38.1	33.3	23.4
Junior faculty members have too little say in the running of my department.	32.8	23.6	24.3	45.3	40.5	28.0	34.2	39.7	28.7	29.0	50.8	47.5	49.9
A small group of senior professors has disproportionate power in decision making in this institution.	46.2	34.6	33.3	56.4	52.9	35.2	44.7	51.0	41.0	42.5	62.5	58.5	60.8
The administration here has taken a clear stand in support of academic freedom.	73.6	80.2	85.4	65.3	70.6	86.0	74.7	68.9	74.7	85.9	66.2	72.7	73.7
Respect for the academic profession has declined over the past 20 years.	59.1	63.2	72.8	55.5	61.9	53.6	61.8	70.5	64.1	78.4	57.4	66.8	67.6
My field is too research oriented.	31.4	26.9	27.6	26.5	28.0	23.2	27.1	19.6	23.7	24.1	30.1	25.0	12.5
Many of the highest paid university professors get where they are by being "operators" rather than by their scholarly or scientific contributions.	55.2	47.9	47.2	51.6	50.6	39.4	49.8	56.0	49.0	56.6	56.0	57.6	62.5
Teaching effectiveness, not publications, should be the primary criterion for promotion of faculty.	72.3	70.9	83.9	78.2	78.6	89.6	77.6	93.0	85.1	91.4	91.0	94.4	96.1
Faculty promotions should be based in part on formal student evaluation of their teachers.	56.6	59.6	54.6	63.0	60.7	63.6	59.1	51.4	52.1	51.6	61.7	60.0	62.6
In my department it is very difficult for a man to achieve tenure if he does not publish.	32.0	33.6	39.6	40.1	38.1	30.3	37.1	8.3	13.3	23.3	32.0	43.7	31.1
Decisions in my department other than personnel matters are normally made by the vote of the whole department including junior members.	69.3	78.9	78.1	62.1	69.0	67.8	70.3	62.4	65.6	75.2	62.7	53.2	59.9

	FOUR-YEAR COLLEGES																Total
Total	PRIVATE																Total
Total	Total	High (Selectivity)							Total	Low (Selectivity)							Total
		Total	Tenure			Nontenure			Total	Total	Tenure			Nontenure			Total
			—35	36–50	51+	—35	36–50	51+			—35	36–50	51+	—35	36–50	51+	
9.6	8.7	4.0	1.9	2.9	6.5	9.0	11.2	6.3	.0	2.5	4.7	4.7	6.5	5.2	5.0	5.8	7.2
40.2	37.4	19.4	13.0	15.6	33.2	30.5	34.0	26.1	10.2	16.8	14.6	31.4	27.4	20.2	23.8	26.6	32.0
54.6	53.1	54.1	59.3	54.7	47.0	48.4	43.2	50.9	44.3	54.6	56.4	44.1	52.6	53.5	50.3	50.7	51.9
49.3	48.4	53.1	53.2	56.7	49.7	53.8	58.7	53.1	50.8	56.7	58.4	48.9	50.0	52.0	52.5	52.9	50.7
32.9	31.8	24.7	21.2	17.8	28.3	30.4	24.4	24.8	19.1	18.8	20.5	28.5	23.2	24.1	23.2	24.3	27.9
40.6	36.5	24.7	18.8	13.0	33.0	28.8	23.7	24.8	21.0	18.4	18.4	29.3	28.0	21.1	24.5	24.7	30.4
52.6	47.6	35.0	27.6	21.7	48.2	41.9	31.2	35.7	41.5	31.9	33.1	50.7	38.4	35.6	39.5	37.0	42.1
72.6	73.9	81.2	84.3	89.4	73.5	72.4	86.3	79.6	80.6	80.9	85.1	65.7	78.2	78.0	76.5	78.5	76.3
66.1	63.4	62.4	58.3	64.6	51.3	60.2	66.7	58.7	58.4	64.3	69.7	55.0	61.8	65.1	62.8	60.1	61.7
24.9	26.3	30.4	26.6	26.6	33.1	26.5	17.9	27.6	26.5	27.7	23.1	30.8	23.6	19.3	26.2	27.1	26.7
55.5	51.8	47.1	42.4	39.6	44.2	48.6	41.5	43.8	38.2	45.0	46.4	48.8	49.8	52.1	47.4	45.1	48.4
91.0	82.5	85.9	84.7	89.9	86.2	88.4	92.8	87.5	96.6	95.1	96.6	95.1	92.7	97.2	95.0	90.1	86.4
57.1	58.3	63.4	59.6	48.2	65.9	61.5	54.2	59.3	60.7	59.5	57.9	68.5	64.8	62.6	63.0	60.6	59.5
27.2	33.5	19.2	22.6	21.5	30.2	28.7	29.5	26.7	6.0	9.8	12.1	16.1	14.4	20.0	13.7	22.1	27.7
63.2	67.7	70.6	79.3	82.0	68.2	61.9	62.0	70.4	78.2	73.5	78.2	68.6	69.9	67.4	71.4	70.8	69.3

Table 7 (cont'd). FACULTY ATTITUDES BY AGE AND TENURE; AND (Percentage

TWO-YEAR COLLEGES

	PUBLIC						Total	PRIVATE					
	Tenure			Nontenure				Tenure			Nontenure		
	—35	36–50	51+	—35	36–50	51+		—35	36–50	51+	—35	36–50	51+

PER CENT OF FACULTY WHO AGREE STRONGLY OR WITH RESERVATIONS WITH THE FOLLOWING STATEMENTS:

Statement	—35	36–50	51+	—35	36–50	51+	Total	—35	36–50	51+	—35	36–50	51+
I have no opportunity to influence the politics of my department.	5.2	3.1	3.4	6.2	7.4	5.9	5.4	14.8	.8	6.5	6.2	9.4	3.8
I have no opportunity to influence the politics of this institution.	13.4	14.9	16.0	30.0	29.6	31.5	23.3	48.4	7.4	11.8	28.6	33.4	28.0
I am in frequent communication with people in my own academic specialty in other institutions.	44.4	57.5	53.6	47.1	49.0	45.1	51.1	66.9	39.6	67.5	27.7	32.2	46.4
The undergraduate curriculum has suffered from faculty specialization.	53.8	52.1	49.3	43.5	47.8	50.4	48.7	67.2	57.4	42.3	57.9	49.4	40.6
The administration of my department is very or somewhat autocratic.	30.5	19.4	17.6	29.0	23.2	32.5	24.0	25.6	2.5	12.9	28.0	25.1	24.6
Junior faculty members have too little to say in running of my department.	25.7	20.4	18.8	31.8	33.0	25.0	26.4	51.4	26.2	28.6	25.2	30.2	16.1
A small group of senior professors has disproportionate power in decision making in this institution.	29.7	22.6	20.6	36.3	34.4	38.4	29.6	34.0	25.7	33.0	29.2	36.1	29.3
The administration here has taken a clear stand in support of academic freedom.	68.9	72.8	78.1	63.1	68.4	76.0	70.4	55.8	94.4	82.0	67.8	69.1	63.8
Respect for the academic profession has declined over the past 20 years.	60.0	66.0	75.4	57.6	70.2	55.3	64.5	40.3	79.5	72.1	74.7	62.0	77.1
My field is too research oriented.	29.7	22.5	18.5	30.6	20.7	23.5	24.3	23.7	16.6	27.6	36.2	25.8	7.6
Many of the highest paid university professors get where they are by being "operators" rather than by their scholarly or scientific contributions.	39.9	41.7	44.8	54.0	52.0	36.1	47.0	51.4	38.4	20.5	47.1	40.0	42.9
Teaching effectiveness, not publications, should be the primary criterion for promotion of faculty.	95.3	95.3	96.3	97.0	98.2	97.4	96.2	100.0	95.4	100.0	98.9	98.9	98.5
Faculty promotions should be based in part on formal student evaluation of their teachers.	67.3	55.0	54.7	69.7	65.6	63.9	62.3	43.5	51.7	58.0	57.7	55.8	47.8
In my department it is very difficult for a man to achieve tenure if he does not publish.	2.5	2.7	2.9	9.2	4.9	15.3	5.8	25.8	10.2	16.6	10.7	11.1	26.9
Decisions in my department other than personnel matters are normally made by the vote of the whole department including junior members.	75.6	79.6	81.2	65.0	67.2	66.3	72.2	80.6	84.1	84.8	67.6	57.3	83.0

SELECTIVITY, CONTROL, AND TYPE OF INSTITUTION
Distributions)

Total	ALL INSTITUTIONS															Total
Total	Total	High (Selectivity)						Total	Low (Selectivity)						Total	Total
		Tenure			Nontenure				Tenure			Nontenure				
		—35	36–50	51+	—35	36–50	51+		—35	36–50	51+	—35	36–50	51+		
6.3	5.6	4.9	4.0	5.1	10.4	10.9	11.4	8.5	6.7	4.4	5.3	9.6	9.9	9.0	8.0	8.3
25.1	23.7	33.9	22.6	23.4	48.6	42.4	44.0	36.4	31.5	26.4	22.6	46.7	40.6	34.4	35.7	36.1
39.8	48.6	65.0	69.8	66.2	52.3	56.1	53.4	60.3	53.9	63.0	64.2	47.1	52.1	47.1	54.8	57.9
51.8	49.4	46.9	51.3	58.5	47.6	53.4	56.9	52.0	50.4	53.6	54.1	47.2	52.4	53.0	51.4	51.8
20.8	23.3	30.4	27.6	24.1	38.2	37.3	28.0	31.9	31.8	27.1	23.7	39.0	30.9	27.6	30.7	31.4
25.4	26.2	31.4	25.3	21.9	43.4	39.1	32.5	33.3	32.1	24.6	23.0	40.6	37.6	28.7	32.0	32.8
31.7	30.1	44.9	36.0	31.5	55.2	50.4	41.2	43.8	38.0	31.8	30.7	50.9	44.5	39.6	40.2	42.3
72.8	71.0	79.3	84.2	89.4	71.2	75.9	84.0	79.6	65.0	69.3	79.4	56.8	66.4	73.5	66.9	74.0
71.2	66.0	53.3	57.8	66.4	52.2	60.1	65.6	58.6	59.8	63.4	70.5	56.9	64.0	67.7	63.2	60.6
22.9	24.0	25.2	22.5	24.9	27.8	24.3	20.3	24.8	26.1	23.4	22.0	29.9	23.1	19.7	24.7	24.7
39.2	45.4	50.0	45.6	43.8	51.1	49.4	42.8	47.7	46.8	47.6	45.8	53.6	49.7	47.2	49.4	48.4
98.4	96.7	60.8	62.1	74.9	71.9	77.7	88.8	71.6	82.8	81.4	87.2	86.6	89.9	96.3	86.6	78.1
53.9	60.4	59.2	56.4	49.7	64.4	60.7	56.8	58.2	57.9	55.1	53.4	64.5	61.3	57.6	58.9	58.5
16.3	8.1	51.2	54.0	53.2	57.4	54.7	48.0	54.7	21.9	26.3	27.1	35.4	31.1	30.0	29.9	44.0
73.7	72.5	67.0	69.7	72.2	59.7	56.9	57.7	63.7	69.9	68.4	73.2	60.2	59.8	66.4	65.0	64.3

Table 8. Faculty Attitudes, Goals, & Interests by Age and (Percentage

	UNIVERSITIES												
	PUBLIC												
	High (Selectivity)						Total	Low (Selectivity)					
	Tenure			Nontenure				Tenure			Nontenure		
	—35	36–50	51+	—35	36–50	51+		—35	36–50	51+	—35	36–50	51+

PER CENT OF FACULTY WHO AGREE WITH THE FOLLOWING STATEMENTS:

Undergraduates should play the following role in faculty appointments and promotions:

Control	.0	.1	.2	.3	.1	.1	.2	0	.2	.3	.1	.0	.0
Voting Power	4.4	2.9	2.1	7.9	4.7	6.1	4.7	4.1	2.4	2.4	8.1	5.1	.8
Formal Consultation	20.3	13.4	8.8	20.2	16.5	10.7	15.2	14.7	9.8	7.1	16.1	12.8	5.7
Informal Consultation	27.8	26.4	23.5	26.3	27.9	23.8	26.0	16.0	24.3	21.3	24.5	21.0	20.4
Little or No Role	47.5	57.3	65.4	45.4	50.7	59.3	53.9	65.1	63.3	68.9	51.3	61.2	73.1

Graduate students should play the following role in faculty appointments and promotions:

Control	.3	.1	.2	.3	.2	.0	.2	.1	.1	.1	.1	.0	.0
Voting Power	8.1	4.9	3.8	13.1	9.4	10.4	8.3	6.6	4.4	2.9	13.1	8.1	3.0
Formal Consultation	23.3	17.4	12.8	25.8	22.4	14.7	20.0	17.3	14.2	12.8	22.8	18.3	11.5
Informal Consultation	27.8	29.6	28.6	25.2	26.8	24.9	27.4	22.5	28.4	25.8	25.4	23.9	33.6
Little or No Role	40.4	48.0	54.6	35.6	41.2	50.0	44.1	53.6	52.8	58.3	38.5	49.8	51.8

Have you known of a case within the past 2 years in which a man's politics affected his chances of promotion or retention?

I know of a case.	14.0	11.5	7.2	16.5	12.4	7.9	12.2	20.7	16.3	8.5	21.7	14.0	9.4
I've heard of a case.	16.4	14.2	10.1	18.6	16.2	12.8	15.1	15.8	14.6	8.8	17.6	15.3	10.0
I don't know of a case.	65.2	67.0	72.8	61.7	67.5	74.5	66.9	59.3	62.8	71.9	58.3	66.5	66.5
I'm sure it hasn't happened.	4.4	7.2	9.9	3.2	3.9	4.8	5.8	4.1	6.3	10.8	2.4	4.2	14.1

PER CENT OF FACULTY WHO INDICATE FIRST PREFERENCE FOR THE FOLLOWING GOALS AND INTERESTS:

What I feel is important:

Provide undergraduates with a broad liberal education.	21.4	21.6	30.4	32.9	28.7	34.3	28.4	21.9	28.7	37.0	34.2	33.9	46.7
Prepare undergraduates for their chosen occupation.	17.8	19.2	23.2	18.8	20.1	23.1	19.9	25.6	25.5	23.3	23.5	23.3	19.5
Train graduate or professional students.	23.6	25.5	20.4	16.5	22.7	17.2	21.1	19.6	23.1	16.6	15.4	18.4	15.0
Engage in research.	25.5	19.0	9.5	20.0	13.2	5.2	16.3	17.6	11.0	5.3	14.6	10.2	2.2
No 1st choice.	11.8	14.7	16.7	11.8	15.3	20.1	14.3	15.4	11.8	17.8	12.3	14.3	16.6

What the institution expects of me:

Provide undergraduates with a broad liberal education.	15.9	15.5	19.2	17.9	16.0	23.3	17.3	17.8	18.9	22.9	18.6	20.9	29.9
Prepare undergraduates for their chosen occupation.	22.2	20.0	18.7	24.4	22.8	23.3	21.5	34.2	29.2	25.1	34.4	31.7	31.9
Train graduate or professional students.	16.1	20.6	17.4	11.8	17.3	16.6	16.6	9.7	16.9	14.4	11.5	15.1	9.0
Engage in research.	33.5	28.6	24.2	32.4	26.7	16.2	28.3	24.0	19.2	14.3	22.3	17.4	5.8
No 1st choice.	12.3	15.3	20.6	13.5	17.2	20.6	16.3	14.3	15.8	23.2	13.2	14.8	23.4

Do your interests lie primarily in teaching or research?

Very heavily in research.	7.2	6.6	4.4	6.7	5.2	4.4	6.0	5.9	6.3	4.1	5.8	5.4	2.2
Both, leaning to research.	44.2	38.1	23.0	33.6	26.7	12.4	31.4	34.8	29.9	16.1	26.3	17.5	9.6
Both, leaning to teaching.	33.6	37.1	40.3	37.0	38.5	32.9	37.5	38.8	42.4	37.9	37.9	37.6	26.0
Very heavily in teaching.	15.0	18.2	32.4	22.7	29.6	50.4	25.1	20.5	21.4	41.9	29.9	39.5	62.3

TENURE; AND SELECTIVITY, CONTROL, AND TYPE OF INSTITUTION Distributions)

UNIVERSITIES — PRIVATE

Total	High Tenure			High Nontenure			Total	Low Tenure			Low Nontenure			Total	Total	Total	Total
	—35	36–50	51+	—35	36–50	51+		—35	36–50	51+	—35	36–50	51+				
.2	.2	.3	.0	.1	.2	.1	.3	.2	.0	.0	.0	.0	.0	.0	.0	.1	.2
4.5	4.6	5.4	3.5	2.2	10.0	7.0	5.1	5.9	.0	4.1	6.2	11.5	13.3	6.7	9.1	6.1	5.0
11.6	13.6	17.0	16.9	10.0	23.5	19.1	10.8	17.3	31.6	16.4	23.0	26.0	12.4	16.3	19.8	17.5	14.6
22.6	24.5	31.5	26.6	24.1	29.3	27.7	25.4	27.0	6.2	23.3	5.1	24.9	10.3	38.8	17.3	26.3	25.0
61.0	57.1	45.7	52.9	63.7	37.0	46.1	58.4	49.6	62.5	56.2	65.7	37.6	63.9	48.1	53.8	49.9	55.2
.1	.2	.3	.1	.1	.5	.2	.0	.3	.0	.0	.0	.0	.0	.0	.0	.2	.2
7.4	7.9	7.5	5.6	4.0	15.2	10.3	8.7	9.2	9.1	6.3	9.0	19.6	15.9	15.2	14.4	9.6	8.3
17.3	18.8	22.6	20.1	12.9	27.6	25.7	16.3	21.8	25.0	24.6	22.5	34.8	11.6	29.3	23.8	21.9	19.6
26.1	26.8	31.2	27.9	28.1	27.1	27.8	26.8	27.9	13.6	24.6	17.4	13.7	17.2	9.8	17.0	27.1	26.9
49.1	46.3	38.3	46.2	54.9	29.3	36.0	48.2	40.9	52.3	44.4	51.1	31.9	55.4	45.7	44.8	41.1	44.9
15.9	13.9	12.8	7.8	4.4	12.6	7.8	3.2	8.2	39.6	19.7	18.1	44.1	28.3	20.4	28.4	9.6	12.7
14.4	14.8	9.8	9.0	6.1	14.3	10.1	6.4	9.8	39.6	17.6	17.5	29.6	12.9	25.5	21.6	10.7	13.7
64.0	65.6	20.1	71.0	74.3	69.0	76.9	81.5	73.3	20.8	62.7	54.8	25.1	57.5	51.0	47.3	71.4	67.1
5.7	5.8	7.3	12.2	15.2	4.2	5.2	8.9	8.7	.0	.0	9.6	1.2	1.3	3.1	2.6	8.3	6.4
33.3	30.6	23.0	20.8	27.0	30.7	23.4	28.8	25.9	6.2	19.6	26.6	39.8	27.4	36.6	30.9	26.3	29.5
23.8	21.7	10.5	10.8	13.1	11.0	11.8	17.3	11.7	39.6	14.0	21.5	13.7	18.4	5.9	16.8	12.1	19.1
18.1	19.7	27.8	30.8	31.8	22.7	30.6	26.0	28.6	14.6	23.8	25.4	20.4	18.9	26.7	20.6	28.0	21.9
10.8	13.9	28.0	23.7	10.1	25.5	18.4	6.0	19.3	.0	7.0	.0	10.0	3.3	3.0	4.9	18.3	15.0
14.0	14.1	10.7	13.8	18.0	10.0	15.8	22.0	14.5	39.6	35.7	26.6	16.1	32.1	27.7	26.8	15.3	14.4
20.4	18.7	24.4	20.7	23.4	22.2	16.2	24.0	21.0	9.1	7.2	23.7	27.8	14.4	35.6	21.9	21.1	19.3
30.7	25.6	9.9	12.1	11.6	14.3	11.8	13.3	12.4	43.2	23.7	23.1	16.7	20.8	21.8	22.3	13.1	22.3
13.7	15.3	19.7	27.6	27.2	19.3	28.2	24.5	25.2	25.0	22.3	19.1	17.4	21.8	15.8	18.7	24.8	17.8
18.8	24.1	32.6	25.0	17.6	32.3	27.1	14.5	25.4	6.8	9.4	5.8	11.7	12.9	6.9	8.7	24.2	24.1
16.4	16.4	13.4	14.5	20.2	11.9	16.8	23.8	16.0	15.9	37.4	28.3	26.5	30.2	19.8	28.4	16.9	16.5
5.6	5.8	10.0	9.1	3.9	8.9	8.5	5.4	7.7	.0	2.9	.0	2.4	4.8	5.6	3.4	7.4	6.2
23.8	28.0	44.7	38.8	27.6	34.5	27.6	13.9	31.9	16.7	15.8	14.8	21.3	23.6	5.6	17.5	30.9	28.7
38.6	38.0	30.5	34.9	38.2	35.4	34.0	29.8	35.0	75.0	58.3	53.8	41.5	34.1	43.5	43.9	35.6	37.3
32.1	28.2	14.8	17.1	30.3	21.2	29.8	50.9	25.5	8.3	23.0	31.4	34.6	37.6	45.4	35.3	26.1	27.7

FOUR-YEAR COLLEGES

PUBLIC

	High (Selectivity)						Total	Low (Selectivity)					
	Tenure			Nontenure				Tenure			Nontenure		
	—35	36–50	51+	—35	36–50	51+		—35	36–50	51+	—35	36–50	51+

PER CENT OF FACULTY WHO AGREE WITH THE FOLLOWING STATEMENTS:

Undergraduates should play the following role in faculty appointments and promotions:

Control	.0	.3	.0	.3	.2	.0	.2	.0	.0	.6	.4	.7	.9
Voting Power	8.8	4.7	3.6	11.3	11.2	1.9	7.6	5.6	4.5	2.7	6.6	4.6	11.1
Formal Consultation	22.1	21.6	14.1	20.1	15.9	16.7	18.5	12.5	7.0	9.1	20.5	13.3	10.7
Informal Consultation	21.7	24.3	24.7	24.2	24.5	23.2	24.0	23.0	19.7	22.4	22.9	26.7	6.9
Little or No Role	47.5	49.1	57.6	44.1	48.2	58.3	49.7	59.0	68.9	65.3	49.6	54.8	70.5

Graduate students should play the following role in faculty appointments and promotions:

Control	.0	.3	.2	.3	.3	.0	.2	.0	.0	.2	.8	.7	.0
Voting Power	11.9	8.0	6.4	17.0	16.8	8.2	12.1	5.6	8.7	6.6	13.5	10.0	13.8
Formal Consultation	22.0	24.3	18.5	24.3	21.3	20.2	22.2	22.5	14.3	14.8	24.8	14.2	14.3
Informal Consultation	23.4	24.4	26.1	24.2	22.1	24.5	24.5	23.6	24.0	26.1	20.6	30.6	30.5
Little or No Role	42.8	43.0	48.7	34.1	39.5	47.2	40.9	48.3	53.0	52.3	40.4	44.4	41.4

Have you known of a case within the past 2 years in which a man's politics affected his chances of promotion or retention?

I know of a case.	19.8	14.8	9.5	18.1	18.7	11.3	15.7	8.2	10.7	12.3	20.7	8.2	3.5
I've heard of a case.	13.8	12.1	10.1	16.9	15.4	8.6	13.8	14.1	13.2	7.9	14.9	13.7	10.1
I don't know of a case.	57.9	61.7	66.5	59.7	59.7	72.0	61.8	71.4	64.0	64.8	61.0	71.2	78.9
I'm sure it hasn't happened.	8.4	11.4	13.9	5.3	6.3	8.0	8.8	6.3	12.1	15.0	3.5	6.8	7.5

PER CENT OF FACULTY WHO INDICATE FIRST PREFERENCE FOR THE FOLLOWING GOALS AND INTERESTS:

What I feel is important:

Provide undergraduates with a broad liberal education.	37.2	43.0	48.1	45.2	47.1	30.4	44.4	39.4	46.4	50.8	50.0	38.9	53.5
Prepare undergraduates for their chosen occupation.	33.0	23.8	22.3	25.5	25.4	28.6	25.0	40.2	30.8	25.2	28.6	30.7	23.0
Train graduate or professional students.	8.2	10.5	8.3	7.8	7.8	12.0	8.9	5.1	5.8	.9	6.4	10.8	3.0
Engage in research.	7.2	7.5	2.6	11.9	6.3	6.0	7.6	2.6	1.3	.0	4.3	.8	.0
No 1st choice.	14.3	15.2	18.8	9.7	13.4	22.9	14.2	12.7	15.7	23.0	10.7	18.8	20.6

What the institution expects of me:

Provide undergraduates with a broad liberal education.	31.6	35.2	40.1	34.3	35.6	34.7	35.5	32.4	36.1	40.0	30.6	33.9	35.0
Prepare undergraduates for their chosen occupation.	43.8	38.2	26.5	42.4	35.7	28.1	37.1	52.9	38.1	36.0	53.5	42.5	34.8
Train graduate or professional students.	2.9	5.6	6.3	4.2	6.7	8.5	5.5	1.5	2.4	.9	4.0	4.8	.7
Engage in research.	7.9	8.5	7.3	10.9	7.4	1.0	8.3	.0	3.1	.8	5.2	.8	.0
No 1st choice.	13.7	12.6	19.8	8.2	14.6	27.8	13.5	13.2	20.2	22.4	6.6	17.9	29.5

Do your interests lie primarily in teaching or research?

Very heavily in research.	4.9	2.5	1.1	3.8	2.0	2.4	2.8	.0	.6	1.1	4.3	2.8	.0
Both, leaning to research.	21.7	19.6	11.1	24.0	16.4	10.7	18.6	13.2	7.2	6.1	8.3	8.3	11.5
Both, leaning to teaching.	36.7	42.2	37.1	40.0	39.9	37.1	39.3	43.6	32.2	29.8	41.1	43.2	32.2
Very heavily in teaching.	36.7	35.7	50.8	32.3	41.7	49.9	39.3	43.3	60.0	62.9	46.3	43.5	56.2

					FOUR-YEAR COLLEGES												Total
	Total							PRIVATE								Total	
Total		High (Selectivity)						Total		Low (Selectivity)						Total	
		Tenure			Nontenure					Tenure			Nontenure				
		−35	36–50	51+	−35	36–50	51+			−35	36–50	51+	−35	36–50	51+		
.4	.3	.0	.0	.0	.2	.1	1.7	.2	.0	.0	.0	.0	.5	.0	.1	.2	.2
5.4	6.8	8.9	3.7	2.5	10.9	7.2	3.4	6.5	5.3	6.4	4.7	11.2	6.7	3.4	7.2	6.8	6.8
12.8	16.4	20.2	20.3	8.8	25.3	16.4	10.1	17.7	15.7	13.1	8.9	19.3	16.6	10.9	14.7	16.7	16.6
22.2	23.3	32.3	29.1	26.6	29.4	27.7	21.2	27.8	31.3	25.3	26.2	30.2	29.7	28.9	28.4	28.0	25.7
59.2	53.2	38.6	46.8	62.1	34.2	48.6	63.6	47.6	47.1	55.1	60.2	39.3	46.4	56.8	49.6	48.3	50.7
.4	.3	.0	.0	.6	.7	.3	.1	.4	.0	.3	.0	.4	.3	.0	.3	.3	.3
10.9	11.6	15.9	7.8	4.9	19.1	11.6	7.7	11.8	8.0	16.4	11.4	18.3	15.3	8.9	14.9	12.8	12.2
17.7	20.6	24.1	24.6	14.2	28.9	22.6	17.3	22.9	25.7	21.7	18.1	28.0	22.4	15.1	22.6	22.8	21.7
24.7	24.6	27.2	27.5	29.0	24.4	26.1	29.5	26.7	28.4	21.5	29.8	25.0	27.0	27.3	26.0	26.5	25.5
46.3	42.8	32.8	40.0	51.3	27.0	39.2	45.4	38.2	37.9	40.1	40.7	28.4	35.0	48.7	36.2	37.5	40.2
13.0	14.7	9.2	7.3	4.6	11.7	8.6	6.6	8.5	8.1	6.3	3.9	14.6	12.1	6.2	9.3	8.8	11.6
12.5	13.3	9.3	7.3	4.0	12.4	9.5	6.8	8.6	9.9	6.4	3.7	11.1	7.2	5.6	7.4	8.2	10.7
66.0	63.3	64.9	59.9	59.4	65.4	68.9	72.6	64.6	53.3	61.5	59.1	62.9	63.5	61.1	61.7	63.6	63.5
8.6	8.7	16.6	25.4	32.0	10.5	12.9	13.9	18.2	28.7	25.8	33.3	11.9	17.2	27.1	21.6	19.4	14.2
47.3	45.4	48.7	54.4	61.8	56.8	53.4	55.4	56.0	69.9	58.7	70.4	57.3	53.2	61.9	60.2	57.5	51.7
28.9	26.4	26.5	23.2	16.6	21.9	20.9	23.8	21.0	19.2	21.5	12.7	25.9	24.8	13.9	20.8	20.9	23.6
5.6	7.6	4.7	6.8	5.4	4.5	7.1	3.4	6.0	.0	1.5	1.6	4.4	5.4	1.9	3.0	4.9	6.2
1.9	5.5	9.4	5.1	1.8	7.6	4.1	2.5	5.0	4.3	2.1	.3	3.3	1.3	.5	1.9	3.9	4.7
16.5	15.0	10.7	10.6	14.4	9.3	14.3	15.0	12.1	6.6	16.2	15.0	9.1	15.3	21.8	14.1	12.8	13.9
35.2	35.4	55.6	62.8	61.0	60.4	50.6	50.1	57.6	69.5	68.7	66.6	65.7	57.9	66.7	64.8	60.2	48.2
43.8	39.6	29.4	18.1	15.0	21.3	26.0	26.7	21.0	19.2	15.9	12.7	20.9	21.0	14.2	17.9	20.0	29.5
2.8	4.5	4.2	6.3	4.7	5.1	6.8	3.1	5.7	3.0	.6	1.8	3.5	2.7	1.3	2.2	4.5	4.5
2.4	6.1	3.1	3.4	2.3	5.0	3.1	1.3	3.5	.9	.9	.0	.9	.2	.3	.5	2.4	4.2
15.9	14.4	7.7	9.4	17.1	8.2	13.4	18.8	12.0	7.4	13.8	18.9	8.9	18.2	17.4	14.6	12.9	13.6
2.3	2.6	1.9	1.6	1.1	2.5	2.3	2.5	2.2	.0	.3	.4	2.4	.0	.5	1.0	1.8	2.2
8.4	14.9	16.7	13.3	8.3	16.7	11.6	5.9	12.6	8.8	5.1	3.3	10.7	9.5	6.2	7.8	10.9	12.8
36.7	38.4	40.8	40.5	28.9	38.3	34.0	23.8	34.9	22.8	30.1	28.4	32.8	35.6	27.2	30.7	33.4	35.8
52.5	44.2	40.7	44.5	61.7	42.5	52.2	67.8	50.3	68.4	64.5	67.9	54.1	55.0	66.1	60.5	53.9	49.2

	PUBLIC						Total	PRIVATE					
	Tenure			Nontenure				Tenure			Nontenure		
	—35	36–50	51+	—35	36–50	51+		—35	36–50	51+	—35	36–50	51+

PER CENT OF FACULTY WHO AGREE WITH THE FOLLOWING STATEMENTS:

Undergraduates should play the following role in faculty appointments and promotions:

Control	.0	.1	.0	.3	.0	.0	.2	.0	.0	15.9	.0	.0	.0
Voting Power	12.5	2.5	5.8	11.1	2.5	4.0	6.3	.0	2.7	.0	5.0	.0	1.1
Formal Consultation	21.4	11.3	6.9	18.2	14.3	9.0	14.2	6.7	.0	9.1	8.0	8.6	1.5
Informal Consultation	19.0	24.2	20.6	24.0	26.1	27.4	23.4	24.0	36.9	6.4	30.8	28.3	15.1
Little or No Role	47.2	61.9	66.8	46.4	57.2	59.6	55.9	69.3	60.4	68.6	56.2	63.0	82.3

Graduate students should play the following role in faculty appointments and promotions:

Control	.0	.1	.0	.3	2.3	.0	.5	.0	.0	.0	1.0	.0	.0
Voting Power	24.7	9.0	14.5	22.9	8.9	1.5	14.8	18.6	2.8	.0	8.4	4.8	4.3
Formal Consultation	20.2	21.7	17.9	22.9	27.1	23.1	22.0	8.9	7.9	19.2	22.1	27.1	8.0
Informal Consultation	16.9	22.8	21.2	23.6	21.0	25.8	21.7	15.4	52.8	28.3	41.3	25.4	16.5
Little or No Role	38.1	46.3	46.4	30.4	40.7	49.7	41.0	57.2	36.5	52.5	27.2	42.7	71.2

Have you known of a case within the past 2 years in which a man's politics affected his chances of promotion or retention?

I know of a case.	12.7	10.2	9.0	13.8	8.3	7.7	10.9	.0	2.0	.0	4.9	7.1	2.3
I've heard of a case.	13.6	8.4	8.7	14.2	7.5	10.7	10.3	.0	8.3	3.2	5.7	6.2	5.3
I don't know of a case.	60.0	62.9	59.9	66.0	71.2	61.1	64.8	90.5	53.5	58.1	62.5	63.2	55.7
I'm sure it hasn't happened.	13.7	18.5	22.4	6.0	12.9	20.6	14.0	9.5	36.2	38.6	26.8	23.5	36.8

PER CENT OF FACULTY WHO INDICATE FIRST PREFERENCE FOR THE FOLLOWING GOALS AND INTERESTS:

What I feel is important:

Provide undergraduates with a broad liberal education.	54.9	46.6	50.8	57.6	41.3	39.2	49.8	50.2	60.2	45.6	54.9	60.2	55.8
Prepare undergraduates for their chosen occupation.	33.4	37.8	32.0	30.7	44.8	31.9	35.2	32.5	16.2	2.1	27.8	36.8	29.7
Train graduate or professional students.	.2	.9	.1	1.3	.2	.0	.7	.0	.0	.0	3.1	.0	.0
Engage in research.	.8	1.1	.3	2.2	.6	.0	1.1	.0	.0	.0	.0	.0	.0
No 1st choice.	10.7	13.6	16.9	8.2	13.2	28.9	13.3	17.3	23.6	52.3	14.2	3.1	14.5

What the institution expects of me:

Provide undergraduates with a broad liberal education.	40.5	40.0	42.7	38.2	37.0	28.0	38.5	54.4	73.2	47.6	48.7	50.0	46.5
Prepare undergraduates for their chosen occupation.	46.9	39.5	35.5	48.9	46.1	36.8	42.8	21.6	6.9	21.1	32.4	42.5	37.7
Train graduate or professional students.	.0	.7	.3	.5	.6	.0	.6	.0	.0	.0	3.1	.0	.0
Engage in research.	2.0	1.4	.3	.9	.2	1.7	1.1	.0	.0	.0	.0	.0	.0
No 1st choice.	10.6	18.3	21.3	11.6	16.2	33.5	17.0	24.0	20.0	31.3	15.8	7.5	15.8

Do your interests lie primarily in teaching or research?

Very heavily in research.	.0	.1	.7	1.2	.2	.6	.5	.0	.0	2.6	.0	3.0	.0
Both, leaning to research.	4.0	2.6	1.3	4.3	4.5	.6	3.7	3.4	1.6	5.4	2.1	2.1	5.9
Both, leaning to teaching.	17.8	18.2	11.3	24.9	24.2	18.5	19.9	6.5	12.0	5.4	14.8	17.1	18.9
Very heavily in teaching.	78.2	79.0	86.8	69.6	71.1	80.2	75.8	90.1	86.4	86.7	83.1	77.7	75.2

Total	Total	High (Selectivity)						Total	Low (Selectivity)						Total	Total
		Tenure			Nontenure				Tenure			Nontenure				
		—35	36–50	51+	—35	36–50	51+		—35	36–50	51+	—35	36–50	51+		
1.9	.6	.1	.1	.1	.2	.1	.7	.2	.0	.1	1.0	.2	.2	.1	.3	.3
1.8	5.3	6.4	3.5	2.5	9.7	7.0	4.3	5.9	7.0	3.2	3.4	8.9	4.5	3.5	5.4	5.7
7.3	12.7	20.2	17.1	10.0	22.0	17.0	11.4	16.9	16.6	9.9	8.1	17.4	13.5	7.5	12.8	15.1
23.4	23.4	27.6	26.5	24.5	27.2	27.2	23.3	26.2	20.0	24.4	21.1	25.4	24.8	21.1	23.5	25.0
65.5	58.0	45.7	52.8	63.0	40.9	48.6	60.4	50.8	56.4	62.4	66.5	48.2	57.0	67.9	58.0	54.0
.3	.5	.2	.1	.2	.4	.2	.0	.3	.0	.1	.1	.4	.7	.0	.3	.3
5.8	13.0	10.2	6.2	4.5	15.6	11.5	8.8	9.9	13.2	7.3	6.8	15.9	9.7	5.8	10.7	10.3
18.3	21.3	23.0	20.6	14.1	26.5	23.1	16.7	21.4	19.5	16.8	15.1	24.2	20.6	15.0	19.3	20.5
31.6	23.7	27.1	27.8	28.1	25.2	26.1	26.8	26.8	21.0	26.7	25.5	24.7	24.8	26.7	25.0	26.0
44.0	41.6	39.5	45.3	53.1	32.2	39.1	47.7	41.6	46.3	49.0	52.5	34.9	44.3	52.5	44.7	42.9
3.3	9.2	14.5	10.6	6.4	15.0	11.5	6.7	11.2	14.3	12.3	8.3	18.2	11.3	6.5	12.7	11.9
5.3	9.2	13.5	11.5	7.9	16.0	12.9	8.5	12.3	13.6	11.6	7.7	15.0	11.2	8.7	11.7	12.0
58.8	63.5	64.1	65.6	69.3	63.6	68.7	75.5	66.9	61.2	62.5	65.4	60.6	67.3	63.0	63.4	65.3
32.6	18.1	7.9	12.3	16.4	5.4	6.8	9.4	9.7	11.0	13.6	18.5	6.2	10.1	21.8	12.1	10.8
55.7	51.1	30.2	31.5	39.1	40.2	36.8	39.3	36.9	42.4	40.1	47.4	46.9	41.4	50.6	44.6	40.3
25.8	33.1	21.9	19.0	19.2	19.3	19.3	22.5	19.3	29.4	28.4	22.5	26.3	30.4	23.2	26.7	22.6
.8	.7	17.2	20.3	18.0	13.4	18.2	14.3	17.1	7.9	11.7	7.8	8.5	9.6	5.0	8.9	13.5
.0	.8	18.6	15.2	6.9	16.7	11.0	4.6	12.9	7.5	5.7	2.3	7.5	4.1	.7	5.1	9.4
17.7	14.3	12.0	13.9	16.8	10.4	14.8	19.3	13.8	12.9	14.0	20.0	10.9	14.5	20.6	14.7	14.2
50.1	41.1	28.0	28.9	32.5	31.6	28.0	34.0	30.3	35.7	34.4	37.6	34.0	34.9	41.0	35.4	32.6
32.3	40.5	26.9	21.7	17.6	25.5	23.2	22.5	22.5	37.8	30.5	26.8	38.2	35.4	30.7	33.4	27.3
.8	.7	11.4	16.5	15.2	10.3	15.5	13.0	14.0	4.4	8.4	6.9	6.3	7.1	2.9	6.6	10.8
.0	.8	21.8	19.3	15.2	21.8	17.6	8.7	18.4	9.5	9.6	6.2	9.9	6.5	2.0	8.1	13.9
16.8	16.9	12.0	13.5	19.6	10.9	15.7	21.8	14.8	12.6	17.2	22.5	11.6	16.0	23.3	16.5	15.5
1.5	.7	6.2	5.5	3.0	5.6	4.7	3.8	4.9	2.1	3.0	2.2	3.6	2.7	.9	2.9	4.1
3.6	3.7	34.0	30.2	19.1	28.1	21.4	10.4	25.0	16.9	15.8	9.0	14.6	10.8	6.3	13.0	19.8
17.3	19.3	35.1	38.3	36.9	37.6	36.5	29.6	36.7	28.9	32.2	28.7	33.4	33.5	24.4	31.5	34.4
77.6	76.2	24.7	26.1	41.0	28.7	37.3	56.2	33.3	52.0	49.0	60.1	48.4	52.9	68.3	52.6	41.8

ALL INSTITUTIONS

✺✺✺✺ Appendix ✺✺✺✺

1940 Statement of Principles on Academic Freedom and Tenure

In 1915, at the time of the founding of the association, a committee on academic freedom and tenure formulated a statement entitled *A Declaration of Principles*. This statement set forth the concern of the association for academic freedom and tenure, for proper procedures, and for professional responsibility. The declaration was endorsed by the American Association of University Professors at its second annual meeting, held December 31, 1915, and January 1, 1916.

In 1925, the American Council on Education called a con-

Reprinted from L. Joughin (Ed.), *Academic Freedom and Tenure: A Handbook of the American Association of University Professors* (Madison: University of Wisconsin Press, 1969), pp. 33–39.

ference of representatives of a number of its constituent members, among them the American Association of University Professors, for the purpose of preparing a statement in this area. There emerged the 1925 Conference Statement on Academic Freedom and Tenure, which was endorsed in 1925 by the Association of American Colleges and in 1926 by the American Association of University Professors.

In 1940, following upon a series of conferences which began in 1934, representatives of the Association of American Colleges and the American Association of University Professors agreed upon a Statement of Principles on Academic Freedom and Tenure and upon three attached "interpretations." The 1940 statement and its interpretations were endorsed by the two associations in 1941. In subsequent years endorsement has been officially voted by numerous other organizations.

The purpose of this statement is to promote public understanding and support of academic freedom and tenure and agreement upon procedures to assure them in colleges and universities. Institutions of higher education are conducted for the common good and not to further the interest of either the individual teacher or the institution as a whole. The common good depends upon the free search for truth and its free exposition.

Academic freedom is essential to these purposes and applies to both teaching and research. Freedom in research is fundamental to the advancement of truth. Academic freedom in its teaching aspect is fundamental for the protection of the rights of the teacher in teaching and of the student to freedom in learning. It carries with it duties correlative with rights.

Tenure is a means to certain ends—specifically, (1) freedom of teaching and research and of extramural activities and (2) a sufficient degree of economic security to make the profession attractive to men and women of ability. Freedom and economic security—hence, tenure—are indispensable to the success of an institution in fulfilling its obligations to its students and to society.

Academic Freedom

(a) The teacher is entitled to full freedom in research and in the publication of the results, subject to the adequate performance of his other academic duties; but research for pecuniary return should be based upon an understanding with the authorities of the institution.

(b) The teacher is entitled to freedom in the classroom in discussing his subject, but he should be careful not to introduce into his teaching controversial matter which has no relation to his subject. Limitations of academic freedom because of religious or other aims of the institution should be clearly stated in writing at the time of the appointment.

(c) The college or university teacher is a citizen, a member of a learned profession, and an officer of an educational institution. When he speaks or writes as a citizen, he should be free from institutional censorship or discipline, but his special position in the community imposes special obligations. As a man of learning and an educational officer, he should remember that the public may judge his profession and his institution by his utterances. Hence, he should at all times be accurate, should exercise appropriate restraint, should show respect for the opinions of others, and should make every effort to indicate that he is not an institutional spokesman.

Academic Tenure

(a) After the expiration of a probationary period, teachers or investigators should have permanent or continuous tenure, and their service should be terminated only for adequate cause, except in the case of retirement for age or under extraordinary circumstances because of financial exigencies.

In the interpretation of this principle it is understood that the following represents acceptable academic practice:

(1) The precise terms and conditions of every appointment should be stated in writing and be in the possession of both institution and teacher before the appointment is consummated.

(2) Beginning with appointment to the rank of full-time instructor or a higher rank, the probationary period should not exceed seven years, including within this period full-time service in all institutions of higher education, but subject to the proviso that when—after a term of probationary service of more than three years in one or more institutions—a teacher is called to another institution, it may be agreed in writing that his new appointment is for a probationary period of not more than four years, even though thereby the person's total probationary period in the academic profession is extended beyond the normal maximum of seven years. Notice should be given at least one

year prior to the expiration of the probationary period if the teacher is not to be continued in service after the expiration of that period.

(3) During the probationary period a teacher should have the academic freedom that all other members of the faculty have.

(4) Termination for cause of a continuous appointment, or the dismissal for cause of a teacher, previous to the expiration of a term appointment, should, if possible, be considered by both a faculty committee and the governing board of the institution. In all cases where the facts are in dispute, the accused teacher should be informed before the hearing in writing of the charges against him and should have the opportunity to be heard in his own defense by all bodies that pass judgment upon his case. He should be permitted to have with him an adviser of his own choosing who may act as counsel. There should be a full stenographic record of the hearing available to the parties concerned. In the hearing of charges of incompetence the testimony should include that of teachers and other scholars, either from his own or from other institutions. Teachers on continuous appointment who are dismissed for reasons not involving moral turpitude should receive their salaries for at least a year from the date of notification of dismissal whether or not they are continued in their duties at the institution.

(5) Termination of a continuous appointment because of financial exigency should be demonstrably bona fide.

Interpretations

At a conference of representatives of the American Association of University Professors and of the Association of American Colleges on November 7-8, 1940, the following interpretations of the 1940 *Statement of Principles on Academic Freedom and Tenure* were agreed upon:

1. That its operation should not be retroactive.

2. That all tenure claims of teachers appointed prior to the endorsement should be determined in accordance with the principles set forth in the 1925 *Conference Statement on Academic Freedom and Tenure*.

3. If the administration of a college or university feels that a teacher has not observed the admonitions of paragraph (c) of the section on Academic Freedom and believes that the extramural utter-

ances of the teacher have been such as to raise grave doubts concerning his fitness for his position, it may proceed to file charges under paragraph (a) (4) of the section on *Academic Tenure*. In pressing such charges the administration should remember that teachers are citizens and should be accorded the freedom of citizens. In such cases the administration must assume full responsibility, and the American Association of University Professors and the Association of American Colleges are free to make an investigation.

Glossary
of Terms

(These brief definitions are intended only to indicate the basic meanings attached to the terms in this report; they of course do not reach to the subtleties and nuances that have characterized the use of the terms in legal and educational discourse.)

Academic Due Process—the assurance, provided by institutional regulations, of procedures to safeguard the fairness of *personnel actions*.* The prevailing assurance in relation to *dismissal* of faculty members provides for an adequate statement of charges followed by opportunity for a hearing before peers; for the right of counsel if desired; for the right to present evidence and to cross-examine; for decision on the record of the hearing; and for appeal from a dismissal judgment. In relation to *nonreappointment*, fair consideration and an established procedure for appeal are provided. Academic due process, an internal

---

* Italicized terms are defined elsewhere in this glossary.

255

institutional procedure, is to be distinguished from due process of law.

Academic Freedom—the right, identified with the purposes of academic institutions, whereby members of the academic community are protected in the privilege to receive, discover, convey to others, and, as generally described in the 1940 Statement of Principles, to act upon knowledge and ideas. Academic freedom should be distinguished from the personal freedoms guaranteed by the constitution, through which it is sometimes reinforced in litigation.

Academic Tenure—an arrangement under which faculty appointments in an institution of higher education are continued until retirement for age or physical disability, subject to *dismissal* for *adequate cause* or unavoidable termination on account of financial exigency or change of institutional program.

Adequate Cause—a basis on which a faculty member, either with *academic tenure* or during a *term appointment,* may be dismissed. The term refers especially to demonstrated incompetency or dishonesty in teaching or research, to substantial and manifest neglect of duty, and to personal conduct which substantially impairs the individual's fulfillment of his institutional responsibilities.

Collective Bargaining Agent—an organization authorized, usually as the result of an election under state or federal law, to represent the personnel in a *collective bargaining unit* in negotiations with an administration over the terms and conditions of employment to be incorporated in a legally binding agreement.

Collective Bargaining Unit—that portion of the personnel of an institution, usually designated by a government agency, whose terms and conditions of employment will be determined through negotiation by a single *collective bargaining agent.* The faculty of a college or university may be such a unit, may be divided into more than one unit, or may be associated with other personnel for this purpose.

Dismissal—action taken against a faculty member during a *term appointment* or while he is on *academic tenure,* whereby his services are terminated for *adequate cause.* Not to be confused with *nonreappointment* or *nonrenewal.*

Grievance Proceeding—a process by which an academic employee seeks correction of alleged error or injustice in a *personnel action*. The process may be defined by institutional regulation or by collective bargaining and may either be wholly internal or permit ultimate resort to arbitrators from outside the institution.

Nonreappointment or Nonrenewal—*personnel action* consisting of a decision not to continue the services of an individual beyond the expiration of a *term appointment*. Not to be confused with *dismissal*.

Personnel Action—official action on behalf of an institution, which affects the status or working conditions of a staff member.

Probationary Period—a period of professional service during which a faculty member on *term appointment* does not hold tenure and is observed by his colleagues for the purpose of evaluating his professional qualifications. At the end of this period, the faculty member either receives *academic tenure* or is not reappointed.

Term Appointment—an appointment for a fixed period, usually from one to five years, as contrasted to an appointment with *academic tenure*. Term appointments may be renewable or nonrenewable.

Selected
Bibliography

General

ALCHIAN, A. A. "Private Property and the Relative Cost of Tenure." In P. D. Bradley, (Ed.), *The Public Stake in Union Power*. Charlottesville: University of Virginia Press, 1959. Pp. 350–371.

ALTMAN, R. A., AND BYERLY, C. M. (Eds.) *The Public Challenge and the Campus Response*. Berkeley: Center for Research and Development in Higher Education, University of California; Boulder, Colorado: Western Interstate Commission for Higher Education, September 1971.

ASTIN, H. S., AND BAYER, A. E. "Sex Discrimination in Academe." *Educational Record*, 1972, *53*, 101–118.

BAHR, H. M. "Violations of Academic Freedom: Official Statistics and Personal Reports." *Social Problems*, 1967, *14*, 310–319.

BLACKBURN, R. T. *Tenure: Aspects of Job Security on the Changing Campus*. Atlanta: Southern Regional Education Board, 1972.

BRESSLER, M. "The American College: Some Problems and Choices." *Annals of American Academy of Political and Social Science*, 1971, *396*, 57–69 (esp. 67–68).

BROOKS, R. "Tenure in Colleges and Universities." *School and Society,* 1934, *19,* 497–501.

BROWN, J. D. *The Liberal University: An Institutional Analysis.* New York: McGraw-Hill, 1969. Part Two, Chapter 2, "Academic Freedom and Tenure."

BYSE, C., AND JOUGHIN, L. *Tenure in American Higher Education: Plans, Practices and Law.* Ithaca, N.Y.: Cornell University Press, 1959.

BYSE, C., AND MERRY, R. W. "Tenure and Academic Freedom." In S. Harris (Ed.), *Challenge and Change in American Education.* Berkeley, Calif.: McCutchan Publishing Corporation, 1965. Pp. 313–332.

CAPLOW, T., AND MC GEE, R. J. *The Academic Marketplace.* New York: Basic Books, 1958.

CARR, R. K. "The Uneasy Future of Academic Tenure." *Educational Record,* 1972, *53,* 119–127.

CARTTER, A. M. "Future Faculty: Needs and Resources." In C. B. T. Lee (Ed.), *Improving College Teaching.* Washington, D.C.: American Council on Education, 1967. Pp. 113–135.

DENNISON, C. P. *Faculty Rights and Obligations in Eight Independent Liberal Arts Colleges.* New York: Teachers College Bureau of Publications, Columbia University, 1955.

d'HEILLY, JEAN-LOUIS. "Needed: A Student Voice on Tenure." *Change,* 1970, *2,* 6–8.

DRESSEL, P. L. "A Review of the Tenure Policies of Thirty-One Major Universities." *Educational Record,* 1963, *44,* 248–253.

EARLE, V. (Ed.) *On Academic Freedom.* Washington, D.C.: American Enterprise Institute for Public Policy Research, 1971.

ECKERT, R. E. "Age and the College Teacher." *AAUP Bulletin,* 1972, *58,* 40–43.

EMERSON, T. I., AND HABER, D. "Academic Freedom of the Faculty Member as Citizen." *Law and Contemporary Problems,* 1963, *28,* 525–572.

ERICKSON, E. K. "An Analysis of Teacher Dismissal Cases in the State of Washington." Unpublished dissertation, Washington State University, 1965.

FUCHS, R. F. "Academic Freedom—Its Basic Philosophy, Function, and History." In L. Joughin (Ed.), *Academic Freedom and Tenure.* Madison: University of Wisconsin Press, 1969. Originally published in *Law and Contemporary Problems,* 1963, *28.*

FURNISS, W. T. "Department and Faculty Profiles: An Aid to Judgment." *Liberal Education,* 1963, *49,* 1–12.

FURNISS, W. T. "Giving Reasons for Nonrenewal of Faculty Contracts." *Educational Record*, 1971, *52*, 328–337.

FURNISS, W. T. "Is There a Perfect Faculty Mix?" *Educational Record*, 1971, *52*, 244–250.

GILLIS, J. W. "Academic Staff Reductions in Response to Financial Exigency." *Liberal Education*, 1971, *57*, 364–377.

GOODE, W. J. "The Protection of the Inept." *American Sociological Review*, 1967, *32*, 5–19.

HILDEBRAND, M. "How to Recommend Promotion for a Mediocre Teacher Without Actually Lying." *Journal of Higher Education*, 1972, *43*, 44–64.

HOFSTADTER, R., AND METZGER, W. P. *The Development of Academic Freedom in the United States.* New York: Columbia University Press, 1955.

HOOK, S. *Academic Freedom and Academic Anarchy.* New York: Cowles, 1970.

HOOK, S. "Ideals and Realities of Academic Tenure." *The Twenty-Eighth Annual Utah Conference on Higher Education.* Salt Lake City: Utah Conference on Higher Education, 1971. Pp. 13–24.

HOOK, S. *In Defense of Academic Freedom.* Indianapolis–New York: Bobbs-Merrill (Pegasus Books), 1971.

JACKSON, F. H. "Tenure and Teacher Effectiveness." *AGB Reports*, 1970, *13*, 3–7.

JENCKS, C., AND RIESMAN, D. *The Academic Revolution.* New York: Doubleday, 1968.

JOHNSON, J. T. "The Restoration of Faculty Ranks." *Educational Record*, 1971, *52*, 251–254.

JONES, H. M. "The American Concept of Academic Freedom." In L. Joughin (Ed.), *Academic Freedom and Tenure.* Madison: University of Wisconsin Press, 1969. Originally published in *American Scholar*, 1959–60, *29*.

KADISH, S. H. "What Tenure Is All About." *California Monthly* (California Alumni Association), November 1971, p. 2.

KUGLER, I. "Whither Tenure?" *Changing Education*, April 1972, Pp. 1–2.

LANE, F. S. *A Study in Role Conflict: The Departmental Chairman in Decisions on Academic Tenure.* Gainesville, Florida: Public Administration Clearing Service, 1967.

LESSARD, S. "The Terms of Tenure: To Have and Be Held." *Washington Monthly*, September 1971, Pp. 11–15.

LEWIS, L. S. "Dismissals from the Academy." *Journal of Higher Education*, 1966, *37*, 253–259.

LUTHANS, F. *The Faculty Promotion Process: An Empirical Analysis of the Management of Large State Universities.* Iowa City: University of Iowa, Bureau of Business and Economic Research, 1967.

MACHLUP, F. "College Teaching: Tenure in Colleges and Universities." In L. C. Deighton (Ed.), *The Encyclopedia of Education.* Vol. 2. New York: Macmillan and Free Press, 1971. Pp. 257–264.

MACHLUP, F. "In Defense of Academic Tenure." *AAUP Bulletin,* 1964, *50,* 112–124. Reprinted in L. Joughin (Ed.), *Academic Freedom and Tenure* (Madison: University of Wisconsin Press, 1969), pp. 306–337.

MARSH, J. F., JR., AND STAFFORD, F. P. "The Effects of Values on Pecuniary Behavior: The Case of Academicians." *American Sociological Review,* 1967, *32,* 740–759.

MASON, H. L. *College and University Government: A Handbook of Principle and Practice.* Tulane Studies in Political Science, Vol. 14. New Orleans: Tulane University Press, 1972.

MC CONNELL, T. R. "The Necessity of Tenure." Statement for the Panel on Tenure at the AAUP Council Meeting, Berkeley, California, March 27, 1971. Washington, D.C.: American Association of University Professors, 1971.

MC GEE, R. *Academic Janus: The Private College and Its Faculty.* San Francisco: Jossey-Bass, 1971.

MC GILL, W. J. Address at the Closing of the Annual College and University Self-Study Institute at the University of California at Berkeley, July 15, 1971.

MC NALLY, A. M. "The Dynamics of Securing Academic Status." In R. B. Downs (Ed.), *The Status of American College and University Librarians,* ACRL Monograph No. 22. Chicago: American Library Association, 1958.

METZGER, W. P., KADISH, S. H., et al. *Dimensions of Academic Freedom.* Urbana: University of Illinois Press, 1969. Includes Metzger's "Academic Freedom in Delocalized Academic Institutions" (pp. 1–33) and Kadish's "The Strike and the Professoriate" (pp. 34–68).

METZGER, W. P. "The Academic Profession and Its Public Critics." In R. A. Altman and C. M. Byerly (Eds.), *The Public Challenge and the Campus Response.* Boulder, Colorado: Western Interstate Commission for Higher Education, 1971. Pp. 71–87.

MILLER, J. P. "Tenure: Bulwark of Academic Freedom and Brake on Change." *Educational Record,* 1970, *51,* 241–245.

MITCHELL, M. B. "The Curious World of University Tenure." *Compact,* August 1968, pp. 31–34.

MOOG, F. "Women, Students, and Tenure." *Science*, December 3, 1971, p. 983.

MORTIMER, K. P. *Accountability in Higher Education*. ERIC Report 1. Washington, D.C.: Educational Resources Information Center, February 1972.

MYERS, R. L. "Some Tenure, Salary and Appointment Policies of Universities, Concentrating on Professional Personnel Supported by Soft Funds." Unpublished report. Cincinnati: University of Cincinnati, Department of Institutional Studies, March 1970.

NEFF, C. B. "Toward a Definition of Academic Responsibility." *Journal of Higher Education*, 1969, *40*, 12–22.

NISBET, R. A. "The Permanent Professors: A Modest Proposal." *Public Interest*, 1965, *1*, 37–50.

O'NEIL, R. M. "The Eclipse of Faculty Autonomy." Address delivered before the Assembly on Goals and Governance, Department of Health, Education, and Welfare, Washington, D.C., 1970.

PARK, D., JR. "A Loyal AAUP Member Says 'Down with Tenure!' " *Change*, March 1972, pp. 32–37.

PARSONS, T., AND PLATT, G. M. *The American Academic Profession*. A Pilot Study, NSF (Grant GS 5B), March 1968.

PERKIN, H. "Academic Tenure." *Association of University Teachers Bulletin*, 1972, *42*, 13–14.

PFNISTER, A. D. "Promotion and Tenure Policies in Undergraduate Colleges." *North Central Association Quarterly*, 1958, *32*, 268–275.

PUNKE, H. H. "Ranking, Tenure, and Sex of Junior College Faculties." *School Review*, 1954, *62*, 480–487.

POTTER, R. A. "Tenure, Or Seven Years to Life in an Institution" 14th Annual Plous Memorial Lecture, University of California, Santa Barbara. *Nexus* (UCSB Student Newspaper), May 26, 1972, supplement.

REINERT, P. C., S.J. *Faculty Tenure in Colleges and Universities from 1900 to 1940*. St. Louis University Studies, 1944. Monolog Series: Social Sciences No. 1, March 1946.

ROCKWELL, L. L. "Academic Freedom—German Origins and American Development." *AAUP Bulletin*, 1950, *36*, 225–236.

ROLNICK, S. "The Development of the Idea of Academic Freedom and Tenure in the United States, 1870–1920." Unpublished doctoral dissertation, University of Wisconsin, 1952.

SALTZMAN, H. "Proposing a National Board to Accredit Tenured Professors." *Chronicle of Higher Education*, November 8, 1971, p. 8.

SHAW, B. *Academic Tenure in American Higher Education*. Chicago: Adams Press, 1971.

SHULMAN, C. H. "The Tenure Debate." In *Research Currents*. Washington, D.C.: Educational Resources Information Center—Higher Education, 1971.

SOULES, J. A., AND BUHL, L. C. "Reviving Promotion and Tenure: A Systematic Approach." *Educational Record*, 1972, *53*, 73–79.

STENE, E. O. "Bases of Academic Tenure." *AAUP Bulletin*, 1955, *41*, 584–589.

STEPHENS, H. T., et al. "The Tenure System in Higher Education— Challenged . . . Re-examined . . . Re-evaluated." *Conversations*, 1972, *8*, 1–20. ARA–Slater School and College Services, Philadelphia, Pennsylvania.

"The Thurstone Plan for Enforcing the Principles of Freedom and Tenure." *AAUP Bulletin*, 1932, *18*, 361–363.

VACCARO, L. C. "The Tenure Controversy: Some Possible Alternatives." *Journal of Higher Education*, 1972, *43*, 35–43.

VAN ALSTYNE, A. "Academic Freedom and Tenure." Address delivered before the Legislative Work Conference, Phoenix, Arizona, December 1971. Boulder, Colorado: Western Interstate Conference on Higher Education, 1971.

VAN ALSTYNE, W. "Tenure: A Summary Explanation and 'Defense.'" *AAUP Bulletin*, 1971, *57*, 328–333.

WILLIAMS, R. C. "Tenure Practices Redefined." *American Junior College Journal*, 1969, *39*, 26–29.

WORCESTER, D. A. "Standards of Faculty Promotion and Tenure: A Pure Theory." *Administrative Science Quarterly*, 1957, *2*, 216–234.

Law

"Academic Freedom and the Law." *Yale Law Journal*, 46, 670–686.

BIERSTEDT, R., AND METZGER, W. P. "Safeguarding Academic Freedom." *Civil Liberties*, March 1972, *285*, 5–6.

BLACKWELL, T. E. "The Tenure Committee and the Courts." *College and University Business*, 1959, *27*, 27–28.

BOLMEIER, E. C. *Teachers' Legal Rights, Restraints and Liabilities*. Cincinnati: W. H. Anderson, 1971.

BRUBACHER, J. S. *The Courts and Higher Education*. San Francisco: Jossey-Bass, 1971.

CHAMBERS, M. M. *The Colleges and the Courts, 1946–1950*. New York: Columbia University Press, 1952.

CHAMBERS, M. M. *The Colleges and the Courts, 1962–1966*. Danville, Ill.: Interstate Printers and Publishers, 1967.

CHANIN, R. H. *Protecting Teacher Rights: A Summary of Constitutional*

Developments. Washington, D.C.: National Education Association, 1970.

COHEN, M. A. "Academic Tenure: The Search for Standards." *Southern California Law Review,* 1966, *39,* 593–608.

"Developments in the Law: Academic Freedom." *Harvard Law Review,* 1968, *81,* 1048–1157.

FELLMAN, D. "Academic Freedom in American Public Law." *Teachers College Record,* 1961, *62,* 368–386.

FELLMAN, D. (Ed.) *The Supreme Court and Education.* New York: Teachers College Press, Columbia University, 1969.

FRAKT, A. N. "Non-tenured Teachers and the Constitution." *Kansas Law Review,* 1969, *18,* 27–54.

KADISH, S. H. "Methodology and Criteria in Due Process Adjudication— A Survey and Criticism." *Yale Law Journal,* 1957, *66,* 319–363.

MURPHY, W. P. "Academic Freedom—An Emerging Constitutional Right." *Law and Contemporary Problems,* 1963, *28,* 447–486.

MURPHY, W. P. "Educational Freedom in the Courts." *AAUP Bulletin,* 1963, *44,* 309–327.

PETTIGREW, H. W. "Constitutional Tenure: Toward a Realization of Academic Freedom." *Case-Western Reserve Law Review,* 1971, *22,* 475–514.

PETTIGREW, H. W., AND HOWARD, L. B. "The Probationary Professor and The Constitution: A Suggested Model Hearing Code for Contract Renewal Cases." *California Western Law Review,* 1971, *8,* 1–74.

RYAN, P. G. "Due Process for All." *Civil Liberties,* 1972, *285,* 5–6.

VAN ALSTYNE, W. W. "The Judicial Trend toward Academic Freedom." *Florida Law Review,* 1968, *20,* 290–305.

VAN ALSTYNE, W. W. "The Constitutional Rights of Teachers and Professors." *Duke Law Journal,* 1970, *5,* 841–879.

Collective Bargaining*

BEAL, E. F., AND WICKERSHAM, E. D. *The Practice of Collective Bargaining.* Homewood, Ill.: Erwin, 1967.

BEGIN, J. P. "Collective Bargaining Agreements in Colleges and Universities: Union Security Provisions." *Journal of College and University Personnel Association,* 1971, *22,* 33–43.

BELCHER, A. L., et al. *Labor Relations in Higher Education.* Washington, D.C.: College and University Personnel Association, 1971.

* For more comprehensive bibliographies, see listings in this section for Gillis, Marks, Mortimer, and Tice.

BLUM, A. A. (Ed.) *Teacher Unions and Associations.* Urbana.: University of Illinois Press, 1969.

BOYD, W. B. "Collective Bargaining in Academe: Causes and Consequences." *Liberal Education,* 1971, *67,* 306–318.

BROWN, R. S., AND KUGLER, I. "Collective Bargaining for the Faculty." *Liberal Education,* 1970, *56,* 75–85.

California State Colleges Academic Senate. "Issues and Answers on Collective Bargaining." Report prepared for Ad Hoc Committee on Collective Bargaining of the Academic Senate, 1967.

DUNLOP, J. T., AND CHAMBERLAIN, N. W. (Eds.) *Frontiers of Collective Bargaining.* New York: Harper and Row, 1967.

ELAM, S. AND MOSKOW, M. (Eds.) *Employment Relations in Higher Education.* Bloomington, Ind.: Phi Delta Kappa, 1969.

FINKIN, M. W. "Collective Bargaining and University Government." *Wisconsin Law Review,* 1971, 125–149.

GARBARINO, J. W. "Precarious Professors: New Patterns of Representation." *Industrial Relations,* 1971, *10,* 1–20.

GARBARINO, J. W. "Creeping Unionism and the Faculty Labor Market." In M. S. Gordon (Ed.) New York: *Higher Education and the Labor Market.* McGraw-Hill, forthcoming.

GARBARINO, J. W. "Faculty Unionism: From Theory to Practice." *Industrial Relations,* 1972, *11*(1), 1–17.

GILLIS, J. W. "Academic Collective Bargaining." *Liberal Education,* 1970, *56,* 594–604.

GILLIS, J. W. "The Continuing Development of Academic Collective Bargaining." *Liberal Education,* 1971, *57,* 529–540.

LIEBERMAN, M. "Professors, Unite!" *Harper's Magazine,* October 1971, pp. 61–70.

LIVINGSTON, J. C. "Collective Bargaining and Professionalism in Higher Education." *Educational Record,* 1967, *48,* 79–88.

MANSON, J. K. "The Impact of Faculty Collective Bargaining on Higher Education." In F. Macchiarola (Ed.), *Critical Issues in Education: The Borton Woolman Distinguished Lectures, 1969–70.* New York: School of Business and Public Administration, Bernard M. Baruch College of the City University of New York, 1970. Pp. 49–56.

MC HUGH, W. F. "Collective Bargaining with Professionals in Higher Education: Problems in Unit Determinations." *Wisconsin Law Review,* 1971, 55–90.

MC HUGH, W. F. "Recent Developments in Collective Bargaining in Higher Education." *College Counsel,* 1970, *5,* 159–208.

MARKS, K. E. *Collective Bargaining in U.S. Higher Education; 1960–*

1971: A Selective Bibliography. Ames: Iowa State University Library, 1972.

University of Michigan. *Report of the Committee on Rights and Responsibilities of Faculty Members.* Ann Arbor, November 1971.

MORTIMER, K. P., AND LOZIER, G. G. *Collective Bargaining: Implications for Governance.* State College, Pa.: Center for Study of Higher Education, 1972.

MOSKOW, M. H. "The Scope of Collective Bargaining in Higher Education." *Wisconsin Law Review,* 1971, 33–54.

REHMUS, C. M. "Collective Bargaining and the Market for Academic Personnel." University of Michigan–Wayne State University Institute of Labor and Industrial Relations, Autumn 1968.

SANDS, C. D. "The Role of Collective Bargaining in Higher Education." *Wisconsin Law Review,* 1971, 151–176.

SHILS, E. B., AND WHITTIER, C. *Teachers, Administrators, and Collective Bargaining.* New York: Crowell, 1968.

SHULMAN, C. H. *Collective Bargaining on Campus.* ERIC Report 2. Washington, D.C.: Educational Resources Information Center, March 1972.

SUMBERG, A. D. *"Collective Bargaining."* G. K. Smith (Ed.), In *The Troubled Campus: Current Issues in Higher Education, 1970.* San Francisco: Jossey-Bass, 1970. Pp. 139–145.

TICE, T. N. (Ed.) *Faculty Power: Collective Bargaining on Campus.* Ann Arbor, Mich.: Institute of Continuing Legal Education, 1972. Contains bibliography, pp. 331–349.

TYLER, G. "The Faculty Joins the Proletariat." *Change,* 1971–72, *3,* 40–45.

VAN ALSTYNE, W. W. "Tenure and Collective Bargaining." In G. K. Smith (Ed.), *New Teaching, New Learning: Current Issues in Higher Education, 1971.* San Francisco: Jossey-Bass, 1971. Pp. 210–217.

Individual Institutions and Systems

California Community Colleges. *Administration of Tenure: Proposed Changes in Policies and Practices in the California Community Colleges.* Special Report to the Board of Governors of the California Community Colleges. Sacramento: Ad Hoc Committee on Tenure and Evaluation for the California Community Colleges, April 1971.

California Coordinating Council for Higher Education. *Academic Tenure in California Public Higher Education.* Sacramento, 1969.

California State Colleges. *Report of the Ad Hoc Committee on Procurement and Retention of a Quality Faculty.* Los Angeles, April 1971.

University of Chicago. *Report of the Committee on the Criteria of Academic Appointment.* University of Chicago, 1972. Reprinted from *The University of Chicago Record,* December 1970 and January 1972.

DE JESUS, A. T. "Factors Associated with the Attraction and Retention of Qualified College Faculty at Indiana University." Doctoral dissertation, Indiana University, 1965. (Microfilm)

Harvard University, Committee on Governance. *Discussion Memorandum on Academic Tenure at Harvard University.* Cambridge, Mass., November 1971.

University of Hawaii Council. *Recommendations on Tenure and Tenure Decisions.* Honolulu, May 8, 1971.

Stanford University. *Decision of the Advisory Board in the Matter of Professor Bruce H. Franklin, January 5, 1972.* Pp. 3–4: "Fundamental Issues and Standards."

Utah State University. *Twenty-Eighth Annual Utah Conference on Higher Education, September 9–11, 1971.* Salt Lake City: Utah Conference on Higher Education, 1971. See especially "Statement on Academic Freedom, Tenure and Professional Responsibility," pp. 95–103.

University of Utah. *The Commission to Study Tenure: Final Report.* Salt Lake City, 1971.

State Council of Higher Education for Virginia. *Those Employed at Virginia's Colleges: State-Controlled Colleges and Universities, 1970–71.* Richmond, December 1971.

University of Wisconsin. *Report of the Regent Subcommittee on Faculty Tenure Criteria.* Madison, 1971.

Policy Statements and Commission Reports

American Academy of Arts and Sciences. *The Assembly on University Goals and Governance—First Report.* Cambridge, Mass., January 1971.

American Association of State Colleges and Universities. *Statement on Academic Freedom and Responsibility and Academic Tenure.* Washington, D.C., 1971.

American Association of University Professors. "Faculty Appointment and Family Relationship." *AAUP Bulletin,* 1971, *57,* 221.

American Association of University Professors. *AAUP Policy Documents and Reports.* Washington, D.C., 1971.

American Association of University Professors. "Statement on Procedural

Standards in the Renewal or Nonrenewal of Faculty Appointments." *AAUP Bulletin,* 1971, *57,* 206–210.

"American Council on Education Conference Statement on Academic Freedom and Tenure." *AAUP Bulletin,* 1925, *11,* 99–101.

Association of American Colleges. *A Brief Comment on Professorial Responsibility in Support of Academic Freedom.* Washington, D.C., 1971.

Canadian Association of University Teachers (CAUT). "Policy Statement on Academic Appointments and Tenure." *CAUT Bulletin,* 1968, *16,* 4–20.

Committee on Faculty Evaluation. *Faculty Evaluation and Termination Procedures: A Special Report of the National Faculty Association of Community and Junior Colleges.* Washington, D.C., 1970.

Committee on Government and Higher Education. *The Efficiency of Freedom.* Baltimore: Johns Hopkins Press, 1959.

Faculty Participation in Academic Governance. Report of the American Association of Higher Education—National Education Association Task Force on Faculty Representation and Academic Negotiations, Campus Governance Program. Washington, D.C.: American Association of Higher Education, 1967.

JOUGHIN, L. (Ed.) *Academic Freedom and Tenure: A Handbook of the American Association of University Professors.* Madison: University of Wisconsin Press, 1969.

National Education Association. *Principles of Academic Tenure for Higher Education.* Statement of the National Education Association to the Commission on Academic Tenure. Washington, D.C., May 1972.

Report of the President's Commission on Campus Unrest. William Scranton, Chairman. *Campus Unrest.* Washington, D.C.: U.S. Government Printing Office, 1970.

Report of the Special Committee on Campus Tensions. Sol M. Linowitz, Chairman. *Campus Tensions: Analysis and Recommendations.* Washington, D.C.: American Council on Education, 1970.

United States Department of Health, Education, and Welfare. *Report on Higher Education.* Frank Newman, Chairman. Washington, D.C.: U.S. Government Printing Office, 1971.

Guide to

Recommendations

These are general descriptions of the recommendations given in the text; they are not intended as official titles for the recommendations. Page numbers indicate where the discussion of a specific recommendation begins.

Index

273